GERMAN
AIR-DROPPED WEAPONS
to 1945

German Air-Dropped Weapons to 1945
© Motorbuch Verlag, 2003, 2004

ISBN 1 85780 174 1

First published 2003 in Germany by
Motorbuch Verlag, Stuttgart

Translation from original Germany text
by Ted Oliver

English language edition published 2004 by
Midland Publishing
4 Watling Drive, Hinckley, LE10 3EY, England.
Tel: 01455 254 490   Fax: 01455 254 495

Midland Publishing is an imprint of
Ian Allan Publishing Ltd.

Worldwide distribution (except North America):
Midland Counties Publications
4 Watling Drive, Hinckley, LE10 3EY, England
Tel: 01455 233 747   Fax: 01455 233 737
E-mail: midlandbooks@compuserve.com
www.midlandcountiessuperstore.com

North America trade distribution:
Specialty Press Publishers & Wholesalers Inc.
39966 Grand Avenue
North Branch, MN 55056, USA
Tel: 651 277 1400   Fax: 651 277 1203
Toll free telephone: 800 895 4585
www.specialtypress.com

Design concept and editorial layout
© Midland Publishing and
Stephen Thompson Associates.

Printed by Ian Allan Printing Ltd
Riverdene Business Park, Molesey Road
Hersham, Surrey, KT12 4RG, England.

Title page illustration:
*A Luftwaffe bomb mechanic holding an
SC-250 Minenbombe (standard Luftwaffe high-
explosive demolition bomb) in a souvenir
photo taken during the early years of World
War Two. The SC-250 was one of the most
important types of German bombs.*

GERMAN
AIR-DROPPED WEAPONS
to 1945

WOLFGANG FLEISCHER

MIDLAND
An imprint of
Ian Allan Publishing

Contents

Foreword

Bombs originally consisted of hollow cast-iron spheres filled with explosives and fuzes. In this form they were used from the end of the 15th century until up to the second half of the 19th century, and fired from smooth-bore field artillery. This term was later adopted to denote explosive charges of various kinds, also for those in connection with treacherous assaults and acts of terrorism. Today, this term is used to denote free-fall air-dropped weapons in attacks from the air.

Fliegerbomben (air-dropped bombs) consist more or less of drop-shaped or cylindrical hollow bodies fabricated of metal, but also partly of cement or synthetic materials (plastics). They possess stabilising surfaces and are filled with high-explosives, incendiary, chemical or propaganda materials whose effectiveness is initiated with the aid of special fuzes and air-dropped from bomb-carrying aircraft. The various types of bombs differ in their filling materials and hence in their destructive effect. The development, manufacture and use of bombs is most closely associated with bomber aircraft, conceived especially for their transport and precisely-aimed release over the target.

During World War Two, their development advanced in accordance with increasing aircraft speeds, range and bombload into a means of destroying wide areas, with whose assistance the war was expanded to affect human life in all theatres. Through their employment, entire cities were obliterated by conventional air-dropped weapons to a degree unimaginable up until then. The preliminary climax was the use of atomic bombs dropped by US bombers over Japan in August 1945, that within minutes destroyed almost all life in the cities of Hiroshima and Nagasaki.

Bombs and bomber aircraft are the means and expression for the conduct of total war. Noteworthy is that although inseparable in terms of application, the two are differently treated in a military and historical sense – a contradiction which cannot be explained from the point of view of the fascination attached to aircraft, which are consistently viewed in connection with aesthetic and technological advancements. Additionally, in relation to their military use which in increasing measure became the object of critical study, such observations have become largely self-understood and directed towards a product of scientific and technical development.

Quite differently considered on the other hand, are the bombs themselves. Their existence, whose purpose is fulfilled with the aid of bomber aircraft, is more often readily suppressed. With the bombs are connected recollections of the indescribable suffering of the victims among the civilian population in the pulverised, burned-to-ashes large cities. Names such as Rotterdam, Coventry, St Lô, Würzburg, Pforzheim, Hamburg, and above all, Dresden, are particular examples. As a result, descriptions are seldom found involving the technicalities, tactics and the history of air-dropped weapons – leaving aside the internal works documents that were prepared within the scope of bomb-disposal activities. This also holds true for German air-dropped weapons until the end of World War Two – the subject of this publication.

At the beginning of the 1960s, in the 'Luftschutz' (Air Defence) document series, Fritz Meinhard took up the subject of conventional Abwurfmunition (air-dropped weapons). A more extensive series of publications in the 1970s, based on regulations of the former Luftwaffe contained in documents, was published by the Publizistisches Archiv Karl W Pawlas which, however, restricted itself to the purely technical aspects. In this connection, the book *Sprengkommandos – Geschichte der Blindgängerbeseitigung* (Detonation Squads – History of Unexploded Bombs Removal) by author Manfred Rauschert, Stuttgart, 1980, deserves attention. In Volume 4 of the series *Die deutsche Luftrüstung 1933-1945* (German Air Armament 1933-45), Koblenz, 1993, author Heinz Nowarra provides only a very brief overall picture of German air-dropped weapons. More detailed is the work of Botho Stüwe on the former Luftwaffe *Erprobungsstelle (Test Centre) Peenemünde-West,* Augsburg, 1998. His interest, however, was confined solely to the technical, but certainly spectacular remote-controlled guided weapons during World War Two.

Bomber aircraft were primarily developed to concentrate the effects of bomb destruction within a limited target area. An important prerequisite for the understanding of aircraft technology as also for air warfare technology and tactics during World War Two, is knowledge of the air-dropped weapons themselves. For this reason the author here seeks above all to satisfy those interested in aviation, and in addition, this book is intended as a work of reference for those involved in unexploded bomb disposal. Because of the wide range and diversity of this topic, an exhaustive treatment had to be refrained from, so that a description of the mines, torpedoes and rockets used by the former Luftwaffe had to be excluded as these are a special theme requiring separate description.

Finally, the author wishes to express his thanks to: Dirk Hensel of the Sächsische Kampfmittelbeseitigung firm (Dresden); Thomas Lange and Joachim Auerswald of the Kampfmittelräumdienst des Freistaates Sachsen; Günter Fricke and Wolfgang Neumann of the Dresdner Sprengschule GmbH (Freital) and to Peter Selinger (Speyer), as well as to his friends Jean-Luc Esnouf (Leinfelden) and Hubert Jülch (Bad Bergzabern). Thanks are also owed to Dr Werner Stang (Güterfelde), Richard Eiermann (Sinsheim-Rohrbach) and Karl-Heinz Caye of the Militärhistorische Sammlung in Kiel-Holtenau. All have contributed by their advice and critical hints as well as providing documents for the presentation and completion of this work on the German air-dropped weapons of World War Two.

The partially reduced quality of the photographs is due to their age and the circumstances under which they were taken.

Wolfgang Fleischer
Freital, January 2003.

Glossary of Terms

Abwurf	Air-dropped, jettisoned, released. As prefix with:
-behälter	Container(s)
-munition	Munitions, bombs, weapons
-waffe(n)	Weapon(s)
Bomb(en)	Bomb(s).* Also as suffix with:
Atom-	Atomic
Blitzlicht-	Illumination flare (for night photography)
Brand-	Incendiary
Beton-	Concrete
Elektronbrand-	Elektron-cased incendiary
Fall-	Free-falling
Fallschirm-	Parachute-dropped
Flamm(en)-	Flaming (oil)
Flieger-	Aircraft-dropped
Flugblatt-	Leaflet
Gleit-	Glide-bomb
Großladungs-	High explosive-content
Hohlladungs(spreng)-	Hollow-charge high-explosive
Kampfstoff-	Toxic chemical
Leucht-	Surface illumination (target marker)
Mehrzweck-	Multi-purpose
Minen-	Standard high-explosive (HE) demolition bomb
Nebel-	Fog or smokescreen
Panzer-	Armour-piercing (A.P.)
Panzerbrand-	A.P. incendiary
Panzerdurschlags-	A.P. high-explosive penetration
Panzerspreng-	A.P. high-explosive
Propaganda-	Propaganda
Proviant-	Victuals, provisions
Raketen-	Rocket-propelled
Roll-	Rolling (for dam-busting)
Schlachtflieger-	Ground-attack aircraft
Schrapnell-	Shrapnel
Splitter-	Splinter, fragmentation
Spreng-	High-explosive
Spreng-/Brand-	Combined HE & incendiary
Streubrand-	Incendiary scatter
Übungs-	Practice, training
Versorgungs-	Troop supplies
Wasser-	Water supply
Zement-	Cement practice bomb
Bombenminen	Air-dropped mine bombs
Bombenvorsatzkörper	Protruding nose attachment
DVL	Deutsche Versuchsanstalt für Luftfahrt (German Experimental Institute for Aviation)
E-Stelle (Erprobungsstelle)	Luftwaffe Test Centre
Flugzeuge	Aircraft, airplane (US). As suffix:
Infanterie-	Infantry (WWI)
Kampf-	Bomber
Riesen-	Giant (WWI)
Schlacht-	Ground-attack, close-support

Sturzkampf-	Dive-bomber (abbr: Stuka)
Granate	Artillery shell. As suffix:
Spreng-	High-explosive
Werfer-	Mortar shell
Wurf-	Projectile, missile
Heer	Army
HWA	Heereswaffenamt (Army Ordnance Office)
Waffenprüfwesen	Ordnance Evaluation Department (abbreviation: HWA Wa Prw, later Wa Prüf)
Wa Prüf 1	Ammunition & Ballistics
Wa Prüf 2	Infantry Weapons
Wa Prüf 3	Engineering
Wa Prüf 4	Artillery Weapons
Wa Prüf 5	Engineers (*Pionier*) Equipment
Wa Prüf 6	Motor & Tank Equipment
Wa Prüf 7	Signals Equipment
Wa Prüf 8	Optical & Observation Devices
Wa Prüf 9	Smokescreen and Kampfstoffe
Wa Prüf 10	Rockets (liquid propellants)
Wa Prüf 11	Rockets (solid propellants)
Wa Prüf 12	Administration & Personnel
Wa F	Forschung (Research)
Wa Fest	Festungswaffen (Fortifications Weapons)
HWK	Hellmuth Walter Werke, Kiel
OKW	Oberkommando der Wehrmacht (Armed Forces High Command)
RfRuK	Reichsministerium für Rüstung und Kriegsproduction (Reich Ministry for Armaments and War Production)
RLM	Reichluftfahrtministerium (German Air Ministry)
GL	Generalluftzeugmeister (Chief of Air Procurement & Supply)
Technisches Amt	Technical Office. Departments included:
LC 7 (Bomben)	Department LC 7 (Bombs)
RWM	Reichswehrministerium (Reich Army & Navy Ministry)
Truppenamt	Armed Forces Office
Treibmine	drifting mine
Zünder	fuze(s) or fuse(s), detonator(s). As suffix:
Aufschlag-	impact or contact or percussion
Doppel-	double or twin
Langzeit-	long time-delay
Sonder-	special
Stör-	anti-removal, deterrent, harassment
Zeit-	time
Zusatz	auxiliary
Voreil-	immediate detonation (WWI)
Nacheil-	delayed-action (WWI)

Named after their manufacturers in World War I were the APK, P.u.W., Karbonit, Skoda and Wöllersdorf bombs.

Chapter One

Basic Characteristics
Types and Methods of Use in Germany

The fundamental difference between Artillerimunition (artillery weapons) and Abwurfmunition (air-dropped weapons) lies in their type of construction. A decisive factor in this difference is the way in which the air-dropped weapons are conveyed to the enemy and the goal of striking enemy targets – often several kilometres away from one's own operating bases – with the highest possible amount of explosives or other chemical materials. Air-dropped weapons (mostly in the form of bombs), are consequently independent of the explosive load as is a necessity of artillery weapons, and are much simpler in their design and manufacture.

Like all other weapons, Abwurfmunition consist of different types:

- Brisanzmunition – *high-explosive weapons*
- Übungsmunition – *practice/training weapons*
- Exerziermunition – *drill or exercise weapons*
- Unterrichtsmunition – *instructional weapons*

Basic construction of high-explosive bombs. Left: the SB-, SC-, and SD bombs. Right: the PC-, PD-, and PC-RS bombs.

A further subdivision and nomenclature of air-dropped weapons denotes their specific purpose and are distinguished as:

I. Sprengbomben
   (high-explosive bombs)
II. Brandbomben
   (incendiary bombs)
III. Sonderabwurfmunition
   (special air-dropped weapons)
IV. Seeabwurfmunition
   (anti-shipping air-dropped weapons)
V. Abwurfbehälter
   (air-dropped containers)

Within these larger groups, a distinction is made of the various explosive effects. The different types comprise:

Sprengbomben (HE bombs)

SB-Bombs (Großladungsbomben)
Bombs of high explosive-content

Characteristic of these is a very thin-walled bomb body whose total weight consists of roughly 75% explosive content. When used against land targets, the bomb is released with the fuze set for immediate detonation

on impact. For attacks on seaborne targets, a delayed-action fuze time setting can be beneficial.
The SB designator is followed by the weight in kg, for example SB-2500.
Colour code: Two yellow bands on each tailfin quadrant.

SC-Bombs (Minenbomben)
Normal high-explosive demolition bombs

Characteristic is a thin-walled bomb body whose total weight consists of roughly 50% explosives content. Emphasis is placed on its explosive effect when used against fixed installations such as buildings. The fragmentation effect is secondary to that of the high-explosive static or 'mine' effect.
The SC designator is followed by its weight in kg, for example SC-500.
Colour code: One yellow band on each tailfin quadrant.

SD-Bombs (Splitterbomben)
Fragmentation or anti-personnel bombs

Characteristic of these Mehrzweckbomben (multi-purpose bombs) is a thick-walled bomb body with a weight up to 500kg

Der grundsätzliche Aufbau der Sprengbomben.

SB-Bombe   SC-Bombe   SD-Bombe   PC-Bombe   PD-Bombe   PC-RS-Bombe

(1,102 lb), of which roughly 30% is the explosive weight. With smaller bombs, the percentage of high-explosive is much less. Particular emphasis is laid on the fragmentation (splinter) effect when used against living and undefended targets.

The SD designator is followed by the weight in kg, for example SD-250.

Colour code: One red band on each tailfin quadrant.

A special group among the Splitterbomben are the SBe-Bomben where Be = Beton (concrete). Here, the explosives-filled cylindrical core is encased within a concrete shell impregnated with iron scrap, which provides a very effective splinter or shrapnel effect.

Colour code: One green band.

PC-Bombs (Panzersprengbomben)
Armour-piercing high-explosive bombs

Characteristic is a thick-walled bomb body made of high-grade steel of high tensile strength and penetration ability. The proportion of high explosives is about 15 to 20% of the total bomb weight. These are used for attacks against armour-protected targets such as warships and fortifications.

The PC designator is followed by the weight in kg, for example PC-1000.

Colour code: One blue band on each tailfin quadrant.

PC-RS Bombs (Panzerdurchschlagsbomben)
Armour-piercing HE penetration bombs

a) These Panzersprengbomben consist of very thick-walled short bomb bodies with less than 15% explosive content, the weapon accelerated by a built-in solid-propellant rocket charge exhausting through several nozzles at the rear, and is only dropped in steep diving attacks. As a result of the higher impact velocity, it exerts a considerable penetration force against armoured targets. Example: PC-500 RS.

b) A similar type, the Panzerdurchschlagsbomben consist characteristically of a very thick-walled slender bomb body with less than 10% explosive content in its total weight. The greatest penetration effect is obtained when released in level flight from heights of at least 4,000m (13,120ft). If dropped in a dive from lower altitudes, the low impact velocity does not bring about the desired effect and is therefore useless.

Colour code: Both variants have a blue band between each of the tail surfaces.

Brandbomben (Incendiary bombs)

The main explosive content of these bombs consists of an enormous heat-generating mass of material or easily inflammable liquid that burns on impact. These are used chiefly against buildings and when employed in mass drops, are expected to cause fires of long duration. These types of bombs differ as follows:

Elektronbrandbomben
(Electron incendiary bombs)

These are of cylindrical shape, stabilised by tail surfaces and consist of an inflammable Elektron casing and internal Thermite incendiary charge. The bomb designator B is followed by its weight in kg, for example B-1 E where E = Elektron (formerly E1) and B-1 EZ where Z = Zusatz (auxiliary) high-explosive charge.

Elektronfreie-Brandbomben
(Electron-free incendiary bombs)

These are cylindrical or mine-shaped bodies filled with incendiary chemical substances. The bomb designator C is followed by its weight in kg, for example C-50, denoting their similarity to the SC Minenbomben in shape and type of suspension on aircraft. Suffix letters such as Na denote the type of explosive filling material, in this case Natrium = sodium. Bomb colour code is a red band encircling the bomb body.

One variant was the Spreng- und Brand C-50 combined explosive and incendiary bomb which contained an internal auxiliary high-explosive charge. Bomb colour code was a red band encircling the bomb body and a yellow stripe on each of the tailfins.

Sonderabwurfmunition
(Special air-dropped weapons)

These types of bombs represented those specially designed to fulfil a particular task. These were individually distinguished by the initial letter of the bomb designation. Where the bomb descended in a stable manner and was released in a similar way to the normal Minenbomben, this was recognisable by its designation, for example C-50. These types of bombs included the following groups:

Bl C-50 Blitzlichtbomben
(lit: lightning-flash) flash-bombs
KC-250 Kampfstoffbomben
(toxic chemical bombs)
LC-50 Leuchtbomben
(lit: illumination bombs) flares
NC-50 Nebelbomben (smokescreen bomb)
ZC-50 Zementbomben
(cement bombs, for practice drops)

Seeabwurfmunition
(Anti-shipping air-dropped weapons)

These were used for attacking seaborne targets and included the following types:
BM Bomben-Minen, for example BM-1000 (mine-type HE bombs)
BT Bomben-Torpedos, for example BT 700 (torpedo-shaped air-dropped bombs)
LM Luft-Minen, for example LM A, LM B (air-dropped mine-type HE bombs)
LT Luft-Torpedos, for example LT F5, LT 10, LT 11 (air-dropped torpedoes)

As these comprise a wide range of special air-dropped weapons, they do not form a part of this narrative.

Abwurfbehälter
(Air-dropped containers)

In World War Two, air-dropped bombs below 50kg (110 lb) in weight were dropped exclusively from jettisonable containers, the latter consisting of a double- or multi-layered hollow shell containing a number of smaller-sized bombs. According to the type of bombing attack, the containers descended for varying distances after release in a closed condition, and at the most appropriate point of descent from the tactical aspect, were opened by a time fuze.

The jettisonable containers, corresponding to their mode of suspension and also partly in terms of shape and ballistics, conformed to that of a particular bomb calibre – signified in the designation, for example AB-250. Within this basic AB category, there were various types of designs, containing in their enclosing casing fittings for low-level attack, or bombs of suitable ballistic shape for high-level attacks. In general, for each type of jettisonable container, various types of bombs could be inserted in them. Special versions were intended to house only one specific type of bomb.

In its simplest form, several small-calibre bombs could be housed as a cluster within the container, dropped from a rack suitable for releasing a single large-calibre bomb, the cluster referred to as an Abwurf-Bündel (air-dropped bundle or cluster).

Markings: The Abwurfbehälter were coated with beige-grey or sand-yellow (RAL 2027), and externally were inscribed for the type of operational use and replenishment supplies. A typical example, would be:

AB 70-1 meant: AB = Abwurfbehälter
50 SD-1 (air-dropped container)
70 = the container calibre
-1 = progressive model no
50 = qty of bombs in container
SD-1 = SD bombs, each of 1kg (2.2 lb) weight

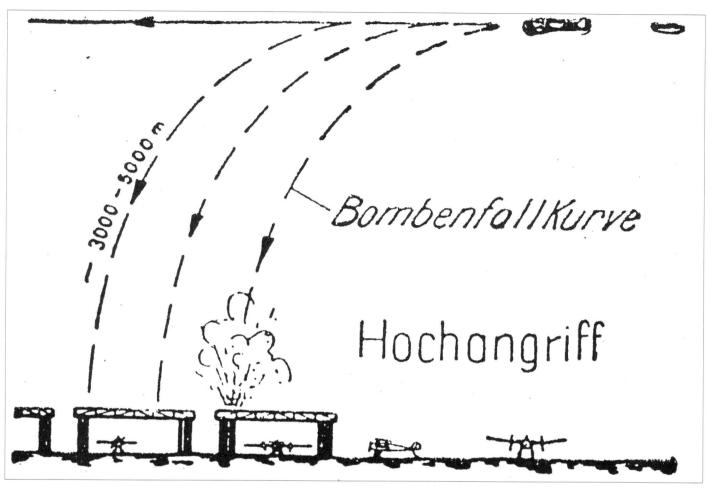

The free-fall bomb trajectories when jettisoned in level flight at altitudes of 3,000-5,000m (9,840-16,400ft).

TA Dornier Do 17E bomber of KG 153 releasing its bombs in level flight at high altitude. It could carry up to ten SC-50 Minenbomben in two magazines or else five SC-50 plus one SC-250 bomb.

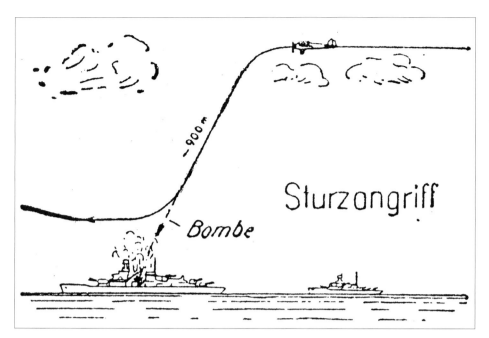

Sturzangriff

Bombe

–900 m

The bombs were dropped either singly, in series, or in mass-drops and differed in the method – ranging from high-altitude level flight to dive-bombing or low-altitude level attack. Just like projectiles fired from gun barrels or rocket batteries by the artillery, air-dropped weapons were likewise subject to natural laws, in this case, the projectile ballistic path. Of particular interest for bomb jettison is the external ballistics, determined by the airflow during its fall and the terminal ballistics which the weapon's effectiveness possesses at the target. Other factors to be taken into account were, the flight altitude, position and movement of the aircraft, any movement of the target being attacked, and the scatter of bombs dropped in series or in clusters.

With the exception of special air-dropped weapons which are excluded, the effectiveness of bombs at the target are measured against their splinter, penetration, and pressure-wave detonation effect. Based on the diameter and depth of the crater that results on detonation, hints can be gained of the size, proportion of explosive content, and the fuze used in the bomb. With a normal high-explosive bomb of 250kg (551 lb) weight, one can reckon with a crater 9.00m (29ft 6⅜in) in diameter and 3.5m (11ft 5⅜in) in depth, and with a 1,000kg (2,205 lb) bomb, a crater of 16m (52ft 6in) diameter and 5m (16ft 4⅞in) depth when fitted with a delayed-action time fuze, the figures for immediate-impact fuzes being somewhat less.

After rupture of the bomb casing, the detonation gases are expelled principally from the sides at velocities ranging from 5,000m/sec (16,400ft/sec) to 9,000m/sec (29,530ft/sec). Air-dropped bombs equipped with a time-delay fuze normally generate a crater of greater size than those fitted with an instantaneous impact fuze. The Splitterbomben (fragmentation or anti-personnel bombs) are the most effective in impacts where they only penetrate insignificantly or else not at all into the ground. It is far more preferable for such bombs to detonate above the surface in order to increase the expansion effect of the bomb splinters. For this reason, like the high-explosive Minenbomben or Großladungsbomben, these are equipped with sensitive super-quick impact fuzes. The latter achieve their destructive effect through large and expansive pressure waves, but leave almost flat craters or shallow basins developing no great splinter or shrapnel effect.

Bomb release in a low-level diving attack.

A Junkers Ju 87B-2 'Stuka' dive-bomber after releasing its under-fuselage SC-250 and four wing-mounted SC-50 bombs.

Right: **A low-level bombing attack together with machine-guns fired at ground targets.**

Below right: **A Messerschmitt Bf 109E-4 dropping an SC-250 bomb in a low-level attack.**

Below: **A bomb trajectory viewed from the ground. AB = bomb flight-path; AE = aircraft flight-path during the fall: Vorhaltewinkel = lead or correction angle; Flughöhe = flight altitude; Zielgelände = target area; Wurfweite BC = jettison distance, and Rücktrittsstrecke CD = distance covered by aircraft at impact.**

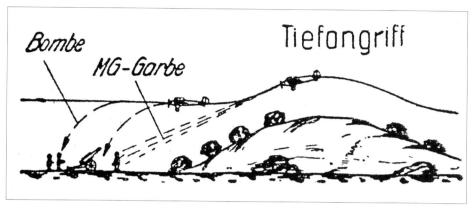

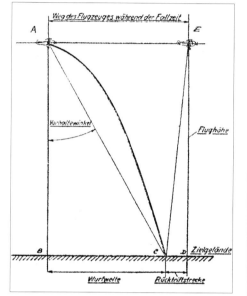

SC-50 bombs in free-fall immediately after release from the aircraft's bomb magazine.

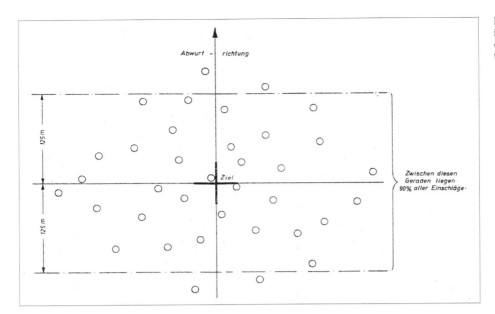

Example of the scatter where 90% of all impacts lie within the upper and lower dotted lines, each 125m (410ft) away from the Ziel (target).

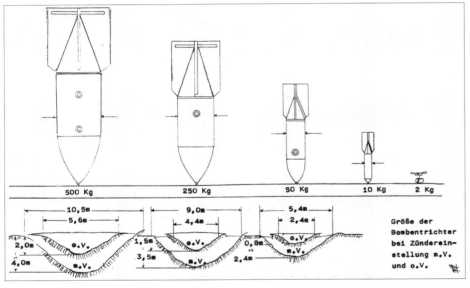

Size comparison of crater widths and depths in metres, of bombs between 2kg (4.4 lb) and 500kg (1,102 lb) weight. The abbreviation o.V. = ohne Verzögerung (without delay) and m.V. = mit Verzögerung (with time-delay) fuze setting.

This bomb crater was made by an SC-500 bomb equipped with an instantaneous impact fuze. Photo taken on the Eastern Front in the summer of 1941.

Chapter Two

The Development of Air-Dropped Weapons to the End of World War One

The idea of dropping bombs from the air originated at a time when aerial vehicles were still lighter-than-air. The term used at that time was aeronautical artillery. It was only after the dirigible, that is the Zeppelin, had made its appearance, that a suitable means of transportation became available for air-dropped free-falling bombs. Later, an alternative means of transportation was offered by the powered aircraft. The first large German aircraft company was the Flugmaschinen Wright GmbH (Wright Flying Machine Co Ltd), established by the AEG or Allgemeine Elektrizitäts-Gesellschaft (General Electric Company) on 19th May 1909.

Despite the rapid improvement in flying performance, the military use of aircraft at this time was still viewed rather sceptically. In issue No 1 of the 1911 Annual of the Army Quarterly publication* concerning military aviation in France, an unnamed author wrote: 'Less significance is apparently given to the dropping of high-explosives on troops and fortifications. Agreeably, it is pointed out from various sources that, compared to means of enormous destruction which we currently possess, the destructive effect of air-dropped projectiles from aircraft will always remain very limited.'

* Vierteljahreshefte für Truppenführung und Heereskunde, Heft 1, Jahrgang 1911.

The aircraft was viewed primarily as a means of communication and observation. 'That future planned battles would ensue in the air, will certainly remain as a flight of fantasy' declared Generalleutnant Friedrich Metzler, a General of the Infantry, in 1912. Despite this statement, the first air-dropped bombs were developed in Germany that same year – a task which the APK or Artillerieprüfungskommission (Artillery Evaluation Commission) had accepted. The ball-shaped cast-iron APK bombs were equipped with an Aufschlagzünder (impact or contact or percussion fuze) and filled with high-explosive, weighed between 5kg (11 lb) and 10kg (22 lb). In the 'History of the German Pyrotechnic Services of the Army and Navy including Materials'† from the year 1936, it was reported that in 1913, the

gunners at the Versuchsschießplatz (Experimental Proving Ground) Kummersdorf, south of Berlin, had acquired a new sphere of activity. By this was meant the dropping of bombs from aircraft and airships, for which purpose the Zeppelin 'Hansa' had been made available, the bombs also being released in practice drops from aircraft in Döberitz. At first, very few of the targets aimed at were actually hit, since the bombs, because of their unfavourable shape and the turbulent airflow around them, presented a large drag surface and like a pendulum, oscillated considerably during their fall. If a hit was achieved at all, as mentioned in a contemporary report, it was purely a matter of luck. In addition, the bomb body itself penetrated deeply into the ground, so that the pressure and fragmentation effect remained marginal. For effective use from the air, the free-falling bombs were hardly suitable and therefore found no use during the First World War. Of interest is that with regard to the unperfected development of these weapons, some accounts published in 1913 in the 'Kriegstechnische Zeitschrift' technical warfare journal regarding the aeronautical artillery in which the installations for the jettisoning of Luft-torpedos (air-dropped torpedoes) or alternatively of high-explosive bombs are related, as also the theoretical and practical problems of bomb releases were discussed.

† Geschichte des Deutschen Feuerwerkswesens der Armee und Marine mit Einschluss des Zeugwesens 1936.

As a result of the tests conducted by the Artillerieprüfungskommission, in collaboration with the Karbonit AG firm, a new type of bomb appeared – the Karbonitbombe. It was produced in sizes varying in weight from 4.5kg (9.9 lb) to 20kg (44 lb), and were used until the end of 1915. Characteristic was its pear- or bulb-shaped bomb body and annular ring tail surface, with the fuze housed at the tail end of the bomb. Trials began with practice free-fall projectiles made of wood, dropped from the fire-brigade training tower at the Schlebusch plant of the Karbonit-Werke, and went

back to the year 1909. The first test drops from aircraft were carried out in 1911 at the Artillery Practice Grounds at Döberitz from a height of 150m (492ft).

From the very beginning, the chief problem with bomb design was to ensure that the contents of the powerful explosive body could be safely transported and in the event of an emergency release, would not explode. Conversely, when jettisoned over the intended target, the bombs had to be primed for detonation during their fall and upon contact, had to be made to disintegrate with optimum results. Such requirements are also fundamental to artillery shells which possessed the advantage that after firing, centrifugal and acceleration forces were used to prime the fuze during the trajectory. These forces were so great that it was possible to design fuzes without any detachable safety devices. With bombs, such forces were not encountered during the fall, so that other means of priming the fuze were required. The development of safe or sure-functioning fuzes during World War One were pushed forward above all in Germany and Great Britain.

Following the outbreak of World War One, the need for effective air-dropped weapons grew. In 23 Zeppelin raids on targets along the British east coast, between January and November 1915 alone, 35 tons of bombs had been dropped. The available Karbonit bombs, to which were added a 1kg (2.2 lb) Splitterbombe, neither the qualitative nor quantitative requirements were satisfied. This held true also for the bombs from other manufacturers, including the Traisen bombs. These existed in sizes of 25kg (55 lb) and 60kg (132 lb), which because of their fuze design, were also designated as Traisen-Voreil or Traisen-Nacheil (instantaneous or delayed-action) bombs respectively. The 20kg (44 lb) and 50kg (110 lb) Skoda bombs and the 40kg (88 lb) Wöllersdorf bombs were also not able to make a name for themselves. Auxiliary assistance was obtained by use of the heavy 42kg (93 lb) 15cm (6in)-diameter howitzer mortar shell that had an annular ring tail surface. Besides these, there were the first models of Leucht- (flare) and

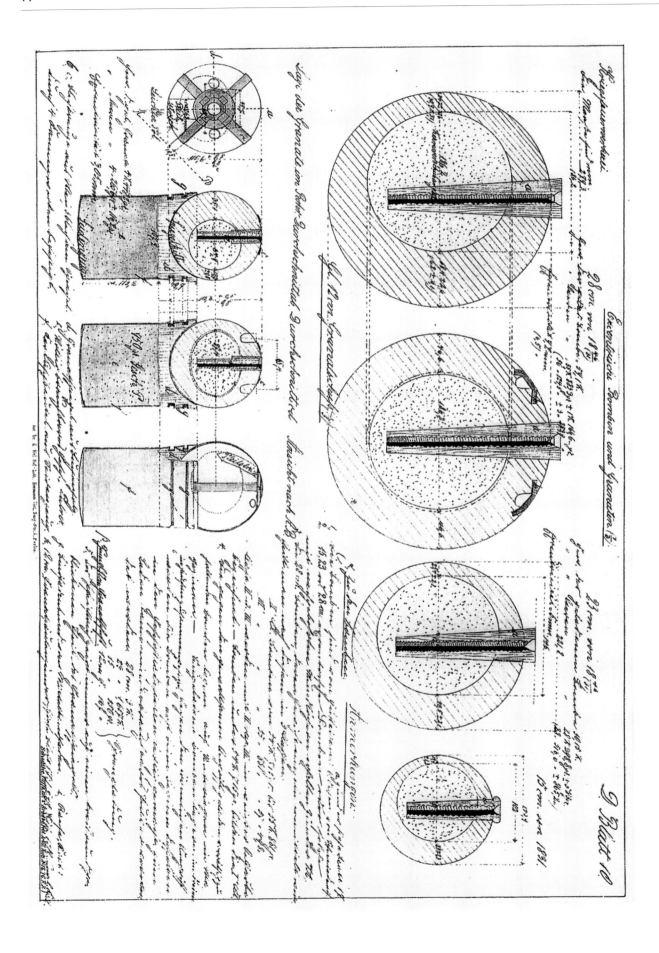

Rauch- (smoke-laying) bombs that were of particular importance to pilots engaged on reconnaissance missions.

During the course of the war, the Karbonit bombs gave way to the more favourably-shaped P.u.W. bombs. Responsible for this development was the military Prüfanstalt und Werft evaluation centre in co-operation with the Goerz firm in Berlin-Friedenau. Trials with the new air-dropped weapons were conducted at the end of 1915, and in 1916, the first P.u.W. bombs arrived at the Front. These existed in sizes of 12.5kg (27.6lb), 50kg (110lb), 100kg (220lb), 300kg (661lb) and 1,000kg (2,205lb). Only the 12.5kg bomb was thick-walled and ejected about 1,400 splinters upon bursting. For launching, racks were mounted on reconnaissance aircraft and day bombers for six of these bombs. With all other sizes, particular value was placed on the destructive effect, for which reason the wall thickness of the bomb casings made in three segments was thinner and the explosive charge proportionally larger. The P.u.W. bombs had to be suspended on two steel cables in the aircraft and thus had no suspension loops or hooks as these would have caused problems with rotating bombs. The centrifugal force-free impact fuzes were installed at the nose of the bombs. By using fuzes with and without a time delay, the effectiveness of the bombs could be influenced according to their type and character. Rotation of the bomb during its fall caused the centrifugal forces to activate the impact fuzes at heights between 30m (98ft) and 1,500m (4,920ft), the rotation ensured by the stabilising tailfins. Any danger to the crew as a result of a crash-landing were as good as none. The disadvantage of this design was that with increasing release altitude and aircraft speed, the stability of the P.u.W. bombs came into question, the critical height lying at 4,500m (14,765ft).

A considerable influence on the effectiveness of the air-dropped bombs were the jettison and target sighting systems in the aircraft. The former consisted initially of tubes, later of simple baskets made of stringers welded together and installed at the observer's position. It was only with the advent of the P.u.W. bombs that it became possible to house the bombs horizontally in or beneath the fuselage or under the wings.

Originally, the bombs were jettisoned without any form of targeting other than visual estimation. But already before the First World War, simple trajectory devices

for bomb-aiming had appeared. Special Lotfernröhre (telescopic bombsights) that enabled a determination of airspeed and correction angle based on the ballistic curve were introduced shortly after the outbreak of the war. These had become necessary since the usual attack altitude of the bombers had increased due to the increased ceiling reached by anti-aircraft defensive armament. Where the altitude had formerly been 800m (2,625ft), by the end of 1914 it had risen to 2,000m (6,560ft).

During the war, the requirement for bombers had risen in terms of range, bombload and operating safety. The most important German bomber was the Gotha G V with a speed of 139km/h (86mph) and a range of 832km (517 miles). Service ceiling was quoted as 6,500m (21,325ft) and bombload 590kg (1,300lb). The Friedrichshafen G III could even carry a 1,000kg (2,205lb) bombload and remain aloft for 5 hours. In addition, there appeared in Germany the Riesenflugzeuge (giant aircraft) – the so-called R-Flugzeuge. They could carry a payload of up to 6,000kg (13,230lb), of which 1.000kg (2,205lb) to 1,500kg (3,307lb) comprised the bombload and enabled altitudes of between 3,700m (12,140ft) and 5,900m (19,350ft) to be attained, as well as a penetration radius of 600-700km (373-435 miles). In increasing measure became the significance of the smaller bombers whose task was to provide close-support of one's own ground troops. These were termed Infanterieflieger (infantry aircraft) or Schlachtflugzeuge (lit: 'battle' or ground-attack aircraft) and in 1916 appeared in strength during the heavy battles in the Verdun area. Together with their machine-guns, they were at first equipped with auxiliary Abwurfmunition (air-dropped weapons) due to the lack of suitable Splitterbomben (anti-personnel bombs). These consisted of Stielhandgranaten (stick-shaped hand-grenades) fitted with time fuzes. Clustered loadings of several hand-grenades, artillery projectiles and the fin-stabilised 1.85kg (4lb)-weight Wurfgranaten were released from the Granatenwerfer 16 ('Priester'-Werfer) artillery shell launchers. It was only in 1918 that small Splitterbomben – the so-called 1kg-Mäuse (2.2lb Mice) also known as the Ifl-Mäuse or Ifl-Bomben (from Infanterieflieger mentioned above) were introduced. Released en masse, good results were able to be achieved with these in funnel-type terrain. A further type of bomb especially used on the German side was the *Brandbombe* (incendiary bomb) of 9kg (19.8lb) to 12kg (26.5lb) weight. Added to these were the Karbonit-*Brandbombe*, the Traisen-*Brandstreubombe* (incendiary scatter) and Wöllersdorf-*Brandbombe*, each of 10kg (22lb) weight. Later, lighter models of incendiary bombs were preferred in

order that a larger number of these could be carried by aircraft. In 1918, design of the B-1 E *Elektronbrandbombe* was concluded. This 1kg (2.2lb)-weight bomb was so designed that it could penetrate through the roof of a normal domestic building and then burn out inside the attic. Its development dates back to a proposal from the firm of Griesheim-Elektron which developed the idea in 1917 of manufacturing small incendiaries comprised of a magnesium-copper alloy for mass drops. The bombs had the shape of a hollow 350 x 50mm (13.8 x 1.97in) cylinder fitted with stabilising fins. In 1918, the Großflugzeuge (large aircraft) of Bombenfliegergeschwader 3 were prepared for the carriage of a few thousand *Elektronbrandbomben*. The operational order for their use had already been written, which in particular envisaged the generation of several small incendiary fires capable of combining into one giant conflagration or fire-storm, but their operational employment was forbidden by Kaiser Wilhelm II.

For providing supplies to indigenous troops on the battlefield, two further types of bombs were introduced in the last year of the war. In June 1918, the *Wasserbombe* (water-bomb) appeared, and three months later, the *Proviantbombe* (victuals or provisions bomb).

During World War One, the organisation, the technology and operational principles of the flying services had made tremendous progress. There existed reconnaissance, fighter, bomber, and ground-attack aircraft which were able to influence events on the battlefield. A comparable development was in that of armament and the airborne equipment carried by bombers. The large variety of bombs and their increasing effectiveness became impressive. There were bombs designed to fulfil different purposes that could be dropped from both high and low altitudes. In Germany, which had lost the war, further expansion of the airborne forces was completely halted by the Treaty of Versailles signed on 22nd June 1919, which had forbidden the existence of a German Air Force. The Reich government gave guarantees to the League of Nations that no secret armament programmes would be pursued on German soil and was prepared to agree to the corresponding sanctions imposed. This resulted in the total dissolution of the Flying Corps from an organisational and technical standpoint. Nevertheless, it led to the further development and evaluation of aeronautical progress by a number of trained air-war experts comprising a secret Fliegerstab (Air Staff) in the Truppenamt (Armed Forces Office) of the Reichswehr (Army and Navy Ministry), a similar modus being pursued by the Navy.

Opposite: **A contemporary illustrated instructional table of eccentric-core 15cm (6in) to 28cm (11in) bombs as well as 12cm (4¾in) grenades for use by siege artillery in the mid 19th century.**

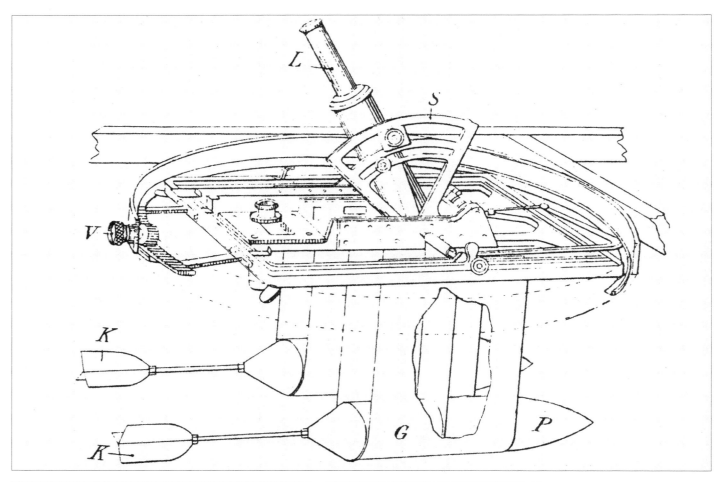

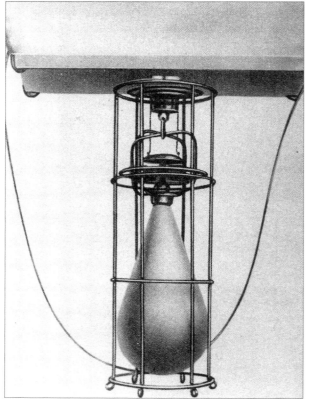

Above: **Jettison scheme of Leutnant Scott, illustrated in the military 'Kriegstechnische Zeitschrift' in 1913. The built-in sighting periscope with cross-hairs is arranged in a Kardan or universal gimbal suspension.**

Far left: **Typical for the Karbonit high-explosive bombs were the pear-shaped cast-iron bomb casing with annular ring tail surface. The bombs were fabricated in weights from 4.5kg (9.9 lb) to 20kg (44 lb); more seldom were the 50kg (110 lb) Karbonit bombs. With bombs from 10kg (22 lb) to 20kg (44 lb) weight, the bomb craters measured from 3 to 4m (9ft 10⅛in to 13ft 1½in) in diameter and 1.5m (4ft 11in) in depth and in terms of explosive and fragmentation effect, were similar to that developed by the 15cm (6in) army artillery shells.**

Left: **Contemporary illustration showing the attachment of a Karbonit bomb to an aircraft.**

Right: **Prior to World War One, the Karbonit firm manufactured simple release-baskets for bombs, the bomb being jettisoned by means of a Bowden cable.**

Centre right: **A pear-shaped 3kg (6.6 lb) *Sprengbombe* (high-explosive bomb). The bomb body had a diameter of 105mm (4.13in), a casing of 2.5mm (0.1in) thickness, and was filled with 150 to 175 shrapnel globules. The explosive weighed 0.6kg (1.32 lb).**

Bottom left: **Sectional view of the 10kg (22 lb) Skoda bomb used against fixed targets, bridges, and the like. The explosive charge weighed from 4.5kg (9.9 lb) to 5.5kg (12 lb), a windmill at the tail end priming the impact fuze located beneath it. Maximum diameter was 171mm (6.73in) and overall length 622mm (24.5in).**

Bottom, centre: **Sectional views of the 25kg (55 lb) Traisen-Nacheilbombe equipped with a time-delay fuze. The thick-walled cast-iron bomb body had a steel nosecap and was filled with 4kg (8.8 lb) of explosive. Fitted with a 3-second delay fuze, this type of bomb was principally used against resilient targets. The example illustrated here had a maximum diameter of 180mm (7.1in) and length 750mm (29.5in). The 60kg (132 lb) Traisen-Nacheilbombe was of similar construction.**

Bottom, far right: **Sectional view of the 40kg (88 lb) Wöllersdorf bomb. As a protection against disintegration upon impact, the nosecap was surrounded by a lead shield. The explosive filling consisted of 12kg (26.5 lb) of Trotyl or 10kg (22 lb) of Dynammon. Maximum diameter was 200mm (7.9in) and overall length 750mm (29.5in). The 18kg (39.7 lb Wöllersdorf bomb was of similar construction.**

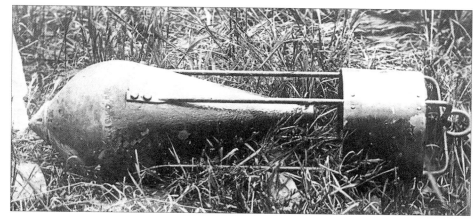

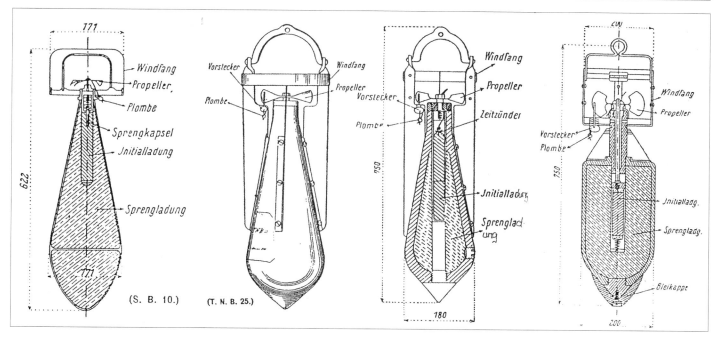

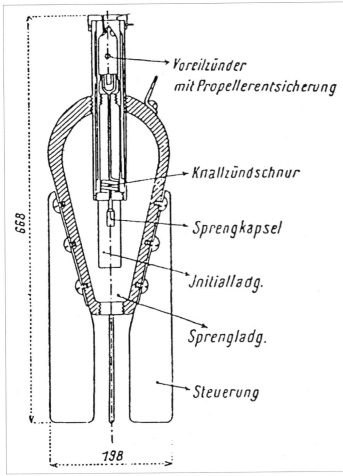

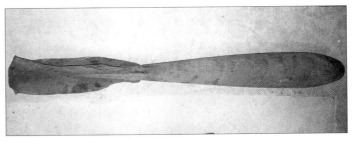

Left: **Sectional view of the 25kg (55lb) Traisen-Voreilbombe. Its Voreilzünder fuze functioned immediately upon impact and caused disintegration of the bomb whilst it was still above the ground. Filled with 5kg (11lb) of high-explosive, it was used as an anti-personnel bomb. Maximum diameter was 198mm (7.8in) and overall length 668mm (26.3in).**

Top: **The 50kg (110lb) P.u.W. bomb. Easily discernible is its slender torpedo shape. The fuzes used without exception were of the impact type with centrifugal-force arming, accomplished by bomb rotation caused by the skew tailfins when the free-fall height was below 1,500m (4,920ft).**

Below: **Introduction of the P.u.W. bombs first permitted horizontal bomb suspension beneath the bomber aircraft's fuselage or beneath the wings. Seen here are 50kg (110lb) and 100kg (220lb) P.u.W. bombs being mounted beneath the wings of a large bomber built by the Gothaer Waggonfabrik.**

Above: **Transporting a 300kg (661 lb) P.u.W. bomb on a special transport carriage.**

Right: **Easily recognisable are large P.u.W. bombs of different sizes suspended on steel cables.**

Far right: **A vertical row of 12.5kg (27.6 lb) P.u.W. bombs in the observer's seat of a twin-engined AEG G IV bomber aircraft. This type of bomb had a thick-walled casing and was produced as a** *Splitterbombe* **(fragmentation bomb) used against living and unprotected targets.**

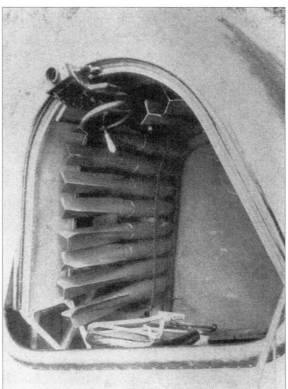

Above: **A horizontal row of six 12.5kg (27.6lb) P.u.W. bombs.**

Left: **In the 1914-1918 war, the crews of the 'artillery aircraft' helped themselves by fitting rifle grenades with an impact fuze and a stabilising parachute.**

Below: **Sectional view of a 10kg (22lb) Karbonit-*Brandbombe* (incendiary bomb). Measuring 175mm (6.9in) in overall diameter and 510mm (20.1in) in length, it contained 4.7 litres of an incendiary mixture of Teer (tar), Benzin (petrol or gasoline [USA]) or Benzol (benzene) and Petroleum (crude-oil or kerosene [USA]).**

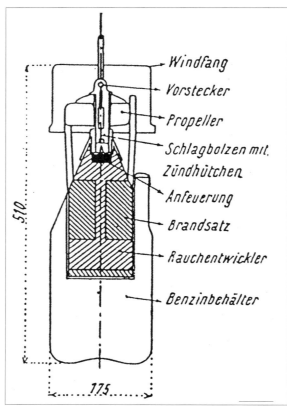

Above: **A 1,000kg (2,205lb) P.u.W. bomb as a size comparison. Except for the 12.5kg (27.6lb) bomb, all were of the thin-walled variety, carried a large proportion of explosive and produced a powerful pressure-wave destructive effect.**

Opposite page:

Top: **The 'artillery pilots' during World War One were equipped with a light MG 14/17 machine-gun with a large ammunition drum, stick hand-grenades with pyrotechnic fuzes in a provisional holder, and signal flares. Towards the end of the war, the so-called Ifl-Mäuse (infantry mice) 1kg (2.2 lb) bombs replaced the hand-grenades.**

Bottom: **For quite some time, the bombs were jettisoned by hand by the observer seen here. A direct hit was a matter of sheer luck.**

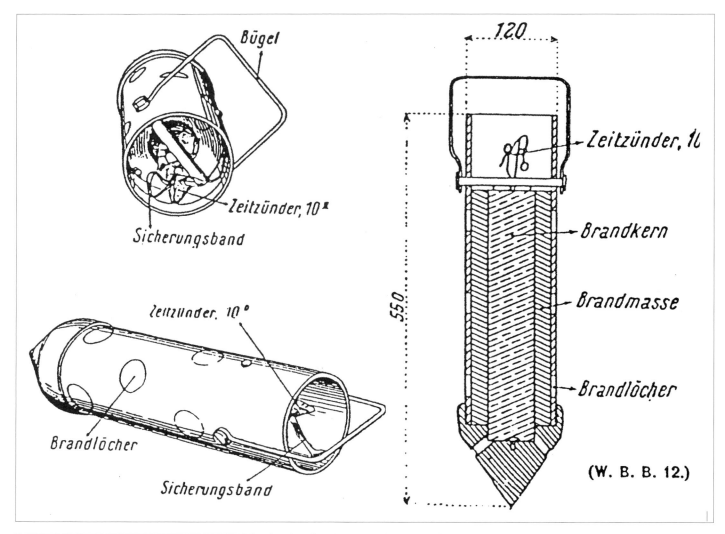

Sectional and perspective views of the 12kg (26.5 lb) Wöllersdorf-*Brandbombe* (incendiary bomb). The incendiary mass was ignited 10 seconds after impact and burned for about 3 minutes.

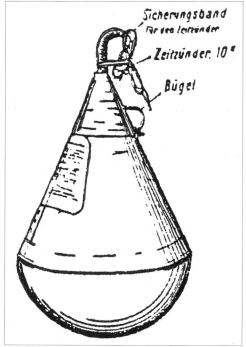

The Traisen-*Brandstreubombe* (incendiary scatter bomb) housed about 100 inflammable pellets of varying combustion time (15 seconds to 2 minutes). The release height was selected so that the bomb should fall and disintegrate at the closest possible distance from the target: at a drop height about 300m (almost 1,000ft).

Chapter Three

Trials under the Reichswehr's Secret Air Armament Programme to the End of the 1920s

The limitations that had been imposed on Germany by the Treaty of Versailles impeded not only possible armaments activity by the Reichswehr, but also that of industry. The sections applicable to aircraft manufacture were set out in new regulations. It thus became forbidden to develop civil aircraft whose external features even hinted at suitability for military use. This concerned possible machine-gun stands and positions for bomb aimers, or even just the locations prepared for such a purpose. Aero-engine power was limited, and multi-

The scenario for the 'aero-chemical war' during an air raid precaution exercise. To portray the poisonous gases, tear-gas, smoke candles and incendiary charges were used.

engined aircraft were not allowed to exceed a total of 500hp. Such aircraft were of course uneconomical and could not compete with civil aircraft built abroad, not to mention being able to satisfy any military requirements. In the event of military usage, it would have entailed making major airframe alterations to civil aircraft to equip them with armament and bomb-jettison equipment. There were also several further design problems involved that hindered such usage. As a consequence of the total dismantling of German armaments industry facilities, there were not even weapons and air-dropped munitions available for trials. Hence, the secret Fliegerstab (Air Staff) in the Truppenamt (Armed Forces Office) were hardly able to conduct practical tests based on development work conducted by industry.

In the mid 1920s, the military leadership in Germany were confronted with another important problem: that of chemical warfare conducted from the air. This had been triggered off by inflammatory reports in illustrated weeklies in which the horrors of such a war had been portrayed to the public. Only a few aircraft would suffice to be able to poison the entire population of large cities, where liquid poisonous chemicals released from great heights would rain down on them as a 'dew of death' sinking into the streets. These descriptions illustrated the operational use of poisonous chemical substances that had first been used by the German side in Flanders in 1917 under the designation Gelbkreuz (Yellow Cross).* This substance proved toxically effective even when the affected area was sparsely occupied over a period of sev-

A contemporary illustration of the spraying of poisonous gases from tanks mounted beneath the wings of a radial-engined biplane.

Scenes intended to mobilise the population as to the correct conduct to be applied in the event of a poison gas attack. (Left): False. To run into the street before it is pronounced safe to do so by the police. (Right): Correct. To remain indoors until the contaminated streets have been cleared by decontamination service personnel.

Falsch!

Vorzeitig den Schutzraum verlassen, ehe die Straßen durch die Polizei freigegeben sind.

Richtig!

In den Häusern bleiben, bis vergiftete Straßen durch die Entgiftungstrupps gereinigt sind.

eral days. Its effects were not only confined to respiratory problems as it also affected the skin. Effective protection was only possible by completely well-enclosed safety clothing. The consequences of this vision of a future war – of an 'aero-chemical war' on Germany in its exposed location at the centre of Europe, appeared unimaginable, especially as suitable aircraft defensive weapons and protective equipment and materials were lacking.

* For an overview of the toxic materials used in such weapons, see Appendix 1 – Translator.

The political and material effects did not go unheeded. One of the most important tasks assigned by the Reichswehr leadership in 1925 to the armament technicians was to evaluate the possibilities presented by chemical air warfare. This, however, could only be executed in connection with practical trials. Under the existing circumstances in Germany, this meant conducting tests with experimental substances at a time when all military flight-testing was forbidden. It was therefore necessary to seek to provide sufficient camouflaging for such activity, even from one's own officialdom and such activity only allowed itself to be conducted by private enterprise. A suitable cover was afforded by forestry, and in 1925, measures were taken in Germany to combat harmful forest parasites from the air. For this purpose, poisonous substances in pulverised form were sprayed from low altitudes onto the forests affected by the parasites. There thus existed the possibility of combating pests by comparison with that of aero-chemical warfare, without having to face the accusation that they were serving a military purpose. In this connection, the main plant of Professor Hugo Junkers received a contract from the Reichswehr's Truppenamt. Junkers developed and produced atomised spraying apparatus for the F 13 and W 33 aircraft, the toxic chemicals being housed in tanks of 200 litres capacity. Practical trials were conducted at the Kurische Nehrung in East Prussia and instead of 'live' chemicals, red or blue-tinted comparable substances were used that accordingly discoloured the areas aimed at. The disadvantage of this atomising method was the loss of chemical concentration of the vapour during the descent and that only a low concentration resulted at ground level. Desirable was a minimum coverage of 5gm/m². An alternative was offered by the use of chemical bombs that could be released from high altitude. Target-aiming was thus made easier, but losses in concentration were suffered by the detonation of the bursting charge that formed part of the bomb's content. These were, however, the sole means of using the Grünkreuz (Green Cross) and Weißkreuz (White Cross) inhalant poisons in air attacks. Always concerned with the necessity for camouflage, the responsible officials of the Reichswehr utilised forestry requirements as a cover for the development and testing of chemical bombs. For example, 'forest fire-extinguishers' were developed which, ejected from aircraft over areas that had been set aflame, were to assist in extinguishing the forest fires. These burst on impact without the use of explosives. Such trials were also conducted at the Kurische Nehrung, this time using a sailplane contest as cover for this activity. Since contest participants expressed doubts about the peaceful use of such 'forest fire-extinguishers', the demonstration was broken off. Renewed trials with chemical bombs were conducted in the autumn of 1926 at the Uchtomskaya airfield 20km (12 miles) southeast of Moscow. Here, as a result of the secret co-operation between the Reichswehr and the Red Army, a secret testing ground was established for the practical use of poison gases dropped from the air. In the initial trials, chemical bombs without fuzes were jettisoned from captive balloons. The focal point of this activity again lay in the dispersion of the sprayed chemicals. For testing, two Junkers aircraft were available: an F 13 and an A 20, capable of carrying the new Type G-125 Kampfstoffbehälter (toxic chemicals containers). These streamlined containers could each hold 125 litres of poisonous chemicals or comparable substances. For dispersion purposes, the undersides were slit open, the surrounding airflow dispersing the chemicals. Later versions used compressed air. In trials, two tanks were mounted beneath the wings of each aircraft.

In the late autumn of 1926, several dispersion tests were undertaken with 'live' chemicals where dogs had been released into the target area. Reports from the Spanish Morocco campaign (1924-1926) in the course of which poison-gas chemicals had been used, encouraged the interest of the Reichswehr's Truppenamt in the work of the meanwhile-established aero-chemical Referat (specialist advisory board). Set-

backs, too, were encountered when in the following winter the entire German installations on the Uchtomskaya airfield were destroyed by fire. On the west bank of the Volga, northeast of the town of Saratov, the Gaskampfschule (poison-gas school) 'Tomka' was established under the leadership of Oberst (retd) Wilhelm Trepper. Following an interruption of several years, tests with poison gases were resumed here. They showed those in responsible circles that aero-chemical warfare was in fact realisable. The basic prerequisites at the beginning of the 1930s, however, were to a large extent still lacking.

In 1927/28, the attention of the Reichswehr's Truppenamt was again drawn to trials with Sprengbomben (high-explosive bombs). A possible partner that appeared to be suitable was Sweden, whose government, following the slow progress of the Geneva disarmament negotiations, had decided to build up its own Air Force. Two factors favoured such an undertaking. The Swedish Bofors firm had obtained the licence rights shortly before the end of World War One for the P.u.W. bombs, with which the two-seater Fokker C V reconnaissance day bombers of the Swedish Air Force were to be equipped. The performance of these aircraft was considerably superior to the bombers of World War One and determination of ballistic data relative to aimed bomb releases was therefore of great interest. A further advantage for the German side was that Sweden had planned to purchase the Lotfernrohr 2 telescopic bombsight from the Carl Zeiss firm. For the trials, personnel and equipment were made available from the DVL. The Reichswehr ministry paid one half of the licence fees from its household funds for the manufacture of one hundred 50kg (110lb) P.u.W. bombs, the rest being furnished by the Bofors firm, with the Swedish Air Force assuming the costs of the flight trials.

Ballistic measurements of the P.u.W. bombs, which had been considered the best at that time, took place from September 1927 until March 1928 at the hands of the Swedish IIIrd Fliegerkorps. Among the most important information gained in relation to ballistics data was that upon jettisoning the bombs at high altitudes, a severe setback had been encountered where it had been least expected: in the design of the P.u.W. bombs. At release altitudes exceeding 4,500m (14,765ft), the 50kg (110lb) bombs burst into several pieces. This also happened later with the 300kg (661lb) bombs, so that only loose high-explosive debris fell to earth. With all the bombs, the breakage point occurred where the tail surfaces had been attached to the conically-shaped rear end. Even the rapidly undertaken strengthening of this section

proved useless. A precise examination showed that it was not the rotational forces that were the cause, but the torsional stresses instead. It should be recalled at this point that in order to prime the fuze, the bomb had to rotate about its longitudinal axis, accomplished by the stabilising fins that were fixed at an angle to this axis. When dropped from 4,000m (13,120ft), the bombs rotated at 3,000rpm, so that the bomb acted like a spinning top or gyro that sought to maintain its stability around its axis, but which resulted in increasing drag during its flight-path. Forces thus acted on the bomb which exceeded the structural strength of the tailfins and caused them to break off. As a consequence of the simultaneously-acting centrifugal forces, the entire bomb body disintegrated. Exactly what importance the experiences gained in the trials Sweden would have for air-dropped weapons design for future generations was not yet recognisable in its entirety in 1928. The trials had nevertheless furnished a sufficient number of measurements for the ballistic tables that were necessary for preparing jettison tables for bomb-aiming instruments, but in a weapons-technical sense, there were still large uncertainties. The Reichswehr's Truppenamt meanwhile demanded from the HWA Waffenprüfwesen 8 the investigation of large Lufthansa civil aircraft for their suitability as auxiliary bombers. The influence could be felt here of the strategic bombing war doctrine favoured by the Italian General Giulio Douhet regarding the employment of a self-sufficient air attack fleet. The procurement of air-dropped weapons having limited possibilities of application under these circumstances, could not be considered as a future solution. Despite this, it was necessary to revert to trials with the tri-motor Junkers G 24 and the Rohrbach Ro VIII 'Roland' as temporary or auxiliary bombers at the Lipetsk Flying School using P.u.W. bombs. The performance of both of these aircraft were no match for the Swedish Fokker C V. For the tests planned in the winter of 1927/28, P.u.W. Splitterbomben of 12kg (26.5lb) weight, and 50kg (110lb) and 300kg (661lb) Minenbomben built by the Maschinenfabrik W Wurl in Berlin-Weißensee were to be used. Parts of these arrived from various plants camouflaged as 'Mittelpufferkupplungen' (central buffer couplings) and as 'Kaminaufsätze' (chimney-stack hoods). The use of a 1,000kg (2,205lb) bomb was dispensed with.

The majority of the 12kg, 50kg and 300kg bombs were filled with a practice-filling material but a few bombs were filled with Trotyl for the purpose of conducting two 'live' drops with each aircraft on the Artillery Proving Grounds at Kummersdorf. For the trials, the fuzes were newly labelled

and brought to the standard of a metric norm. Standard fuzes did not exist at the time, as trials of these had shown during World War One without satisfactory results. Bombs and fuzes were transported from Stettin via Leningrad (St Petersburg) to Lipetsk, where the two aircraft that had previously fitted with mechanical bomb-release fittings stood ready. With the Junkers G 24, a night-bomber version with a weak defensive armament, the suspensions were comparable to those used for the P.u.W. bombs of World War One. These consisted of two cables beneath the centre fuselage on which 3 x 300kg P.u.W. bombs or alternatively 14 x 50kg bombs could be suspended. In contrast, the Rohrbach Ro VIII 'Roland' could carry 2 x 300kg bombs beneath the wings and 5 x 50kg bombs in a niche in the fuselage floor.

Five further bombs could be carried on a movable trolley in the fuselage for reloading purposes, a feature which took 15 minutes to accomplish, during which time the aircraft had to circle over the target area. To ward off fighter aircraft, it was equipped with strengthened defensive armament. With both aircraft, bringing the bombs into place was rather difficult as they hung up to 3m (9ft 10⅛in) above the ground.

In Lipetsk, after they had been suitably equipped for this purpose, both aircraft undertook flight-testing for the Weapons and Bombs Referate of the HWA Wa Prüf 8. For the trials, a 40 Hectar (0.4km²) area had been leased near Lipetsk. In the middle of these test grounds was a 30cm (12in) high thick concrete platform on a 1.5m (59in) high stone base that served for testing the structural strength of the bomb bodies.*

The use of toxic gas by agricultural spraying aircraft at the beginning of the 1920s followed principles that resembled military usage. The scene shows Junkers W 33 aircraft being loaded with poison-gas containers, those involved wearing gas masks.

A specially-equipped Junkers W 33 dispersing toxic gases over a forested area, photographed in 1923.

*In the book: *German Secret Flight-Test Centres to 1945* (Midland Publishing, 2002), Chapter 4, p.59, author Hanfried Schliephake stated that the bomb proving ground measured 2 x 2km (1.2 x 1.2 miles) or 400 Hectares, the area for the bomb drops measuring 50 x 50m (165 x 165ft) at the centre of which was a 50cm (20in) thick concrete platform – Translator.

For the trials with the 12kg P.u.W. bomb, intended to be used solely by reconnaissance and day bomber aircraft, the Junkers A 35 was used as the launching craft. Besides 6 x 12kg bombs, it could also carry 2 x 50kg bombs. The latter, like the 300kg bombs, when jettisoned from heights up to 5,000m (16,400ft), displayed the same problem that had occurred in the tests undertaken in Sweden. There were set-backs even with the 12kg bombs. Several horizontal impacts occurred where the majority of the bombs did not explode. From the multiple launchers, the bombs sometimes unintentionally released themselves, a factor that had led to losses in World War One. For future use, the 12kg P.u.W. bombs were to be housed in magazines containing 5 bombs in vertical stacks, whereas the 50kg bombs, as before, had to be suspended beneath the wings.

In low-level releases with the 50kg bombs, further defects came to light. These proved unsuitable for low-level drops since the bomb bodies shattered on impact on the concrete platform before the all-ways 30-second-delay time fuze became effective to detonate the charge. The 12kg and 50kg P.u.W. bombs had also been tested with uncanted stabilising fins and the new electrical bomb fuzes that had been developed by the Rheinmetall-Borsig GmbH in Sömmerda. This firm was later to play an important role when newer types of bombs were introduced. The non-rotating P.u.W. bombs fell just as unstably as those with the canted stabilising surfaces. Despite all deficiencies, the Reichswehr's Wehramt (Ordnance Office) informed the HWA Wa Prüf 8 on 13th February 1929 that development of the 12kg, 15kg and 300kg bombs had been concluded. By that was meant that the modifications already mentioned above to the old-type P.u.W. bombs, were available for immediate use in high-altitude drops by the auxiliary bombers of lesser performance. Urgent tasks for the future were:
1. The development of *Spreng-* (high-explosive) and *Brand-* (incendiary) bombs including the necessary fuzes and practice fuzes for them.
2. The development of standard fuzes for bombs and further development of bomb bodies and fuzes.

The development of *Blitzlicht-* (flash) bombs had been set aside. In May 1929, the Truppenamt renewed its demand for toxic chemicals dropped from the air and their use in bombs. Instead of the special G-125 containers, the S-125 Sprühgerät (spray device) had appeared working with compressed-air. In order to utilise the Gelbkreuz (Yellow Cross) poison-gas in high-level attacks, a time-fuzed bomb of 200 litres capacity was developed and tested. For detonating the thin-walled bomb body, only a small quantity of high-explosive was sufficient, so that the oily chemical substance did not burn. Trials were undertaken with releases from 4,000m (13,120ft) altitude, the detonation occurring 200-300m (656-984ft) above the target. The poison gas hence formed a roughly 200m (656ft) vertical column that descended earthwards according to the wind direction and contaminated a 50m (165ft) wide and a 300-400m (984-1,320ft) long carpet of ground. One problem was the use of these poison-gas bombs when the wind direction was variable.

For the time fuze, a modified clockwork flak (anti-aircraft) fuze was used, which was activated by pulling out a plug upon release. The time-delay setting was accomplished when the poison-gas bomb was installed in the bomb-release gear. With the S-125 Sprühgerät and the 200 litre *Zeitzünderbombe* (time-fuze bomb), a particular technical conclusion had already been attained in 1929 for their use with air-dropped poison gases. Further trials in Tomka were in relation to the substances themselves and their effects.

Also in 1929, trials commenced in Lipetsk with the new *Elektronbrandbombe* (Electron incendiary bomb) that weighed only 1kg (2.2 lb). It was dropped from a Junkers G 24 that had been equipped with an experimental fitting that enabled the bomb to be released in salvoes of 10 to 20 bombs at a time. The B-1 E, as it was designated, had already been completely designed in 1918. A planned operational use of it, to release the bomb over a city in July 1918 with the aim of creating a fire-storm following the outbreak of small fires caused by several scattered incendiaries, was not able to be conducted. Hardly any experience with the behaviour of *Elektronbrandbomben* was therefore available. Tests already conducted had merely revealed problems with the stabilisation. Concerning destructive effects, there existed partially fantastic expectations. These were now to be finally put to the test. The B-1 E possessed one distinct advantage: it consisted almost entirely of inflammable material.

Trials revealed that the 1kg *Elektronbrandbombe* functioned perfectly. Loading the magazine in the aircraft's fuselage, however, took too long. The focal point of further development lay in the housing and jettison equipment and the design of suitable containers that could be installed in the aircraft without considerable modification efforts in place of the high-explosive bombs. Dispersion of these small bombs was so large that even with a salvo of 40 to 50 bombs, concentration at the target was not as compact as desired.

The 1kg *Elektronbrandbomben* were designated in Germany as *Streubrandbomben* (scatter incendiary bombs) since, because of their dispersion, could be dropped in large numbers on a closely-knit target. In contrast, the C-50 *Brandbombe* introduced at a later date with a thickened incendiary fluid, was called an *Intensivbrandbombe* (intensive incendiary bomb). This type of bomb was capable of igniting even fire-resistant targets.

Trials with *Elektronbrandbomben* at the end of the 1920s in the sphere of *Brandbomben* had reached a particular conclusion in their development. With the *Sprengbomben* (high-explosive bombs) on the other hand, the wide-ranging tests led to no satisfactory results. Replacement of the old-type P.u.W. bombs with modern designs became one of the primary tasks to be tackled in the years that followed.

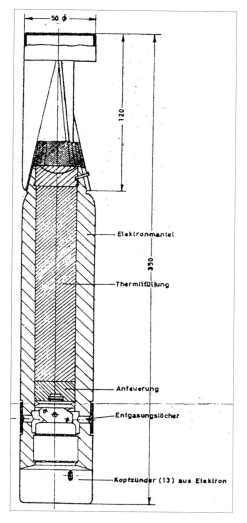

Cross-section of the Thermite-filled B-1 E Electron incendiary bomb with principal dimensions. It was intended for use in large numbers against towns and industrial installations. Total weight was given as 0.83kg (1.83 lb).

Chapter Four

New Developments in the Sphere of Air-Dropped Weapons up to 1933

From the winter of 1929/30, the Reichswehr leadership's interest concentrated on the evolution of newer *Sprengbomben* (high-explosive bombs) as well as on *Aufschlag-* (impact or contact or percussion) and *Zeitzünder* (time fuzes). Tests carried out with the P.u.W. bombs up to this period of time had revealed unambiguous defects with this type of air-dropped weapon. Added to that was the difficulty expected to be encountered in accommodating future models in the fuselage of a bomber aircraft due to the unusually great length of the bombs. The 50kg (110lb) P.u.W. bomb of 180mm (7.1in) diameter was moreover 1,700mm (66.9in) in length. For the 300kg (661lb) P.u.W. bomb, diameter was 350mm (13.8in) and length 2,800mm (110in). Air-dropped weapons with 9.5 or 8.0 calibre lengths – three times that of artillery projectiles and which had an extremely slender torpedo shape, were very complex in their construction and could only be manufactured with considerable effort. The thick-walled 12kg (26.5lb) P.u.W. bomb had an instantaneous-action nose fuze, all others having a nose fuze with a short time-delay. Functioning of the large bombs was ensured by the addition of a base fuze and all models of fuzes, like artillery projectiles, were activated by centrifugal force.

In an HWA document of 17th January 1930, the tasks to be solved within the scope of the Reichswehr's Department Wa Prüf 1 (Ballistics and Munitions) development programme, was consolidated. A distinction was made in the development proposals relative to emergency armament, ideal solutions, and future developments as follows:

EMERGENCY ARMAMENT

Air-dropped Bombs
- New cylindrical bombs of calibres 10kg (22lb), 50kg (110lb) and 300kg (661lb) C-bombs.
- 10kg (22lb) of cast-steel fabrication
- Bombs and cylindrical tubes
- *Brandbomben* (incendiary bombs)
- *Gasbomben* (gas-filled bombs). [Details to be established between the Abteilungen (Departments) Wa Prüf 1 and Wa Prüf 8 based on continuing special reports.]
- *Leuchtbomben* (illumination flares)

Fuzes
- *Zeitzünder* (time fuzes) for air-dropped bombs
- *Aufschlagzünder* (impact fuzes) for air-dropped bombs
- Substitute materials for various fuzes
Ideal Solutions – Air-dropped Bombs
- A 1,000kg (2,205lb) bomb

Future Developments
- Electrical fuzes for the artillery, mine-throwers, and air-dropped bombs.

Previous developments on high-explosive bombs in Germany hardly took into account the wishes of the combat aircrews. Work was directed chiefly by artillerymen who were members of the Artillerieprüfungskommission (Artillery Evaluation Commission) until 1918 and thereafter in the Reichswehr's Heereswaffenamt (Army Ordnance Office). There were also comprehensive and partly negative experiences with their use in World War One and from trials conducted in the 1920s, whose evaluation, based on gunnery knowledge, was insufficient. These experiences influenced the tactical and technical requirements that had been placed on the types of air-dropped weapons to be developed. The requirements were:

1. Two different types of *Sprengbomben* (demolition bombs), small *Splitterbomben* (fragmentation bombs) and larger *Minenbomben* (normal HE bombs)
2. An increased mine-type of effect.

At an early date, it had already been recognised in Germany that stationary targets were destroyed more due to the pressure waves generated when a bomb burst, rather than from pieces of explosive debris flying around. Hence, interest was concentrated on thin-walled bombs which had a higher explosive or mine effect. The most favourable possibilities of housing the necessarily large high-explosive charge (c30%

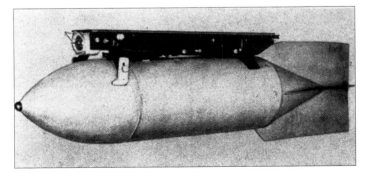

A modern German C-bomb in its horizontal suspension. The 50kg (110lb) bomb shown here was essentially similar to the 250kg (551lb) bomb.

The horizontal suspension for two 50kg (110lb) bombs.

Vertical magazine for ten 10kg (22 lb) *Splitterbomben* (fragmentation bombs). To avoid mishaps upon release, the magazine was equipped (at centre of photo) with a reloading mechanism which ensured that each bomb would be led to the lowest release position.

Magazine for five 50kg (110 lb) bombs.

of the bomb's total weight) was afforded by a short, cylindrical-shaped bomb body. Not ignored in this connection was the task of minimising the overall drag, consisting of the bomb's form drag and frictional drag of the external surface. Relevant precedents for such bomb shapes had already been ascertained in the USA.

3. Taking into account manufacturing interests. This was achieved where the C-bomb body length had been reduced to one-third in comparison to the P.u.W. bombs that were much simpler to manufacture. They consisted of the original nose portion, the cylindrical centre section, and the short tail end plus stabilising tailfins.

With regard to the dimensions of the centre section, predetermined figures were specified that conformed to the seam-free tubes manufactured in German rolling-mills, so that their production capacity could be utilised for bomb production.

4. Suspension lugs for the vertical and horizontal suspension of C-bombs in the fuselage or beneath the aircraft's wings, such that the previously tiresome dependence on suspending the bombs on cables could be eliminated. This type of suspension, however, presupposed the use of rotationally-independent fuzes whose arming was not dependent on the use of centrifugal forces.

5. The vertical suspension of C-bombs by the nose end, and not as in the USA, by the tail end. With this form of suspension, the bombs were pushed away rearwards when released from the magazine. The stabilising fins on contact with the direction of the airflow, led them to follow along the longitudinal axis of the bomb. This had the advantage that the bombs would not somersault or steer with constant pendulum movements into the free-fall trajectory.

6. Fundamentally new technical solutions in

connection with fuzes due to the vertical suspension of the bombs at the nose end. Electrical impact and time fuzes, for various reasons that shall be covered presently, were predestined for use in air-dropped bombs. From the economic aspect, such fuzes offered a series of advantages. Their planned production in enterprises engaged in the manufacture of electro-technical apparata in the event of war, helped to utilise additional production capacity available in the armaments industry in wartime. It was to be expected that the precision-tool industry, with contracts for mechanical artillery fuzes, would become overtaxed.

Electrical impact fuze developments were conducted by the Rheinmetall-Borsig AG in Sömmerda, and were prepared for service use in collaboration with the HWA Wa Prüf 8 and the Chemisch-Technische Reichsanstalt establishments. This work took years to accomplish and was able to be successfully concluded. Only the 10kg (22 lb) *Splitterbombe* was equipped with a mechanical impact fuze that displayed the unmistakable characteristics of an

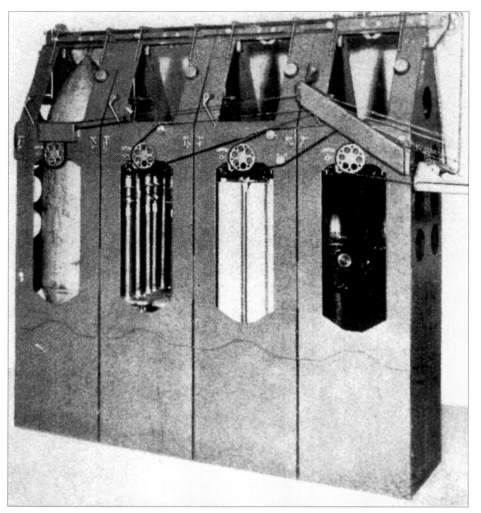

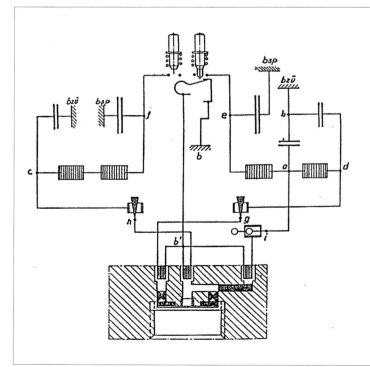

1 Zdr-Körperunterteil	13 Isolierring	25 Kontaktfeder
2 Zdr-Körperoberteil	14 Filzring	26 Widerstand
3 Gewindering	15 oV-Kontaktstift	27 Kondensator
4 Unterer Gewindering	16 mV-Kontaktstift	28 Brückglühzünder
5 Einsatzstück	17 Isolierstück	29 Verdrehsicherung
6 Gewindering	18 Aufnahmestück	31 mV-Verzögerung
7 Oberer Gewindering	19 Hartpapierscheibe	32 Verz. 0,4 s
8 Abschlußplatte	20 Kontakt	33 Verz. 8,0 s
9 Bodenschraube	21 Spiralfeder	34 Kontaktbuchse
10 Pulverkorn	22 Isolierstift	35 Lötfahne
11 Papierscheibe	23 Körperschl.Kontakt	36 Kontakthülse
12 Zündladungskapsel	24 Hohlniet	37 Kontaktfeder

This page bottom and opposite page bottom: **Circuit diagram and cross-sectional views of the El.AZ (15) electrical impact fuze formerly designated C-50. An all-ways impact fuze, it could be set in flight to function as o.V, m.V. or VZ, and was used in the 50kg (110 lb), 250kg (551 lb) and 500kg (1,102 lb)** *Minenbomben.* **There were different fuze switches for the Do 23, Ju 86, He 111 and Do 17E. The fuze terms mean: o.V. = without delay, m.V. = with delay, and VZ = safety-delay fuze.**

Opposite page:

Top left and right: **A single empty bomb container vs the quadruple set in the other photograph.**
For moderate aircraft speeds, bombs could also be housed vertically within the fuselage. For this purpose, the ESAC-250/IX <u>E</u>lectrische <u>S</u>enkrecht <u>A</u>ufhangung für <u>C</u>-bombs (electrical vertical suspension) was developed in conjunction with the RAB-14C <u>R</u>eihen<u>ab</u>wurfautomat (series-ejection automat) and the Lotfe C-7A or B <u>Lotfe</u>rnrohr (telescopic bombsight) used in the Heinkel He 111 bomber. The advantage was that in the magazine, it was possible to house bombs of different sizes and weights, such as 4 x SC-50 and 32 x SC-10 bombs simultaneously.

Right: **A training or practice** *Aufschlagzünder* **(impact fuze) AZ C.10 (h.u.t.), later designated as the Zünder 3 fuze. A live fuze of this type consisted of a non-detonable mechanical impact fuze designed for a minimum jettison altitude of 300m (984ft). Its development was taken up at the end of the 1920s and its use followed in the SC-10 and later, in the SD-10 bombs.**

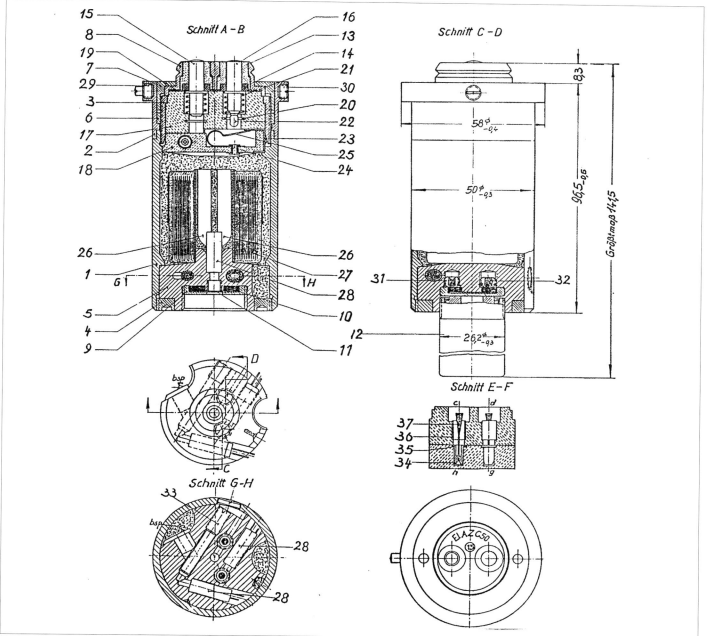

granted. These concerned mainly artillery
fuzes, and only a few could be applied to
air-dropped weapons. In some of the proposals, generators and airscrew-type vanes
were to be used to develop electrical
energy, whereas with others this was
accomplished by acceleration after release
or by the delay upon impact. All of these
designs were complicated, and their preci-
sion left much to be desired. In 1926, on the
other hand, the possibility existed of making fuzes with condensors (capacitors), to
supply them with electrical energy and to
use them as reservoirs up to the point
where the fuze was activated. Electrical
means of ignition were likewise known.
These existed in the mining industry since
1910 and later by the military.

Up to the beginning of 1929, the Development Department in Sömmerda was able
to provide proof of the fundamental utiliz-
ability of electrical bomb fuzes. In February
of that year, the first 20 experimental fuzes
were delivered to the HWA Wa Prüf 8 and
tested in the following summer. They had
been manufactured for use with and without a delay-time facility, whereby the
switching function could be effected by
electrical or mechanical means. The set-
backs already mentioned with these fuzes
when 'live' bombs were jettisoned in summer 1930 pointed to the need for further
work. It was only with the trials conducted
in summer 1932 that the HWA showed
complete satisfaction. In spring 1933, new
problems again occurred, this time however, because of the low durability of the
ignition capsules based on acetylene.
Despite this, mass production of electrical
bomb fuzes continued in January 1934 at
the Rheinmetall-Borsig AG in Sömmerda.
An improvement to the storage qualities,
however, was first realised as a result of further tests conducted with the involvement
of the Chemisch-Technische Reichsanstalt,
and was successfully concluded in 1935.
Up to the end of World War Two, electrical
impact and time fuzes were dominant in
the realm of air-dropped weapons used by
the Luftwaffe. Their multifarious development and application possibilities were set
out in 85 patents which Rheinmetall-Borsig
alone had applied for up to the end of 1939.

Electrical bomb fuzes, also called *Kon-
densatorzünder* (condenser or capacitor
fuzes), besides an electrical igniter, are
able to make use of a storage battery and an
ignition condenser. The storage condenser
was first charged at the moment of release
and offered several advantages, as follows:

artillery fuze. It was shown to be a failure
and was the cause of several, partly severe
accidents that occurred with air-dropped
bombs.

In the autumn of 1929, the Reichswehr's
Truppenamt made available Reichsmarks
RM 30,000 as a special funding from its current budget for development and testing of
the new C-bombs. For this purpose, orders
were placed for 200 SC-10, 100 SC-50, and
25 SC-250 bombs. Following their delivery
in the summer of 1930, the bombs under-
went practical trials in Lipetsk, for which
two single-engined Junkers W 23 aircraft
were suitably prepared. All of the test
bombs were jettisoned perfectly, even better than the P.u.W. bombs. The vertically-
housed SC-50 bombs also showed a very
favourable ballistic trajectory. A few problems, however, were experienced with the
bomb fuzes as well as with the SC-10
mechanical nose fuzes and the electrical
nose fuzes of the SC-50 and SC-250. Most of
the bombs were released as practice

rounds with a non-detonable filling material. At the end of the test cycle, a few of the
bombs were filled with Trotyl and jettisoned, revealing that the experimental
electrical fuzes possessed an undesirable
delayed-action so that the bomb shattered
after it had penetrated deep into the
ground. This of course, had a noticeable
influence on its optimal destructive effect.

At this juncture, the development of electrical bomb fuzes in Germany will be discussed in more detail. Characteristic of this
type of fuze was that an electrical trigger, as
opposed to mechanical triggering that
reacted to an impact force, used electrical
energy to achieve detonation. This required
a connection to an electrical source in
order to function. As early as 1926, engineer
Herbert Rühlemann at the Rheinmetall-
Borsig GmbH was assigned the task of
examining the development possibilities of
electrical fuzes. In his paper entitled 'The
Electrical Fuze' he stated at this time that 12
German patents were known to have been

1. During transport and handling, there was no possibility of ignition. This meant transport and handling safety.
2. If a bomb was inadvertently dropped whilst an aircraft was taxying or on take-off, ignition could not take place (presupposing that the main switch to the fuzebox was switched off). This meant safety during movement on the ground.
3. The main fuze switch was switched on just before jettisoning took place. The ignition storage condensor was first loaded after jettisoning and a short distance traversed in flight. This guaranteed safe release.
4. The voltage in the fuze condensor first became large enough to prime the fuze after a time delay. This meant that the bomb only became 'live' after it was released from the aircraft. Contact was made with the ignition charge upon impact, which resulted in bomb detonation.
5. In emergency landings, the bombs could be jettisoned 'blind' when the main fuze switch was in the 'off' position.
6. Fuze delays could be achieved with the aid of pyrotechnic charges ignited via the electrical means of ignition.
7. Condenser time-fuzes functioned with a voltage-dependent installation, the electrical spark tubes. Up to a particular voltage, they allowed no current to flow through, but were thereafter electrical conductors. The desired time-delay for bomb detonation could then be set with the electrical *Langzeitzünder* LZtZ (17) long-duration time fuze, for up to 72 hours.

Besides the work with fuzes, practical trials of bombs were carried out at Lipetsk. In the summer of 1931, the focus lay on the horizontally-loaded SC-250 *Minenbombe*. Because of the already-mentioned problems with experienced with the mechanical fuze of the 10kg (22 lb) *Splitterbombe*, a vertical suspension had also been adopted for this larger calibre also. The Arado Ar 65 fighter and the Heinkel He 46 close-range reconnaissance aircraft were fitted with racks for the series-release of 5 bombs. In order to prevent the bombs from sinking into the ground, they were jettisoned by using a low-level attack without the stabilising fins, in which case the fuzes were set for a 3-second delay. The vertically-mounted SC-50 bomb was primarily used in the twin-engined Dornier Do 11 (Do F) night bomber which the Luftwaffe was to take over as its first auxiliary bomber. For the smaller aircraft, the horizontal method of suspension for the SC-50 bomb was important, as they had insufficient space to accommodate the bombs within the fuselage. In addition, it was not known at the beginning of the 1930s how vertically-suspended bombs would behave at higher flying speeds.

In 1931, the Reichswehr's Truppenamt required bombs to be dropped in low-level attacks below 100m (328ft), if possible without fuze alteration. The concrete platform on the Proving Grounds at Lipetsk served, under this new aspect, for checking the structural strength of the bomb casings. Although the new C-bombs could be manufactured only in welded form, they proved that their sturdy method of construction was highly durable. Following the dropping of secrecy, it was planned to produce the bomb casings with the help of modern production systems cut in one piece, either moulded or drawn, in order to further increase their durability.

Added to the testing activities in 1932 were trials with the 'over-dimensioned' SC-500 *Minenbomben*. These were suspended horizontally beneath the Do 11 and like the SC-250, had two fuzes. This aircraft was also equipped with a mechanically-operated release mechanism. In their place, without time-consuming conversion efforts, a GR 4 C-10 cradle for 10kg (22 lb) *Splitterbomben* or BSK 36 *Schüttkästen* (multi-bomb containers) for 1kg (2.2 lb) *Elektronbrandbomben* could be installed. Carriage of mixed loads was also possible, so that all types of mission possibilities were catered for. Unfortunately, neither the Do 21 nor its Do 23 successor turned out to be suitable and resulted in the Junkers Ju 52 becoming their replacement. Likewise tested were bomb-aiming devices. In the Do 11, it was the Goerz Fl 219 mechanical night-sighting device, and in the He 59, the optical automatic Goerz/Boykow Fl 213 sighting periscope.

In the sphere of 'aero-chemical' warfare, all had become quiet at Tomka following the conclusion of testing. Parallel to the development of new *Sprengbomben*, there were design proposals for *Kampfstoffbomben* (toxic chemical bombs), similar in external shape to the SC-250, with a 1mm thick casing holding 100 litres of chemicals. Based on Russian precedent, large spraying devices for 200 and 300 litres of chemicals were tested. Lack of clarification concerning their tactical use led to an interruption in this activity.

On 30th January 1933, the National Socialists assumed power in Germany. In the aftermath of this event, the WIVUPAL or Wissenschaftliche Versuchs- und Personalausbildungsstelle (Scientific Test and Personnel Further Education Centre) in Lipetsk was dissolved. Among the most important achievements during its many years of activity were:

1. Development and testing of a whole series of *Sprengbomben* and fuzes as well as the examination of all types of attack and their effectiveness.

2. The successful testing of bombing equipment for various makes of aircraft.
3. Evaluation of the applications of *Kampfstoffen* from spraying devices and in bombs.

Fundamental problems of a tactical and technical nature were able to be cleared up, and in addition, a core of specialists was established whose experiences were of high value for the approaching tasks within the scope of the new rearmament programme.

The ZC-50C dummy or practice *Zementbombe* (cement bomb) was used for air-drop training. To enable its trajectory to be followed more easily after release, a flare was mounted in the tail. Among firms that manufactured the bomb were Johannes Dörnen, and the Brückenbauanstalt (Bridge-building Institute) in Dortmund-Derne which had the bomb coding 'enk'.

Chapter Five

Decisive Years: Development until the Re-attainment of Military Sovereignty in 1935

What influences did the armed forces have on military differences of opinion?

How could they be effectively employed and their utilisation be organised? These questions could not be fully answered in the first half of the 1920s. There were air-warfare experts whose views were oriented upon the theory of the decisive role that air forces would exert in wartime, whilst others perceived the air forces as a type of auxiliary arm completely subordi-

Bomb-jettison from a Heinkel He 111 bomber equipped with the vertical ESAC-250/IX electrically-operated suspension canisters. Development of this type of vertical suspension magazine had already begun at the end of the 1920s.

nated to the land and naval forces. In Germany, the opinion prevailed that land and air forces should strive together to bring about a rapid and decisive outcome of a war. It was only under a particular set of circumstances that the independent use of the Luftwaffe was favoured. These theoretical discussions influenced the development of bombers and consequently, the task of creating suitable air-dropped weapons was at first excluded. The workplan laid down at the end of the 1920s was in pursuance of this specialist field. To ensure continuity, the aviation specialists of the HWA Wa Prüf 8 were taken over by the Technisches Amt (Technical Office) of the RLM that had been established on 1st May 1933. The tasks to be resolved were:

1. Assigning of development contracts to industry and supervision of the status of development.
2. Testing of equipment in the Luftwaffe Test Centres in Rechlin and Travemünde. Live bomb releases could only be carried out on Artillery Proving Grounds, camouflaged by simultaneous shooting trials by the artillery. In 1933/34, this was only possible in Jüterbog (south of Berlin) and even then, for only one to two weeks in each quarter of a year. The continuity of development and testing of air-dropped weapons thus suffered accordingly.
3. Organisation of large-scale production of bomb casings and tail surfaces that had been evolved in the HWA design offices and whose fabrication was mostly undertaken

Top: **In order to house 4 x SC-50 bombs in the ESAC-250 /IX magazine, the bombs had to first be fastened together in a Schlossplatte 4 C-50 brace and then** inserted. **This brace belonged, like the 2 C-50 fuze primer, to the fittings used by the Heinkel He 111H and He 111P.**

Above: Luftwaffe bomb mechanics with the LWC-500 transporter holding an SC-500 bomb. In the background is a line-up of Junkers Ju 87 dive-bombers.

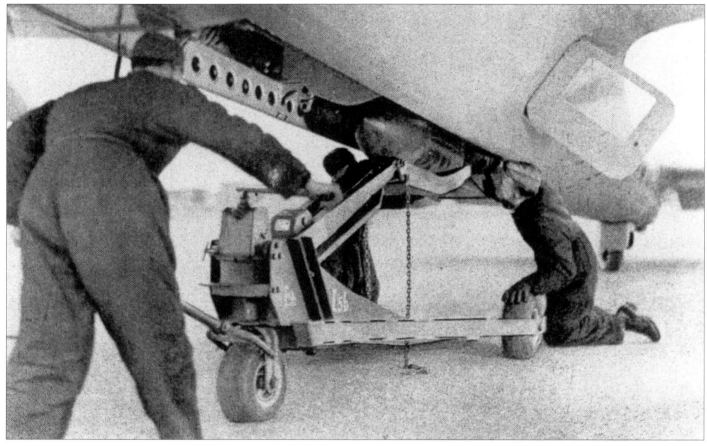

Loading a bomber with the aid of the LWC-500 bomb transporter.

in smaller engineering plants. The filling with explosives had been taken over by personnel of the Kummersdorf Versuchsschießplatz (Experimental Shooting Range) in existing filling facilities. In 1933, firms were sought that were able to manufacture larger quantities, but both the Krupp and Bofors concerns refused. The Rheinmetall-Borsig AG in its main plant in Düsseldorf was prepared to manufacture SC-50, SC-250 and SC-500 bombs as one-piece casings using the compression and extension methods. A further contractor gained was the Vereinigte Oberschlesien Hüttenwerke (United Upper-Silesian Smelting Works) which had already made bombs in World War One. Here, the SC-10 *Splitterbombe* was further developed. The sole manufacturer of *Elektronbrandbomben* was the Hagenuk firm in Kiel, which took over further development of this air-dropped incendiary bomb.

Bomb fuzes came from the Rheinmetall-Borsig AG in Sömmerda, whose production capacity was initially sufficient to cover the Luftwaffe's needs. Bomb target-sighting devices were produced solely by the Carl Zeiss firm in Jena, after they had taken over the Friedenau plant of the C P Goerz Optical Institute in Vienna. Carl Zeiss provided the Luftfernrohr 6 automatic telescopic

bombsight which, unlike earlier models, not only showed the moment of bomb release but also activated the electrical contact for bomb jettison.

At the beginning of April 1933, a consultation took place at the offices of the Reichskommissar für Luftfahrt (Reich Commissioner for Aviation) concerning the course to be adopted for airborne rearmament. It had wide-ranging consequences, including the erection of an independently-operating Air Fleet '... *to whom the task of harassing and destroying neighbouring enemy air forces would be delegated* ...' In May/June 1933, further details were laid down in the so-called '1020 Programme' for the risk-oriented Air Fleet. Up to the year 1935, 1,000 bombers and bombs sufficient 20 air-drop sorties were to be made available.

As already related, the bombers were to consist of the Do 21 and Do 23 but which proved unsuitable and led to the Ju 52 civil aircraft being considered. In the tri-motor Ju 52/3m g3e version, it was fitted with the ESAC-250 for the vertical suspension of 6 x SC-250 *Minenbomben*. The release of 24 x SC-50 or 90 x SC-10 bombs was also possible, as well as 864 x B-1 E Electron incendiary bombs in the BSK-36 cluster canister. Until 1938, the Ju 52 was used as a temporary or auxiliary bomber, and those

machines still on hand were reconverted for use as civil transports.

The hasty build-up of Bomber Groups in conjunction with the availability of air-dropped weapons sufficient for 20 sorties suddenly resulted in a shortage of bombs. At the time, large-scale series production of these were in the preparation stage. Attention was focused on the 10kg (22 lb) and 50kg (110 lb) *Minenbomben* and the 1kg (2.2 lb) *Brandbomben*. The 250kg (551 lb) *Minenbombe* was only available in the welded version, the later Quality Classification, Grade, or Class III (Güteklasse III). In order to overcome the deficit in bombs, the Reich government supported the production of auxiliary (emergency) bombs made out of compressed-air bottles that were to be filled with explosives and auxiliary fuzes.

Further development of *Abwurfmunition* (air-dropped weapons) was to be pursued in parallel. Considerable importance was attached to comprehensive trials for which the most important test aircraft up to 1935/36 remained the Ju 52 launching craft. The most important test objectives were:

1. Ballistic measurements of vertically-jettisoned SC-250 *Minenbomben*.
2. Correct determination of the fuze time-delay with *Minenbomben* release. This was important in order to achieve a maximum destructive effect against various targets that were approached in high- and low-level attacks. The requirement remained unaltered for all *Minenbomben*, if possible, to use only one fuze. A fuze time-delay of 0.1 second, as had been demonstrated in trials, was too long. So as to be able to determine the correct value, a target building measuring 10 x 40m (32 x 131ft) was erected in the summer of 1933 on the Artillery Proving Grounds at Jüterbog, erected to resemble an industrial armaments production plant. The requirement was that the *Minenbomben* would detonate on the ground floor and blast the building walls outwards. Bomb calibre to be used depended upon the size of the target: 50kg (110lb) bombs for 2-storey buildings, 250kg (551lb) bombs for 4- and 5-stories, and 500kg (1,102lb) bombs for even larger buildings. The target building amply fulfilled its purpose. After a long series of tests, the time-delay for the electrical El.AZ (15) impact fuze was fixed at 0.08 seconds. Besides the functions termed o.V. = ohne Verzögerung (without delay), m.V. = mit Verzögerung (with delay), the fuzes were also provided with a VZ = Verzugszündung (safety delay time) setting of 14 seconds for low-level attack since it had been demonstrated that 5 seconds was too short when the bomb impacted with the ground, followed by the passing of the aircraft overhead.
3. Determination of a practical *Brandbombe*. It needed to be established whether the B-1 E *Elektronbrandbombe* developed during World War One was still capable of fulfilling the newest demands and whether it could be taken over unaltered. From England came a report of the existence of a *Flammstrahlbombe* (lit: flame-jet, or flamethrower bomb). Was this better than the German Electron incendiary bomb? To be able to answer this and other questions, tests had to be carried out. For this purpose, in 1934 and again on the Artillery Proving Ground at Jüterbog, buildings with tiled and sheet-metal roofing with various angles of slope were erected and whose attic flooring was filled with trash or junk specially delivered from Berlin.

Bomb mechanics positioning an SC-250 *Minenbombe* in the electrically-operated vertical suspension magazine. With the aid of a special hoist, the bomb was raised to the height where it could be secured to the suspension lug of the Schloss C-250 locking mechanism.

In Germany, one did not want to dispense with the *Elektronbrandbombe*, since it was simple to manufacture. What had still to be determined was the correct size for this type of bomb. Besides the B-1 E, 10,000 examples of the B-0.2 E of merely 200gm (0.44lb) weight and also 200 examples of the B-4 E bombs were produced. The B-4 E had the same shape as the SC-10 *Minenbombe*, had a mechanical AZ (3) impact fuze and was dropped in salvoes of four bombs from the 4 C-10 fittings. Two hundred examples of the B-0.2 E fitted into a transport canister, and its safety transportable fuze feature was a considerable improvement over that of the B-1 E bomb.

During the course of trials conducted in

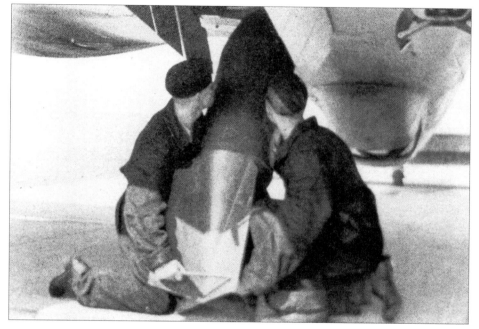

1934, the B-4 E was discarded due to insufficient concentration at the target impact point and effectiveness. In comparison with the B-1 E, the B-0.2 E proved more favourable as fires generated by these bombs could only be extinguished with much effort and trials were to be continued under realistic conditions. To serve as targets from the beginning of 1934, cottages and harvester barracks of the former Gut Leppin estate became available that were given up due to expansion of the Rechlin Test Centre. Within a few months, the entire estate was expanded into an ideal air-raid protection area. The roof beams of the buildings were impregnated with a fire-resistant substance, the floors being fitted

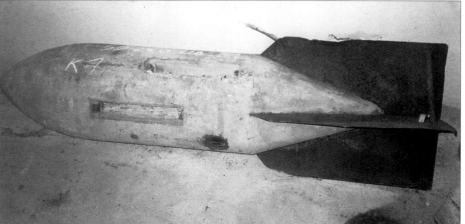

Easily recognisable on this SC-250 *Minenbombe* of pre-war manufacture (later Quality Class III), are the two fuze positions. Among others, the El.AZ (25) fuze was used in conjunction with other fuzes, or alternatively, the ZusZ (40) auxiliary fuze. The suspension lug normally at the centre, is missing on this bomb.

The ZC-250A cement bomb (found here on the ground) was used for training purposes. Glass phials were inserted in 6 lateral openings that, after release, produced either red or white smoke that marked the impact point.

with concrete reinforcements and the masses of furniture removed. Not a single building or house caught fire when incendiary bombs were dropped, so a decision on the question of *Brandbomben* was again postponed. As a postscript, the buildings on the Gut Leppin estate were first able to be destroyed on 22nd June 1935 following the destructive effects of SC-50 *Minenbomben*.

As a new, larger targeting object, the possibility was offered by the meanwhile uninhabited village of Schillersdorf that consisted of 30 to 40 houses in the middle of the bomb dropping grounds located east of Rechlin. There are differing statements with regard to the time when large-scale trials with *Brandbomben* commenced, but presumably took place at the end of October 1935. From a height of 1,200m (3,940ft), some 2,000 B-1 E and about 4,000 B-2 E bombs were dropped from Heinkel He 111 aircraft flying in formations of four. The small *Elektronbrandbomben* bounced off the more sharply inclined roofs, and otherwise produced hardly any effects. The fires that had been started by these bombs expanded only slowly, even when the glowing bomb bodies had been covered with sand. The task of extinguishing the fires was interrupted by the renewed approach of the aircraft dropping high-explosive bombs.

The majority of the Schillerdorf village was burned down, and with this, the decision fell in favour of the B-1 E bomb, whose procurement in large numbers could now be instituted with only minor improvements. Further trials, roughly involving the use of irritant capsules and small black-powder explosive charges, did not bring about the desired success to hinder the work of fire-fighting personnel. It was only during World War Two that the combined *Brand-* (incendiary) and *Sprengbomben* (high-explosive bombs) first affected the moral resistance of the fire-fighters.

From the spring of 1935, trials with *Abwurfmunition* were able to be continued uninterrupted on the Proving Grounds that lay east of Rechlin.

Right: **Loading an SC-50 bomb with the loading-stick.**

Below: **Following-on from the Do 23 and Ju 52 auxiliary bombers, the He 111J-1 shown here became the Luftwaffe's first standard bomber.**

Bottom left: **Various types of** *Elektronbrandbomben* **are seen here: the B-1 E, Ex, B-1 E, B-1 EZ, and B-1.3 E incendiaries.**

Bottom right: **Test set-up showing the joint work of the RLM Abteilung LC 7 (Bomben) and the Inspektion (Inspectorate) L In 14 (Ziviler Luftschutz), showing the effects of an Electron incendiary bomb on a wooden staircase.**

Chapter Six

Organisation and Activities of the RLM Technisches Amt Abteilung LC7 (Bomben)

The further development of *Abwurfmunition* (air-dropped weapons) and associated equipment was the task of Department LC 7 (Bombs) in the RLM Technical Office in Berlin. For conducting tests, the newly-erected E-Stellen (Test Centres) in Rechlin and Travemünde were at its disposal. The Abteilung LC 7 (Bomben) was subdivided into five groups:

Gruppe I   Zünder (fuzes)
Gruppe II   Bomben (bombs)
Gruppe III Abwurfeinrichtingen
            (jettison equipment)
Gruppe IV   Kampfstoffgerät
            (toxic chemical devices)
Gruppe V   Einbau (installations)

The Luftwaffe leadership staff drew up the tactical and technical requirements for the air-dropped weapons and passed them on for further handling to the head of Department LC 7 which determined the organisation of the tasks to be performed. Development contracts were then given to industry by the appropriate specialists in the subdivisions which controlled the progress of development work, the manufacture of samples, and participated in important tests. If design work was brought to a conclusion, the results had to be submitted to the responsible department head who then confirmed acceptance of official testing. Expert advice was provided by the technical specialists to Luftwaffe leader-

ship staff, above all, when doubts existed on the tactical use of the development model submitted. The order to conduct official tests was then passed to the E-Stellen whose personnel were likewise instructed on the on-going development tasks. If these proceeded favourably, the equipment or device was demonstrated to the Operations Staff who then made the final decision for its introduction into the

The scatter pattern of individual bombs aimed under identical conditions at a railway embankment with bridge and railtracks on a test structure at a Bomb Proving Ground near Rechlin.

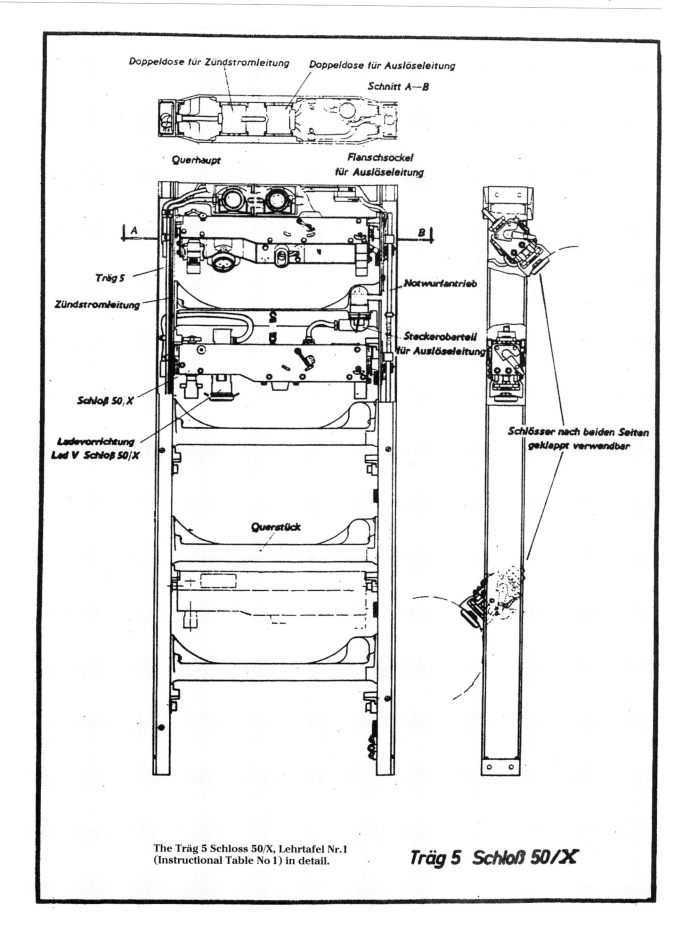

Doppeldose für Zündstromleitung   Doppeldose für Auslöseleitung

Schnitt A—B

Querhaupt

Flanschsockel
für Auslöseleitung

A   B

Träg 5

Zündstromleitung

Notwurfantrieb

Steckeroberteil
für Auslöseleitung

Schloß 50, X

Ladevorrichtung
Lad V Schloß 50/X

Schlösser nach beiden Seiten
geklappt verwendbar

Querstück

The Träg 5 Schloss 50/X, Lehrtafel Nr.1
(Instructional Table No 1) in detail.

Träg 5 Schloß 50/X

In addition to air-dropped bombs and fuzes, supporting apparata were also tested at Luftwaffe Test Centres. Among them was the Träg 5 Schloss 50/X shown here that was introduced in the second half of the 1930s. The abbreviation stood for Trägergerüst (supporting frame) with 5 foldable clasps for bombs of maximum 50kg (110 lb) weight, followed by the development year (Roman X).

The bomb magazines shown beneath a Dornier Do 17E bomber.

Luftwaffe inventory. From the head of Abteilung LC 7, the RLM norms and manufacturing standards sections received timely information so that upon the successful progress of test and development, documentation outlining series production were made available.

Parallel to the trials conducted with air-dropped weapons, there was a useful co-operation between Abteilung LC 7 (Bomben) and the Inspektion L In 14 (Ziviler Luftschutz = civil air defence) in the RLM. For example, the Inspectorate arranged the erection of several multi-storied buildings as well as an air-raid shelter on which bombs were to be dropped on the Bomb Proving Grounds in Rechlin. The results of trials were then made available for evaluation by both departments.

Close co-operation also existed with the Marinewaffenamt (Navy Ordnance Office) as it was also interested in knowledge gained on the effects of bombs used against ships of all types. It was thus shown that in explosives tests on the former liner Lothringen (in French: Lorraine), the SC-250 Minenbombe with its large explosive content of 125kg (276 lb) or 50% of the total weight, was more effective than the 38cm (15in) Sprenggranate (high-explosive shell)

of 400kg (882 lb) weight that held only 69kg (152 lb) of explosive. Practical trials were carried out in the Lübecker Bucht (Bay of Lübeck) with a trading vessel of 7,700 tons displacement purchased from Great Britain. The effectiveness of the SC-50 Minenbombe was minimal, and it was only through a direct hit by the SC-250 that the ship ran aground.

On the Kampfstoffversuchsplatz (Toxic Chemicals Testing Ground) in Munster Nord, trials of these substances were again renewed for the first time since 1931. Stationed at the E-Stelle Munster Nord were a Fliegerstabsingenieur (air staff engineer-chemist), two Referenten (specialist advisors) and two pilots who for administrative purposes were subordinated to the Luftwaffe E-Stelle in Travemünde.

During World War Two, a further wide-ranging sphere of activity appeared that involved evaluation of captured enemy air-dropped weapons by Abteilung LC 7 (Bomben) and its E-Stellen in Rechlin and Travemünde, a task that was mastered together with Industry. Comprehensive and also time-consuming were the trials in the so-called Sprenggärten (high-explosive gardens) which served to determine the quantity of bomb splinters, their compactness,

and their dispersion. It gained in importance in 1942 with the demand for small Splitterbomben in large numbers and in several variants. Also investigated was the degree of penetration by Panzersprengbomben and Panzerdurchschlagsbomben as well as the shock-proof safety of the high-explosive fillings of Minenbomben and Großladungsbomben.

When the steel quality grades for large-calibre bombs had to be reduced in 1942, it became necessary to test their sturdiness when they impacted on hard surfaces, for which purpose outstations in Norway and Italy were prepared. In the spring of 1944, trials were also conducted with glide-bombs in France. The E-Stellen situated in the eastern part of the Reich only first terminated their activities at these locations in the spring of 1945 due to the advance of Soviet forces.

Opposite page:

Instructional illustrations for the ESAC-250 vertically-housed bomb magazines that could house one SC-250 or a cluster of four SC-50 bombs.

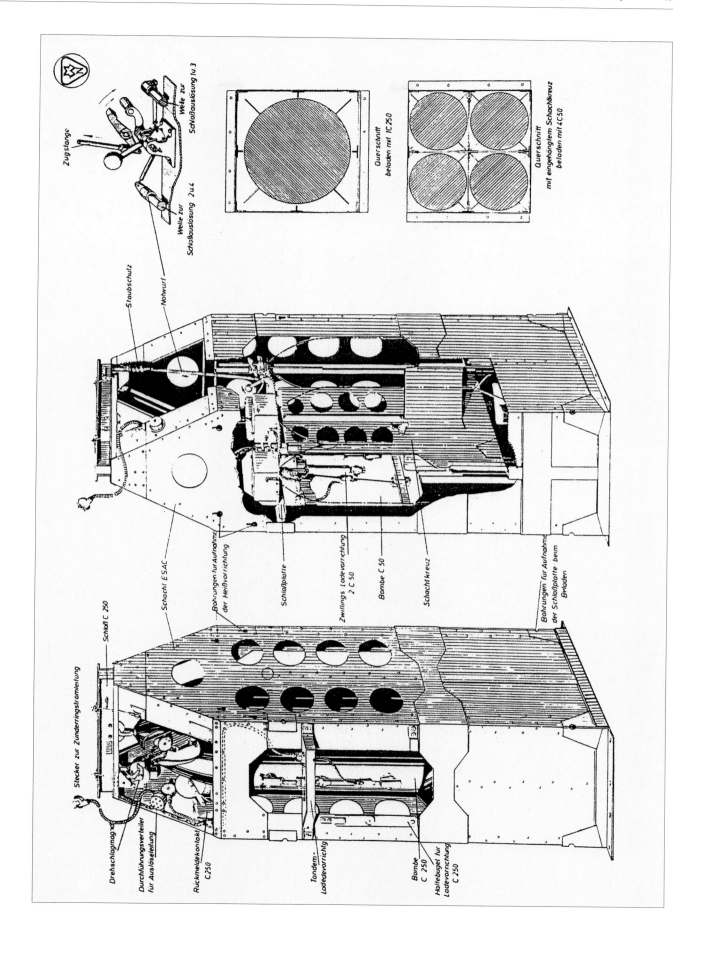

Left and Below: **Evaluation of captured enemy bombs was undertaken within the sphere of responsibility of the GL or Generalluftzeugmeister (Chief of Air Procurement & Supply) who assigned this task to Department LC 7 in the RLM Technisches Amt (Technical Office) as well as to other Departments and to Industry. Technical experience gained was utilised in the development of German bombs.**

Opposite page:

A 20kg (44 lb) Russian chemical bomb to 1/6th scale, from an instructional sheet issued by the RLM GL, document number Br.B. Nr. 4425/41 LT Ang. (LWB/IIIA) dated 15.9.1941. Overall dimensions of this anti-personnel bomb were: diameter 240mm (9.45in) and length 630mm (24.8in). The effectiveness of its contents was unknown, as the bomb was found devoid of its filling. Bomb marking was a single white band aft of the welded seam near the nose.

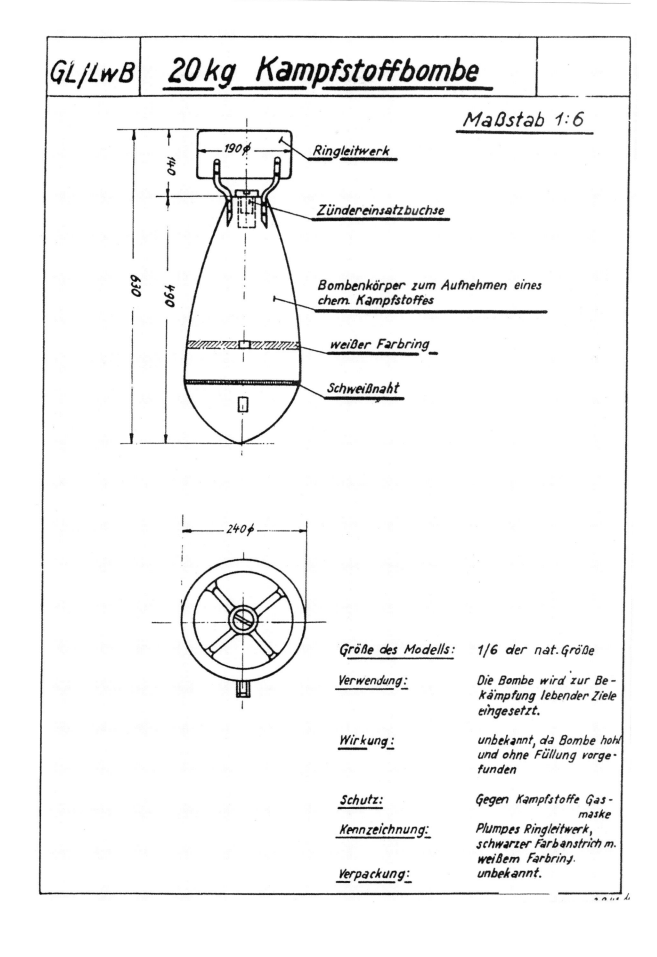

GL/LwB | 20 kg Kampfstoffbombe

Maßstab 1:6

190 ⌀

Ringleitwerk

140

Zündereinsatzbuchse

630   490

Bombenkörper zum Aufnehmen eines chem. Kampfstoffes

weißer Farbring

Schweißnaht

240 ⌀

Größe des Modells:	1/6 der nat. Größe
Verwendung:	Die Bombe wird zur Bekämpfung lebender Ziele eingesetzt.
Wirkung:	unbekannt, da Bombe hohl und ohne Füllung vorgefunden
Schutz:	Gegen Kampfstoffe Gasmaske
Kennzeichnung:	Plumpes Ringleitwerk, schwarzer Farbanstrich m. weißem Farbring.
Verpackung:	unbekannt.

Chapter Seven

Air-Dropped Bomb Development from the mid-1930s up to the Outbreak of War

In the mid-1930s, the Luftwaffe had available some 1,600 bombers, of which over 700 were the Dornier Do 21 and Do 23, as well as Junkers Ju 52 auxiliary bombers. On 1st December 1933, the Reichsminister für Luftfahrt (Aviation Minister) Hermann Göring had required that up to 1st October 1935, 15 Bombergeschwader and 5 Behelfs-(auxiliary) bombergeschwader be made operationally ready to spearhead a long-range war. In 1933/34, the conceptual and constructive prerequisites for a new generation of bomber aircraft had been created. Of the three types envisaged, the Ju 86 and the Do 17 had been proposed as commercial aircraft, but in their design, had provision

for conversion into bombers. The likewise twin-engined Heinkel He 111 was also conceived from the outset as a bomber. In order to save space, it was capable of housing a maximum of 8 x 250kg (551 lb) bombs suspended vertically in the fuselage. Further features were a fully-glazed cockpit canopy, beneath which was located the bomb-aimer equipped with an optical Lotfe 7 telescopic bombsight and a multiple-jettison automat, the pilot and bomb-aimer having full-vision capability on approach to the target. The bombs that had already been developed were successfully tested with this aircraft.

Other new aircraft were the Junkers Ju 87

dive-bomber, for which the tactical and technical requirements had already been set out prior to 1932, and the Henschel Hs 126 reconnaissance aircraft. For the dive-bomber especially, in connection with its intended role, there were a particular set of requirements for its use by the Navy in relation to its bombs and fuzes. With little pressure exercised, the development of four-engined bombers capable of long

The Heinkel He 111H bomber. Easily recognisable is the location of the ESAC-250/X vertical bomb suspension canisters (No 37).

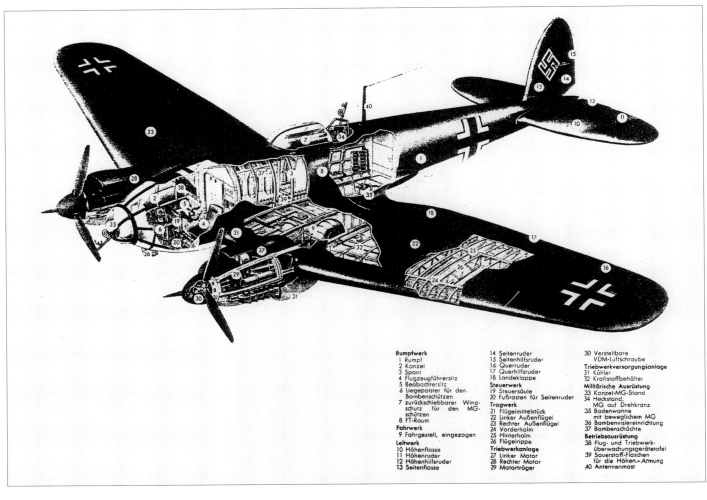

Rumpfwerk	14 Seitenruder	30 Versteltbare
1 Rumpf	15 Seitenhilfsruder	VDM-Luftschraube
2 Kanzel	16 Querruder	**Triebwerkversorgungsanlage**
3 Spant	17 Querhilfsruder	31 Kühler
4 Flugzeugführersitz	18 Landeklappe	32 Kraftstoffbehälter
5 Beobachtersitz	**Steuerwerk**	**Militärische Ausrüstung**
6 Liegepolster für den Bombenschützen	19 Steuersäule	33 Kanzel-MG-Stand
7 zurückschiebbarer Windschutz für den MG-schützen	20 Fußrasten für Seitenruder	34 Heckstand, MG auf Drehkranz
8 FT-Raum	**Tragwerk**	35 Bodenwanne mit beweglichem MG
Fahrwerk	21 Flügelmittelstück	36 Bombenvisiereinrichtung
9 Fahrgestell, eingezogen	22 Linker Außenflügel	37 Bombenschächte
Leitwerk	23 Rechter Außenflügel	**Betriebsausrüstung**
10 Höhenflosse	24 Vorderholm	38 Flug- und Triebwerk-überwachungsgerätetafel
11 Höhenruder	25 Hinterholm	39 Sauerstoff-Flaschen für die Höhen.-Atmung
12 Höhenhilfsruder	26 Flügelrippe	40 Antennenmast
13 Seitenflosse	**Triebwerkanlage**	
	27 Linker Motor	
	28 Rechter Motor	
	29 Motorträger	

The Junkers Ju 87A-1 'Stuka' dive-bomber was able to carry an external 500kg (1,102 lb) bomb beneath the fuselage. When released in a dive, the bomb was first lowered to clear the propeller disc.

range (the 'Ural Bomber') was pursued. Due to technical problems – especially based on experience gained in the Spanish Civil War and because of changed tactical and technical perspectives, its operational use by the Luftwaffe was pushed into the background. Two such aircraft had been completed up to the beginning of World War Two: the Ju 290 and the He 177, the latter capable of carrying a 7,200kg (15,875 lb) bombload.

Problems with the newer aircraft and their air-dropped weapons were first encountered when the He 111H-1 appeared, engined with the more powerful Jumo 211 motors that enabled a speed of 350km/h (217mph) to be attained. Upon ejection from the vertical, the bombs stuck fast in the airstream. Because of the meanwhile primed electrical fuzes, this presented a great danger for the aircraft. To prevent this happening, an extendable airflow-interruptor was added from the

He 111H-3 variant onwards. This diverted the airflow and enabled the bombs to fall unhindered.

The cylindrical shape that had been selected for bombs in Germany as the fundamentally correct path of development was confirmed by US high-explosive bombs that had arrived in Germany in the 1930s. These had been brought over by Ernst Udet who had made a name for himself with his daring stunt-flying demonstrations and by this means, had gained access to circles in the USAAF, at that time still a part of the US Army. The design drawings were handed over to the Rheinmetall-Borsig AG. The bombs consisted of *Minenbomben* of welded construction and were of low structural strength in comparison to German models.

In 1936, the experimental workshops of the Rheinmetall-Borsig AG in Düsseldorf made the first one-piece SC-50 and SC-250 *Minenbomben* with greater structural rigidity than the welded-construction bombs of these calibres. They were soon adopted as the standard bomb type and were later raised to Quality Classification I (Güteklasse I) standard. This new method of manufacture was also adopted for the SC-500.

To investigate the high quality of the bomb casings, Rheinmetall-Borsig on its company-owned Proving Grounds at Unterlüß in the Lüneburger Heide (Lüneburg Heath) erected a special field gun called the Körperwerfer 38 (Projectile Launcher 38) with which the rigidity and effectiveness of the bombs independent of the weather and availability of aircraft could be tested against concrete roofs and the armoured decks of ships. A prerequisite for the optimum effect of air-dropped weapons was that the shell of the bomb remained whole and that the electrical fuzes remained functional. Although minor deformations were acceptable, the bomb body itself had to remain intact, otherwise a portion of the high-explosive content would be lost. The Körperwerfer 38 later gained in importance, especially in connection with the development of armour-piercing bombs and checking the structural rigidity of bomb casings stemming from replacement or 'substitute manufacture' that had become necessary after the outbreak of the war.

There were also other opportunities for examining the effectiveness of air-dropped weapons. At the instigation of the Luftwaffe

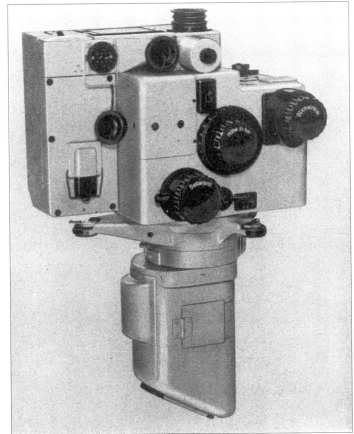

Opposite page:

Top left, top right and bottom left: **For bomb-aiming, the He 111H was equipped with the Lotfe C-7B sight manufactured by the Carl Zeiss firm in Jena. The example seen here bore the Equipment No 127-25 and Werknummer (constructor's number) 51 300 37.**

Opposite page, bottom right, and this page, top and above: **Important knowledge and stimulation for the tactics and technology of air-dropped weapons was gained by the operational use of German aircraft in the Spanish Civil War of 1936-1939. Seen here with a stack of SC-50 and SC-250 bombs are He 111E-3 bombers of the 'Condor Legion' on a forward airfield in Spain.**

General Staff, as early as August 1935, a series of so-called 'tactical targets' had been erected in the neighbourhood of the Fliegerhorst Fassberg air station in the Lüneburger Heide. Forming part of these were buildings with concrete roofs of varying thicknesses, an aircraft hangar made of concrete, and a steel bridge with a concrete foundation. The Abteilung LC 2 in the RLM Technisches Amt even mentions in a document dated 13th August 1936, ammunition depots covered over with earth which contained old P.u.W. bombs that had been set up as targets. These targets were bombarded several times as the aiming points in training sorties for bomber crews, and enabled an assessment of the large number of hits achieved to be made.

The experiences gathered by the 'Condor Legion' during the Spanish Civil War between 1936 and 1939 centred principally on missions flown by aircraft in low-level attacks that led to the demand for more effective *Splitterbomben* to be placed at the forefront. In addition to this, in the Spanish war theatres, dive-bombers had been used for the first time in the winter of 1937/38.

A favourable opportunity for testing air-dropped weapons presented itself by the signing on 29th September 1938 of the Munich Treaty, which compelled Czechoslovakia to cede immediately those areas of predominantly German population in Bohemia close to the German border – the Sudetenland. As a result, almost all existing modern fortifications in that region were

An SC-50 *Minenbombe* pictured immediately after release in a high-level attack.

was mentioned, with whose assistance poison-gas was expected to be disseminated. The KC-250 *Kampfstoffbombe* filled with Gelbkreuz and equipped with an electrical impact fuze, was able to assert itself. In a discussion on 21st November 1933 between the HWA and the Luftwaffe, it was agreed that production of the KC-250 bombs would be increased up to May 1940 to 10,000 Gelbkreuz (Yellow Cross), 3,000 Weißkreuz (White Cross) and 800 Grünkreuz (Green Cross) bombs per month.

The results of tests conducted up to the end of 1938 in Rechlin, Fassberg and Travemünde, which mirrored the judgement of air-dropped weapons before World War Two were summarised by General (Ing.) Ernst Marquardt who, during the war, was head of Abteilung LC 7 (Bomben) in the RLM Technisches Amt as follows:

a. The B-1.3 E *Elektronbrandbombe* (with steel nosecap) for fire generation. Penetration and air-dropped concentration from the BSK *Schüttkasten* (cluster-bomb container), good.

b. The SC-10 *Splitterbombe* disadvantageous in low-level attack due to bouncing of the bomb. Effects as anti-personnel bomb good, especially in high-level releases. The splinters are in general too minute to cause enduring destruction of aircraft. Manufacture of this bomb was held pending, and the new development taken up of a 1.2kg (2.6 lb) *Schlachtfliegerbombe* (ground-attack bomb) and a 50kg (110 lb) *Mehrzweckbombe* (multi-purpose bomb).

c. The SC-50 *Minenbombe* has a sufficiently destructive effect only on small buildings. Militarily important targets on airfields, on railway installations and armament industrial complexes require an increase in calibre to around 1,000kg (2,205 lb) in order to be properly destructive.

d. The SC-250 *Minenbombe* is the most important of all *Sprengbomben*, with the exception of large hangar-type buildings; its high-explosive content is sufficient to destroy all envisaged buildings, bridges and transport ships by direct hits. A one-piece type of casing manufacture is absolutely necessary whereby the extrusion and compression methods have preference before completion of joint-less steel tubes. Assuming this takes place first, bomb casings with gradually-reducing wall thickness towards the rear should be produced so that the same structural strength pertains at each point of the bomb. Whilst bombs made of tubes dovetailed into each other are of course easier to produce,

lost to the Czechs. These bunkers of various thicknesses offered the Luftwaffe ideal opportunities for evaluating the destructive effects of their air-dropped weapons on fixed reinforced targets. Horizontal attacks by the bombers showed an insufficient number of hits with the 500kg (1,102 lb) and later, the 1,000kg (2,205 lb) *Minenbomben* on strong fortifications, which attained penetration depths of between 150mm (5.9in) and 350mm (13.8in) only. These merely destroyed the shatterable outermost layer and laid waste the proximity near the bunker. More effective were attacks performed by dive-bombers where a direct hit could be achieved with an SC-250 bomb on a light fortification of the Type 180, Baureihe 37 (Construction Series 37) model, rendering it completely unusable. Impacts right

next to the target were also effective due to the increased air pressure that exercised fatal results on the bunker crews.

The testing of *Kampfstoffmunition* (toxic chemical weapons) for the Luftwaffe once more gained prominence. Just as before, trials were centred around the use of various Gelbkreuz (Yellow Cross) compounds, but had shifted the focus from the tactical aspect more towards attack. In this connection, the effects of suffocating vapours were now favoured for their use on living targets. Contamination of the area itself, which had previously been a requirement, was now pushed into the background. Several types of bomb bodies filled with chemicals were now examined. In a report as early as May 1933, a *Schwel-Flammbombe* (smouldering inflammable bomb)

their durability upon impact is strongly influenced due to the lower wall thickness between the nose and the cylindrical body.

e. The SC-500 *Minenbombe* is envisaged for use only against sea transports of over 10,000 tons and modern large aircraft factory buildings.

f. The delay-time of 0.08 seconds is in general correct for land targets; against floating targets, the time has to be doubled. Electrical fuzes have asserted themselves well, also under service conditions due to their handling safety and the setting possibilities of o.V. = without delay, m.V. = with delay, and VZ = safety ignition-delay.

g. For combating armoured targets such as ships and fortifications, the new development of *Panzerbomben* is essential.

h. The bomb jettison mechanisms of the aircraft tested up to the present serve their purpose. In view of increasing aircraft speeds, only the horizontal suspension method for bombs and electrical triggering of same is to be used.

i. The focal point of air warfare is shifted from combating area-targets to the point-target that can be attacked in diving flight. The development of multi-engined dive-bombers with the appropriate fittings is to be taken up at a greatly accelerated pace. With regard to bomb-aiming devices, priority is to be given to pure 'Stuka-sights' ahead of combined target-sighting devices.

These experiences formed the basis for the tactical and technical requirements for the year 1939 which the Luftwaffe leadership had put to the RLM Technisches Amt.

The KC-250 Gr *Kampfstoffbombe* had a loaded weight of 156kg (344 lb) with a self-destruction charge of 3.2kg (7 lb) of Fp 02 (TNT) and a filling of c100kg (220 lb) of *Lost* (dichloroethylenesulphide) or *Winterlost*. The bomb dimensions conformed to that of the C-250 *Flammbombe*. This chemical-filled toxic bomb was ignited by the El.AZ (26) electrical impact fuze. Bomb body diameter was 368mm (14.5in), overall length 1,650mm (65in) and tailfin span 512mm (20.2in). [The colour code for the KC-250 III Gr. filled with *Tabun* (ethyldimethylamine-phosphorocyanidate) consisted of two sets of three green bands around the bomb casing, different from the example shown here – Translator].

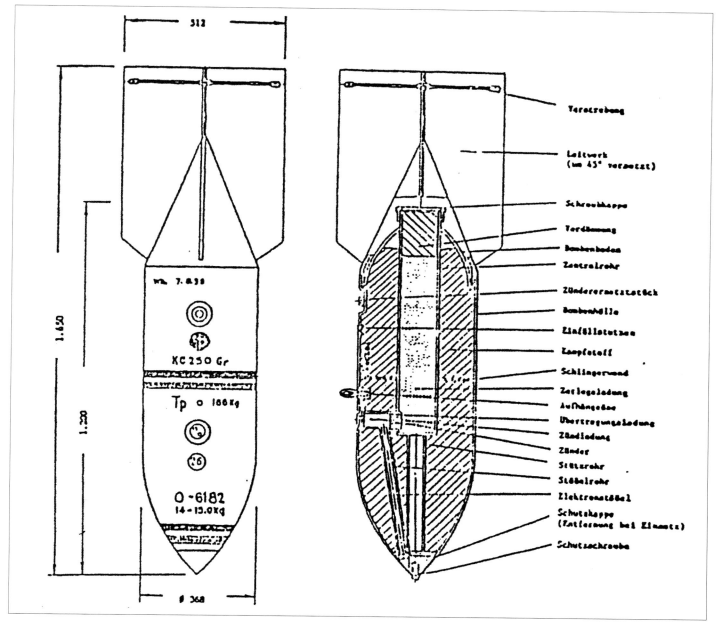

Chapter Eight

Experiences During the Initial War Years 1939-1941

In the early morning hours on 1st September 1939, Luftwaffe bombers attacked targets in Poland. At that time, there were exactly 2,093 aircraft available. The Luftwaffe was to fulfil three basic tasks that had been defined in 1935 in the Luftwaffe Service Regulation 16 (L.DV. 16) as follows:

1. To gain and retain air superiority in close co-operation with the Army and Navy.
2. To combat the military might of the enemy's armed forces.
3. To conduct air war operations against forces in the enemy hinterland, which should only be pursued under particular conditions, especially before and after decisive ground operations.

The German side was able to achieve its concept of air warfare during the campaign against Poland, partly due to its numerical superiority. Poland possessed only 436 bombers. The total of Luftwaffe losses in September 1939 have been quoted as 120 aircraft – losses that could be replaced within a very short time. Much more significant is the fact that in the three weeks of the campaign, almost all 50kg (110 lb) and 250kg (550 lb) bombs had been used up. Shortly before the outbreak of war, stocks of these were not much more than 20,000 bombs. At the end of September 1939, only the 1kg (2.2 lb) B-1 E *Brandbomben* and the 10kg (22 lb) *Splitterbomben* were still available in sufficient quantities. As noted in a report, the Luftwaffe had dropped the B-1 E

and the B-1.3 E bombs rather aimlessly over the Polish capital Warsaw, which had been declared a 'fortress'.

Experiences with air-dropped weapons were extremely varied. This concerned, among others, the 10kg *Splitterbombe* which, after the appearance of the SD-50, was now designated SD-10 that was dropped in large numbers without stabilising tail surfaces. Immediately before the war began, a few Staffeln that had been equipped with Dornier Do 17E bombers, were modified to accept magazines con-

The stock of SC-50 *Minenbomben* on a forward airfield at the beginning of the Second World War. Camouflage measures at this time were still often neglected.

taining SD-10 bombs without stabilising fin surfaces. These bombs did not penetrate into the ground, so that their splinter effect was able to expand quite effectively as a result, and was one of the experiences already accumulated during the Spanish Civil War. The aim in September 1939 was to render the parked Polish aircraft unusable through fragmentation effects whilst at the same time, preserving the runways and and aircraft hangars for later use by the Luftwaffe. The bombs detonated with a delayed-action fuze after 5 seconds, so that the launching aircraft would not be affected by flying bomb splinters. Despite this, the success rate remained low. This was shown not only by the attacks on Krakow airport, but also from bombs dropped on Polish army columns on the move, and was primarily due to three causes:

1. Some of the SC-10 bombs bounced far off the targets after impact.
2. With bombs that detonated horizontally, one third of the splinters penetrated into the ground beneath. For the SD-10, this gave a figure of 170 fragments each of over 5gm weight.
3. The fragmentation distribution was very uneven.

These deficiencies with the SD-10 were a known factor and were accepted in the occasional drops carried out in low-level attacks. But these were now critically evaluated and were to lead to development of a new *Splitterbombe*, the SD-2.

In the spring of 1939, a new multi-purpose 50kg (110 lb) bomb under the designation SD-50 was introduced. Its development was likewise based on experiences gained by the 'Condor Legion' during the Spanish Civil War. The thick-walled bomb bodies were cast as one piece out of steel and upon detonation, produced around 1,200 to 1,400 splinters with an average weight of 13gm (0.5oz) each. There were also bomb casings made of moulded steel and steel tubing which asserted themselves successfully during the Polish campaign against troops, equipment of all types, conventional buildings with up to three floors, against domestic houses, and tooling machinery in industrial installations.

The SC-50 *Minenbomben*, which could be fitted with El.AZ (15), (25), and (38) electrical impact fuzes with or without time-delay, were too weak in their effectiveness against the majority of the targets. It was too late for the transition to an 800kg (1,764 lb) *Minenbombe*, as the suspensions on the aircraft would all have had to be modified.

In Poland, there were only a few resilient targets, so that the welded bombs still available in appreciable numbers proved adequate to satisfy the requirements regarding their structural strength. The SC-250 *Minenbombe* achieved good results when dropped on airfields and factory installations when the time fuze was set for delayed action. The fuze setting without delay was especially effective against railway installations where the air pressure and fragmentation effects were distinctly advantageous. The SC-250 is characterised as a thick-walled high-explosive *Sprengbombe* with a minimum casing thickness of 6mm (0.24in). Its effectiveness lay chiefly on the gas pressure waves generated upon detonation of the explosive. Its splinter effect was lower due to the thick-walled construction. Bombs manufactured in peacetime were generally filled with 125-130kg (276-287 lb) of Füllpulver Fp 02 (TNT) filling powder, whereas in wartime, several

A bomb loading crew handling SC-250 *Minenbomen* in preparation for a sortie.

types of explosive fillings were used. More details on this subject, as also concerning the various Quality Classifications or Grades (Güteklassen) are covered later on in this chapter. Various fuze combinations were also possible.

The SC-250 bombs were capable of vertical mounting in the ESAC-250/IX, or horizontally in the Schloss 500/XII, ETC-500/IX, and L-Rost 2 C-500A for jettisoning. In order to achieve an additional effect other than detonation of the high-explosive itself, auxiliary devices were utilised. One of the first of these was the 'Jericho Trumpet' that consisted of a cardboard tube in the shape of an organ reed that developed a loud whistling howl during the fall of the bomb. Four such 'Jericho Trumpets' were fastened to the bomb, one to each tailfin, and if not needed, could be easily removed.

For generating an additional incendiary effect, in place of the 'Jericho Trumpet' it was possible to attach four B-1 E *Brandbomben* without their tailfins to the bomb.

With tailfins of reduced size or even completely without any, SC-250 *Minenbomben* were used to combat submerged submarines. These bombs were fitted with the all-ways El.AZ (38) electrical impact fuze, and from December 1942 onwards, were filled exclusively with Trialen explosive.

To effectively destroy large factory buildings, recourse had to be made to using SC-500 *Minenbomben*. Their resulting more frequent employment meant a correction to production planning. The SC-500 differed only essentially in terms of its dimensions and explosive content from that of the SC-250, where its explosive weight formed roughly 50% or 250kg (551 lb) of the bomb's weight. It was equipped with the El.AZ (25) B and C, (38) and (55) electrical impact fuzes. This make of bomb also exhibited differences in regard to the explosive preparation and manufacturing quality of the bomb casings. In the course of fabrication, the four tailfins were replaced by an annular ring-tail. Besides the Trialen-filled

version for use against submarines, there was also the SC-500 MB that had two lateral suspension clips for attachment to naval aircraft.

The SC-250 and SC-500 *Minenbomben* of Güteklasse I were also delivered to meet special requirements by being fitted with an annular protruding ring near the nose of the bomb, which for attacks made on shipping with an impact angle of over 20°, would separate after entry into the water.

In documentary reports, the high moral effectiveness of napalm-type Flam C-250 *Flammenbomben* was mentioned. With this type of bomb, the casing of the KC-250 *Kampfstoffbombe* was filled with 80 litres of petrol. The detonation charge, consisting of the short C/98 igniter and an explosive cylinder housing 1 kg (2.2 lb) of Fp 02, was detonated via a highly-sensitive El.AZ (26) electrical impact fuze. The incendiary content developed a fireball of up to 20m (66ft) in diameter, which however, rapidly declined in extent. It was only during the

war that it became possible to extend the fireball effect by using a 74kg (163 lb) heavy incendiary mixture consisting of 30% Benzin (petrol) and 70% Rohöl (crude-oil) in the model C-250 C *Flammenbombe*. Another still larger *Flammenbombe*, the C-500 C was developed and produced during World War Two.

Already at the beginning of the Polish campaign, Luftwaffe operational crews had exercised criticism of the safety of the electrical fuzes used. Upon the release of bombs, on several occasions detonations were observed directly beneath the aircraft that had led to their total loss. It could be unequivocably established that this was due to poor combat training of the aircrews. Even so, as further accidents during the course of the war showed, the com-

Comparative sectional views of the SC-50 *Minenbombe* (upper) and the multi-purpose SD-50 *Splitterbombe* (lower).

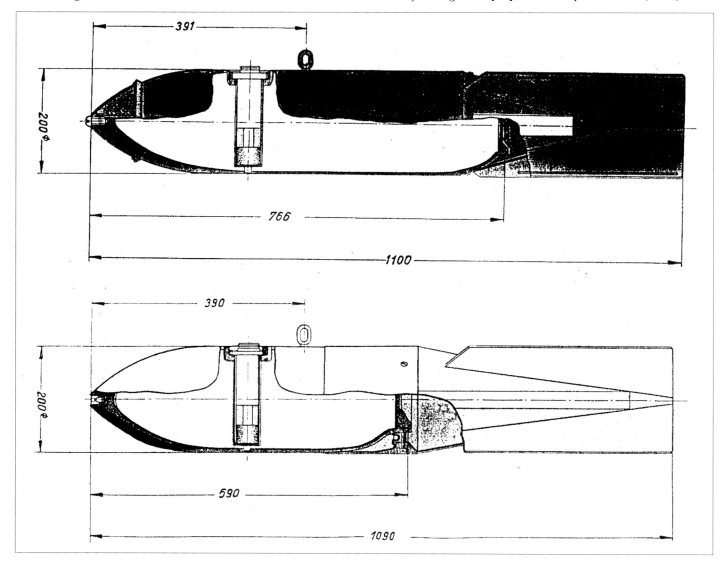

plaints could not be easily dismissed. The safe functioning of the moisture-sensitive electrical impact and time fuzes depended upon the low energy that became effective, particularly upon the stability of all electrical factors. Even minor deviations were sufficient to produce catastrophic results, and it was hoped that with improved quality control, carried out within the scope of acceptance from the manufacturer and the military, that these could be prevented.

By far the greatest problem from the point of view of the military and political situation in the winter of 1939/40 was the low stocks of air-dropped weapons for the Luftwaffe's flying formations. To fill the empty Luftwaffe munitions depots, extraordinary efforts were called for in the industrial armaments plants. These were faced with the problem that there were insufficient manufacturing facilities for making one-piece *Minenbomben*. A requirement of the Generalluftzeugmeister Ernst Udet from the spring of 1939, envisioned that beginning only in 1941 would an adequate production capacity for a monthly output of 20,000 SC-250 and SC-500 *Minenbomben* be attainable. Bomb production in summer 1939 was suddenly accorded the highest priority, when a monthly production of 100,000 SC-250 bombs was demanded, the electrical fuze also receiving a supply requirement for one million per month. In this connection it was determined by the Luftwaffe General Staff that one tenth of this figure should consist of the complicated and high-grade multi-purpose Mehrzweckzünder (25) fuze, and an enormously larger proportion of the simplified El.AZ (55) electrical impact fuze with time-delay function. Their development and manufacture had already been prepared before the war in expectation of manufacturing bottlenecks. Under the conditions of the production now strived for, the quality classifications for fuzes, and especially the strength qualities of the bomb casings and the effectiveness of the explosive fillings had to be compulsorily reduced. With the explosive there was a further bottleneck – related in another section of this chapter.

To increase production quantities of the bomb bodies, the various manufacturing methods were initially studied. The fewest number of problems were encountered with the 50kg (110 lb) bombs, whose supply requirements for this small calibre could be almost completely fulfilled by the tube-manufacturing industry that was additionally able to supply a large proportion of the SD-50 multi-purpose bombs ordered. A further relief came when the rolling-mill production lines that had been relocated from the Saarland from the front of the war theatre to less affected areas could again resume production. This whole account

Following favourable experiences gathered at the beginning of the war with the air-dropped Flam C-250 *Flammenbombe*, the larger Flam C-500 was introduced. The latter weighed 225kg (496 lb), was filled with 157kg (846 lb) of petrol (gasoline) and crude oil, and was used with the super-quick El.AZ (26) electrical impact fuze.

shows how advantageous were the decisions taken at the end of the 1920s to gauge the dimensions of this bomb calibre to match the pertaining standards in the steel-tube industry. In addition, manufacture of the SBe-50 *Splitterbombe* was begun. This consisted of a double-walled concrete casing impregnated with steel splinters. In the course of time, there were six variants of this bomb, which in their effectiveness approached that of the SD-50 bomb.

Of greater severity were the problems that appeared with the increase in output of the 250kg (551 lb) bombs. Here, in addition

to the manufacture of one-piece moulded and welded bomb bodies, three further manufacturing processes crystallised as being realisable. The larger rolling-mills in the Rheinland and Westphalia were capable of manufacturing a small proportion of the SC-250 out of a single cylindrical tube. A further increase occurred when a manufacturing process was developed in which two tubes with a ductile/pliable nose and tail piece could be welded together. Later bombing trials showed that penetration was around 20% less than bombs made in one piece.

Industry was first able to commence mass-production after permission had been granted for the SC-250 *Minenbomben* to be fabricated out of three sections welded together: the nose cap, body, and the tail end. These three components were produced in several small firms and put together in a newly-erected bomb assembly plant. This method of assembly first enabled an annual increase in output of

Above: **A Junkers Ju 87 that made an emergency landing, showing the advantages of the electrical bomb fuze. The force of impact dislodged the SC-50 *Minenbomben* out of their electrical ETC 50/VIII suspension racks without causing the bombs to detonate.**

50,000 SC-250 bombs to be achieved. An advantage was the experience gained during the testing phase of German air-dropped weapons that was able to be called upon during the development of this method. Disadvantages in terms of quality of the bomb casing had to be accepted, where it had only 40% of the penetration capability compared to pre-war standards. Instead of penetrating 50mm (2in) of steel, these now achieved only 20mm (0.8in).

The outbreak of war interrupted all the planning measures. In order to fill the gaps in supplies of the SC-250 *Minenbomben*, the Luftwaffe reverted to *Zementbomben* that had otherwise been used as practice bombs. In 1939, von Velsin-Zarweck, the works head of the Berginspektion Rüdersdorf, had proposed to the RLM that *Splitterbomben* be developed based on Swiss patents. In autumn 1939, this proposal was turned into reality. In order to manufacture the bomb casing, concrete had to be encased in a wire mesh and mixed with finely-chopped steel rubble. The explosive content weighed only 6kg (13.2lb). Between April and June 1940, 2,000 SBe-250 *Splitterbomben* were produced in Betonwerk 2 (Concrete Plant No 2) in Rüdersdorf and during the course of the year, a further 330,000 examples followed, including 500kg (1,102lb) bombs in this total. General (Ing.) Dipl.-Ing. Ernst Marquardt considered the *Splitterbetonbomben* as completely unacceptable. With regard to their effectiveness, they compared at best with that of a 50kg (110lb) bomb and their release in air-drops was only possible with a fuze no-delay setting. In high-level drops, the concrete crumbled, and cement and sand clouds covered the target. On the subject of the ceasing of production, various statements are available. One sure fact is that in the 'Luftwaffe Service Regulation No 4200, German Air-dropped Weapons, June 1943 Edition', the SBe-250 is already no longer mentioned.

Nothing more pointedly emphasizes the dearth of air-dropped weapons in the Luftwaffe than the fact that, following the end of the campaign against Poland, bombs captured there as well as those of Czech

origin were modified with supporting straps and German bomb suspension lugs. In this way, a complete Stuka-Geschwader was equipped with bombs sufficient for 50 sorties. This was repeated in 1940 with French bombs and in 1943 with Italian bombs.

As previously mentioned, the scarcity of explosives was a further bottleneck to increasing bomb production. Due to the unexpected tenfold increase, the Luftwaffe became the greatest user of high-explosives in the autumn of 1939. Production of Füllpulver 02 (Trinitrotoluol), the most-used military explosive, was closely related to the production of coke, and hence on coal

output which could not be increased to any desired figure. The expansion of plants for the multiple-step nitration of Toluol advanced at only a slow pace, being in the controlling hands of the Army. Equally affected was the manufacture of Amatol, another common explosive used, where a sufficient number of filling plants were not available. For these reasons, recourse had to be made to powder-type substitute explosives such as the Ammonals.

The Luftwaffe High Command now had to introduce introduce additional letters for the different types of bombs that were chiefly in use, for example, the SC-50, SC-250 and SC-500, and still later, the SD-500

Opposite page bottom and this page:
In their external shape and dimensions, the *Minenbomben* resembled the multi-purpose *Splitterbomben*. A precise identification of the bombs shown here as being the SC-250 was possible purely because of the yellow stripes on each of the tailfins. In the background is a Junkers Ju 87D which was used in the dive-bombing and ground-attack role. Note that the bombs in the lower photo are each fitted with the 'Jericho Trumpet' whistling organ-reed-type cardboard cylinders on the tailfins.

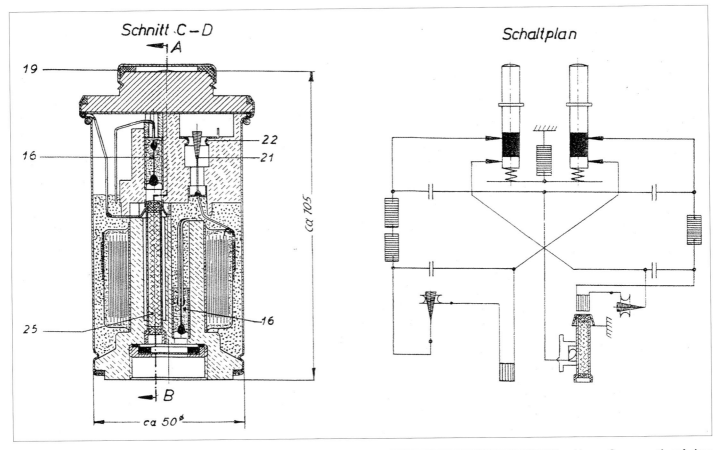

Schnitt ·C – D

Schaltplan

Above: **Cross-sectional view
and circuit diagram of the
El.AZ (55) electrical impact
fuze. The all-ways
percussion fuze was
suitable for being dropped
in high-level, low-level, and
dive-bombing attacks. Its
type of setting (from
instantaneous to delayed-
action) could be set during
the flight.**

Left: **Transporting
Minenbomben on a combat
airfield in the East. The
vehicle used to tow the
bomb transport sleds was
a captured tracked STZ-
NATI 1 TA of the Red Army.**

Above: **A Heinkel He 111H-16 carrying a *Minenbombe* on an external rack beneath the fuselage.**

Right and below: **For bombing-up crews on forward airfields on the Eastern Front, it meant heavy work. Seen here are some of them resting between SC-250 and SC-500 *Minenbomben*. Note the white stencilled markings on the bomb in the foreground.**

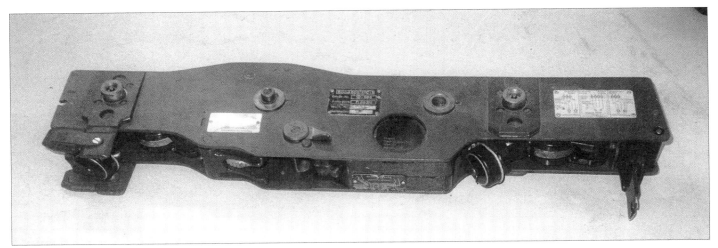

Opposite page:

Top: **An example of a bomb release clasp, the ETC-500/XII C-1 (Gerätenummer 18,586, Fl.-Nr. 50310). Manufacturer was the Sachsenwerke Licht und Kraft AG in Radeberg in Saxony, whose product bore the code 'edr'.**

Centre and bottom: **The 'Hercules II' (Geratenummer 20277, Fl-Nr. 66726) hydraulic transport and bomb loading dolly had a lifting range from 15cm (6in) to 200cm (78¾in) and was designed to carry a load weighing up to 2,500kg (5,512 lb). The example seen here was converted after the war into a vehicle lifting jack.**

This page:

Loading a *Minenbombe* with the transportable hydraulic LWC-500 lifting dolly. In ready-to-use condition, it weighed 315kg (694 lb).

because of the various production methods. These additional letters were applied as suffixes to the bomb designation, for example SC-250 K. Since manufacturing differences had an affect chiefly on the strength of the bomb casing, within a particular type of bomb category, a distinction in their Quality Grading (Güteklasse) resulted. The SC-250 existed in Güteklassen I, II and III. The aim was that at the Front, bombs of Güteklasse II would be mainly used, as they were adequately suitable for employment against the majority of targets.

Bombs of the other two quality grades were more seldom available and could only be used for special purposes. These were against shipping targets for use with fuzes having long delay-times and interference-hindering features, or when it was known beforehand that the bombs with safety-delay fuzes were to be dropped. A bomb of Güteklasse II possessed around 80%, and that of Güteklasse III, about 40% of the structural strength of a Güteklasse I bomb.

Characteristic for the development, test, and procurement of air-dropped weapons up to the year 1939 was their targeting against a European continental opponent. The results took shape in the form of diverse *Splitterbomben*, *Minenbomben* and *Mehrzweckbomben* becoming available by the outbreak of the war. From 1938, attention was concentrated on the development of armour-piercing and concrete-piercing bombs that would be dropped by dive-bombers against fixed fortifications having a wall thickness of 2m (6.56ft), against steel bridges and armour-plated warships. A specific orientation was against France as the possible opponent in war whose eastern border was protected by enormous defences: the Maginot Line. A further opponent envisaged by the Luftwaffe was Great Britain as a sea power possessing a numerical superiority in its naval fleet of armour-plated warships. In a future war whose contours were already sketched out at this time, it was faced with the task, together with the other armed forces branches – the Heer (Army) and the Kriegsmarine (Navy), of principally attacking resilient point tar-

gets. In such cases, high-level horizontal attacks with bombers would have little chances of success, since no bomber fleet anywhere in the world was capable of conducting precision-bombing. With the concept pursued in Germany of employing small groups of dive-bombers for destroying selected targets, it was hoped to achieve greater efficiency as opposed to the mass release of bombs in high-level attacks. This in itself correct concept was later overtaken by events. Expansion of the dive-bombing capability to almost all bombers led to technical difficulties and hindered the formation of strong and far-ranging level-bomber fleets.

The use of dive-bomber formations especially, required particularly high-grade air-dropped weapons capable of higher penetration. For solving this task, various paths of development were pursued, namely:

1. Rocket-powered projectiles which fired hollow-charge or armour-piercing high-explosive warheads. At the beginning of November 1939, the RLM Technisches Amt together with the HWA performed calculations for an armour-piercing shell of 500kg (1,102 lb) weight, of which 30kg (66 lb) consisted of the explosive with which a much higher impact velocity was expected. Tests with prototypes took place four months later in Tarnewitz.
2. Based on the Davis Principle, the Rheinmetall-Borsig AG in Düsseldorf designed a recoil-less 35cm (13¾in) aircraft cannon shell weighing 650kg (1,433 lb) –

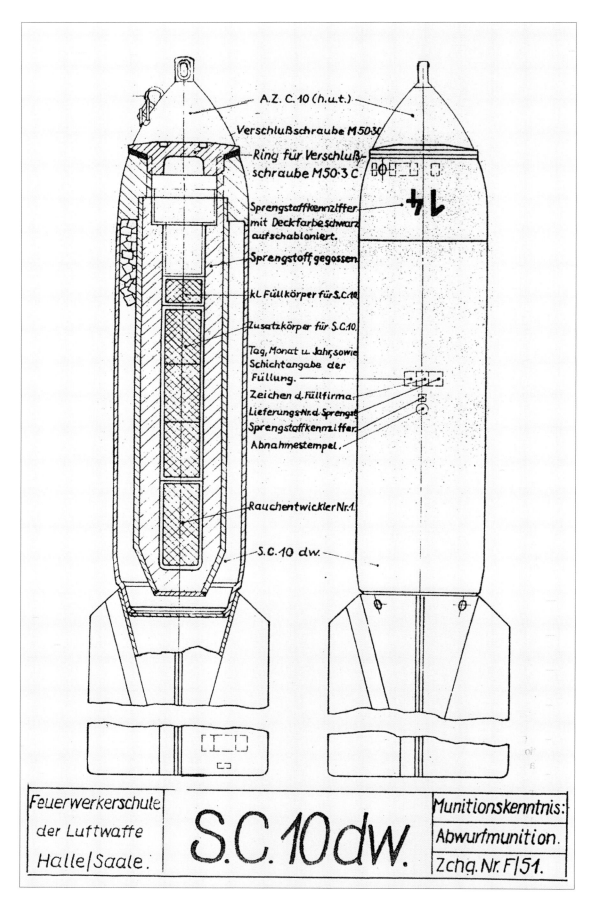

A.Z.C.10 (h.u.t.)

Verschlußschraube M50.3C

Ring für Verschluß-
schraube M50.3 C

Sprengstoffkennziffer
mit Deckfarbe schwarz
aufschabloniert.

Sprengstoff gegossen.

kl.Füllkörper für S.C.10.

Zusatzkörper für S.C.10.

Tag, Monat u. Jahr, sowie
Schichtangabe der
Füllung.

Zeichen d. Füllfirma.

Lieferungs-Nr. d. Sprengst

Sprengstoffkennziffer.

Abnahmestempel.

Rauchentwickler Nr.1.

S.C.10 dw.

Feuerwerkerschule der Luftwaffe Halle/Saale.	S.C.10dw.	Munitionskenntnis: Abwurfmunition. Zchg. Nr. F/51.

The SC-10 dw *Splitterbombe* consisted of a double-walled sheet-metal shell filled with concrete impregnated with steel splinters between the two layers, and an inner compartment containing 0.9kg (1.98 lb) of Fp 60/40 (Trotyl and Ammonal saltpetre) explosive mixture. It was equipped with the Zünder (3) impact fuze formerly designated C-10 (h.u.t.).

the Gerät 104. This forward-firing single-shot weapon at the moment of firing ejected a cartridge of equal weight in the opposite direction.

3. Development of bombs with hollow-charge warheads. It was only in 1942 that the Luftwaffe discontinued co-operation with the HWA. Its first independent developments were the SD-250 HL and SC-500 HL *Hohlladungsbomben*. The problem that surfaced with these was to maintain the correct distance from the target's armoured layer in order that the hollow-charge warhead would exert a maximum destructive effect. This could only be evaluated by the experimental detonation of the explosive charge, which revealed that the SC-500 HL penetrated armour-plated decks of 60mm (2.4in) thickness.

4. Shortly before the outbreak of war, in the design offices and experimental workshops of the Rheinmetall-Borsig AG in Düsseldorf, the development of the PC-500 and rocket-propelled PC-500 RS *Panzersprengbomben* was conducted, intended to be used by the Junkers Ju 88 dive-bombers. Both types of bombs were successfully jettisoned. In spite of this, the Luftwaffe High Command demanded an even larger *Panzer-sprengbombe* of over 1,000kg (2,205 lb) weight. Within a very short time, the PC-1400 thus made its appearance.

Initially, in spring 1940, only a few PC-500 and PC-1400 *Panzersprengbomben* as well as the rocket-propelled PC-500 RS were on hand for attacks against resilient point targets. These had been preceded in development by armour-piercing air-dropped bombs weighing 50kg (110 lb), 150kg (330 lb) and 250kg (551 lb) to which must be added Panzersprenggranate (armour-piercing high-explosive shells) of 15cm (6in), 21cm (8¼in), and 28cm (11in) calibre used by warships and combined with a multi-nozzle blackpowder rocket motor. This development ran under the codename of 'Ballastbeschleuniger' (Ballast Accelerator). In order to achieve higher impact velocities, even more powerful rocket motors were necessary, which were developed in great

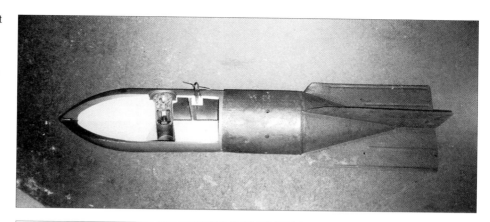

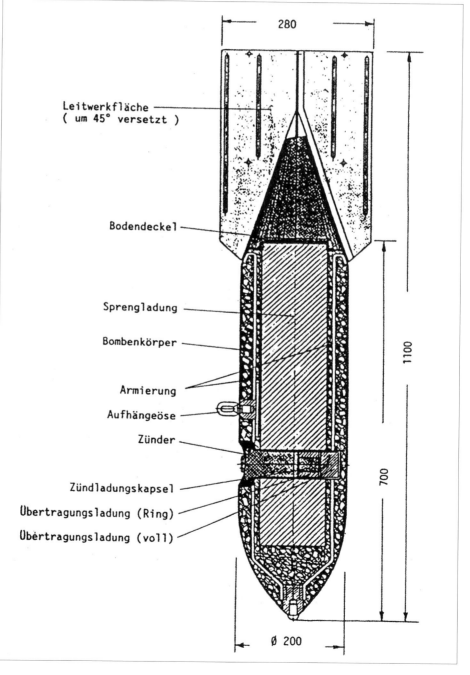

Leitwerkfläche
(um 45° versetzt)

Bodendeckel

Sprengladung

Bombenkörper

Armierung

Aufhängeöse

Zünder

Zündladungskapsel

Übertragungsladung (Ring)

Übertragungsladung (voll)

280

1100

700

Ø 200

Cutaway model of the SD-50 *Splitterbombe*. Fuzes that could be used in this bomb were the electrical impact fuze El.AZ (25) B and C, the El.AZ (55), and the super-quick eAZ (55)A fuze.

Sectional view of the SBe-50 *Betonsplitterbombe*. During the war, there were five other variants which differed principally in their tail surfaces and their method of attachment to the concrete-cased bomb.

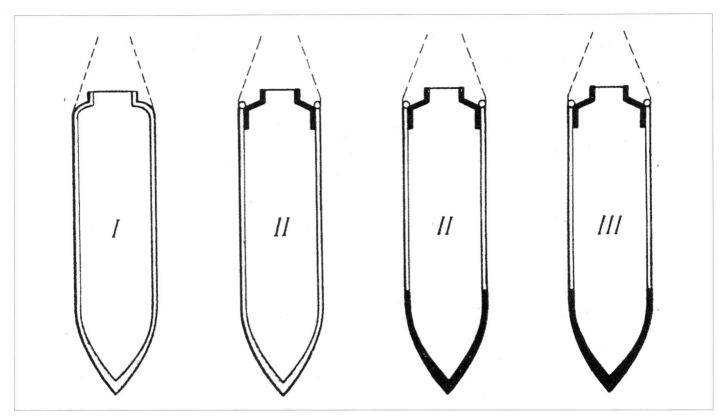

haste. These resulted in the first rocket-propelled armour-piercing bombs, the first test model being the PC-200 RS and the previously mentioned PC-500 RS that was also only built in small numbers and were followed by the first SC-1800 *Minenbomben*. During the fighting for the forts in the Lüttich (Liège) area of Belgium in May 1940, the Luftwaffe experimentally used a few of their large bombs. The PC-500 RS was unable to penetrate the fortification walls of several metres of thick concrete. Even the PC-1400 *Panzersprengbombe* and the SC-1800 *Minenbombe* achieved no material effectiveness on the structures lying 60m (200ft) below the surface. They only penetrated to a depth of 15m (50ft) into the earth, but when they detonated, produced earth tremors that had a noticeable morale effect on those beneath. A short while later, the crews of the two forts east of the Maas capitulated.

During the Western Campaign, the Luftwaffe achieved the greatest effects in May and June 1940 with the SC-250 and SC-500 *Minenbomben*. Both were most often used, especially in dive-bombing attacks. Besides the SC-50 and SD-50, SBe-50 *Splitterbomben* were used operationally above all against airfields. The latter bomb had such meagre success that production was temporarily halted as early as June 1940. *Brandbomben* were only dropped in small numbers, and partial success was registered in setting factory installations ablaze

with *Minenbomben*. Noticeable success too, was achieved with the Flam C-250 *Flammenbomben* dropped blindly against fortified installations. Their thin-walled bomb casings shattered on impact, the Benzin (petrol or gasoline) eked through cracks and crevices into the interior of the structures and were then set ablaze by bombs equipped with instant-detonation fuzes that were dropped immediately thereafter.

In the generous development programme for air-dropped weapons which the Generalluftzeugmeister laid before the Luftwaffe General Staff in 1940, a high rating was placed on the abovementioned *Panzersprengbomben* and *Minenbomben* weighing up to 1,800kg (3,968lb).

This latter weight corresponded to the maximum bombload of the twin-engined He 111H-4 bomber. With this aircraft model, there were no limitations regarding bomb dimensions. In the space originally designed for vertically-housed SC-250 *Minenbomben*, fuel tanks were installed to extend the aircraft's range and as a result, the bombs had to be carried beneath the fuselage, with consequent aerodynamic disadvantages.

In the Luftwaffe High Command, great hopes were placed on the effectiveness of the SC-1000 and SC-1800 *Minenbomben*. Fifty percent of their weight consisted of explosive (Fp 60/40 or 60/10 plus additives, or Trialen 105). At this time, the Luftwaffe

had no underwater torpedoes, whose lack was to have been somewhat compensated by using the larger-calibre bombs. The pressures produced by detonation of the bomb impacting directly beside the target was able to break the underwater protection of large warships which could be sunk by this means. Hermann Göring ordered the accelerated development of large-calibre air-dropped weapons for use against ship targets, this task being outlined in the so-called 'Y-Programme' and included all heavy bombs with weights greater than 500kg (1,102lb).

An alternative to attacks with *Minenbomben* was presented by the use of *Panzersprengbomben* which in direct hits, penetrated the warships' armour-plated decks, for which purpose the PC-1000 became available from 1940. At a minimum impact angle of 60°, they could penetrate 110mm (4.3in) of armoured steel. For detonating the 320kg (705lb) weight of high-explosive, the El.AZ (25) B and C electrical impact fuze and El.AZ (28)A and B fuze with additional accelerated ignition, or the El.AZ (35) fuze with an intermediate ignition component were used. In October 1941, the Luftwaffe Supply Office took on charge 357 PC-1400 bombs. The total quantity rose by 1st February 1942 to 6,011 bombs and 479 empty bomb casings. The originally very high manufacturing target set of 500 per month was reduced to 25 in August 1942 and then stopped thereafter. In its

Opposite page:

The Quality Classifications (Güteklasse I, II and III) as shown for the SC-250 *Minenbomben*. The Roman numerals stencilled on the bomb casing were 80mm (3.15in) high.

This page:

Bomb loading personnel preparing SC-250 *Minenbomben* before a sortie. Both photos show welded bomb casings of Güteklasse III. In 1940, the GL had issued a multi-part Luftwaffe Service Regulation, the L.DV 143 entitled 'Vorschrift für das Fertigmachen von Bomben' (Regulations for the Preparation of Bombs).

place came the PC-1600 *Panzersprengbombe*. At a minimum impact angle of 60°, it could penetrate 180mm (7.1in) of armoured steel. When used against battleships, it was dropped from heights between 4,000m (13,120ft) and 6,000m (19.685ft). When released in a dive, its penetration capability was reduced by 50%, added to the ricochet danger. Jettisoning this bomb from such heights presupposed the presence of high-grade bombing targets.

At the end of May the first large-scale operations with large-calibre armour-piercing and *Minenbomben* as well as with rocket-accelerated *Panzerdurchschlagsbomben* took place. The Luftwaffe attacks were aimed at British naval concentrations that lay at anchor in Suda Bay on the southern coast of the island of Crete, and represented the opening phase of the 'Mercury' paratroop landing operation whose goal was the occupation of the island. The warship contingent, consisting of two protected cruisers, four unprotected cruisers, a range of torpedo boats and some 20 supply ships, were able to be destroyed without any losses worth mentioning. The armour-piercing bombs penetrated the structures of the unprotected cruisers and detonated in their machine rooms or ammunition storage magazines. Enormous destruction was achieved and the ships were rendered unmanoeuvrable.

Significant experiences were gathered in the realm of air-dropped bombs in the 'Battle of Britain'. This had begun with the evacuation of British troops from Dunkirk at the end of May 1940 and reached its zenith with the issue of Hitler's War Directive No 17 bearing the document number OKW/WFA/L Nr. 33 210/40 g.Kdos. Chefs on 1st August 1940. The Reich Chancellor and C-in-C of the Armed Forces, Adolf Hitler, specified that the Luftwaffe should, by all the means at its disposal, destroy the Royal Air Force as soon as possible. The actual text in the Führer Directive was as follows:

Above: **Bomb loading personnel taking a break. The ZC-250 *Übungsbomben* (cement practice bombs) served as pillows. The version shown here had a self-destruction load of 75gm (2.65oz)) of high-explosive, detonated by the El.AZ (5) electrical impact fuze that was formerly designated as the AZ C(50).**

Below: **The crew of a Junkers Ju 88A-4 preparing for a sortie. In the foreground (right) are SC-50 and (left) SC-250 bombs equipped with the 'Jericho Trumpet' on the tailfins. Made of cardboard, these organ-type reeds made a loud whistling sound during the fall of the bombs.**

1. ...'The forefront of the attacks are to be directed against the flying units, their ground organisation and supplies installations; further, against the aviation armaments industry including the anti-aircraft weapons manufacturing industry.' *

* This was followed by five further paragraphs outlining other vital targets to be attacked. For the Directives numbered 1 to 75, licence-published by Karl Müller Verlag, 2nd Edition 1983, see Walter Hubatsch: Hitlers Weisungen für die Kriegsführung 1939-1945, Copyright Bernard & Graefe Verlag, Bonn – Translator.

Air superiority in terms of time or region were to be strived for. The battles that had up until then been concentrated on enemy warships and merchant vessels lost their significance at this time. Following the bombardment of Scapa Flow and Malta by the Luftwaffe using large-calibre *Panzer-sprengbomben*, the British became very respectful of these bombs and kept their warships outside the range of German bombers. A clear example of the intensification of the air war over Great Britain, due to the effectiveness of the British anti-aircraft defences, was the increasing adoption of night raids of varying intensity by the Luftwaffe. Towards the turn of 1940/41, air battles had subsided. Dominant at this point were 'nuisance' raids.

The great majority of the air-dropped bombs over Great Britain in the summer of 1940 consisted of SC-50, SC-250 and SC-500 *Minenbomben*. Due to the deficit in high-grade bombs, SC-250 bombs of Güteklasse III had to be dropped on resilient targets. The bombs often shattered in side impacts and ejected their explosive contents before the delayed-action electrical impact fuze could come into effect. For this reason, the aircrews demanded a thick-walled 250kg (551 lb) *Mehrzweckbombe* (multi-purpose bomb). The reduced quantity of explosive filling was taken into account in favour of greater structural strength and increased fragmentation damage. In 1940, the plant in Langendreer near Bochum which had been erected for mass-production of SC-250 *Minenbomben* of Güteklasse III, was completely converted within a few weeks to producing the newly-developed bomb designated SD-250. This bomb casing, produced in four variants, was filled with 80kg (176 lb) of Fp 60/40 or Amatol 39 explosive. Test-drops against semi-destroyed factory buildings of the Schneider-Werke in Harfleur near Le Havre indicated the suitability of the SD-250 bomb, especially for low-level attacks. They were released for use against industrial, railway, and rail terminal installations. The SD-500 that was likewise introduced a short time later, differed in its type of construction, for instance moulded or cast steel and steel-tube.

In September 1940, the Luftwaffe diverted its attacks away from military and armaments targets and concentrated more strongly on night attacks on area targets. As a rule, these involved domestic housing areas and less resilient buildings, which eased the existing lack of availability of Güteklasse I *Minenbomben*. In parallel, several of the newer large-calibre *Minenbomben* and *Panzersprengbomben* were dropped on targets in Great Britain. For land-based targets of relatively low structural sturdiness, the electrical impact fuzes of the *Panzersprengbomben* had too great a time-delay and penetrated too deeply into the ground after impact. The large SC-1000 and SC-1800 *Minenbomben* tended to shatter upon impact. When used against hardened targets, they were equipped with the El.AZ (28) B/6, B/2 or B/0.7 electrical impact fuzes which initiated detonation prior to the disintegration of the thin-walled bomb casings. The fuze setting was normally set for a delay of 0.12 seconds. If upon impact a particular braking force was exceeded, immediate detonation was made to occur via the special fuze contact which came into operation without the delay mechanism.

As a replacement for the *Großladungsbomben* that were still in course of development, the Luftwaffe dropped sea mines attached to parachutes over Great Britain,

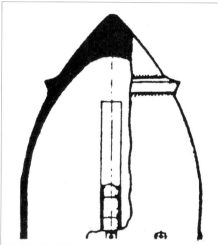

Top: **Close-up of the 'Jericho Trumpet' attached to each tailfin of an SC-50 bomb.**

Above: **If required, *Minenbomben* of Güteklasse I were also supplied with an annular nose ring.**

these being detonated by a built-in emergency fuze. Its effectiveness was overestimated by the bombing crews due to its bright explosive flame from the aluminium content of its Navy-used Schießwolle 18 high-explosive.

In late autumn 1940, a beginning was made to manufacture SB-2500 *Großladungsbomben*, each made up of three LBM sea mines in preparation for operational use. In Luftwaffe Service Regulation L.DV 4200 of June 1943, it is classified as a '*bomb with the greatest possible pressure-wave destructive effect when used against towns*

and industrial complexes.' There were two variants: one with a bomb casing made of cast aluminium and the other of welded sheet steel. The 'heaviest pressure-wave effect' referred to, was secured by the 2,000kg (4,409 lb) or alternatively 1,570kg (3,461 lb) filling of Fp 60/40. The bomb was equipped with electrical impact fuzes like the other large-calibre *Minenbomben*, in conjunction with the all-ways AZ (24) A mechanical impact fuze. A few hundred SB-2500 bombs were dropped on London in the winter of 1940/41, their pressure-wave destructive effects being most impressive.

Bombing raids on Great Britain almost came to a standstill with the commencement of Operation *Barbarossa* – the attack against the Soviet Union on 22nd June 1941. Projects for developing a concentrated-load bomb consisting of 4,000kg (8,818 lb) of explosive in the shape of the SA-4000 were given up in favour of the SB-1000 *Großladungsbombe* that could cause significantly more damage with its 735kg (1,620 lb) of explosive when four of these bombs were dropped instead of a single SA-4000 bomb.

In connection with the introduction of large-calibre bombs, it is of interest to relate the changes in the bomb loading capacities of the bomber aircraft themselves. The variability attained was the result of the diverse types of equipment fitted, which in turn were subdivided into a multiple of load-carrying conditions. For the He 111H-3, its bombload could consist of eight vertically-housed SC-250 bombs or 1,152 B-1 E or B-1.3 E *Brandbomben*. The He 111H-4 was only able to carry a single SC-1800 *Minenbombe* or one PC-1400 *Panzerspreng-*

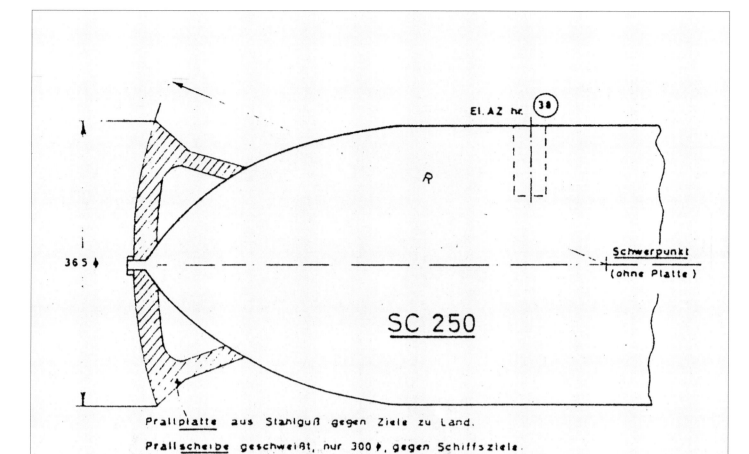

El. AZ. nr. (38)

R

365 ⌀

Schwerpunkt
(ohne Platte)

SC 250

Prallplatte aus Stahlguß gegen Ziele zu Land.

Prallscheibe geschweißt, nur 300 ⌀, gegen Schiffsziele.

M. 1 : 1000

ohne Scheibe

Bombenbahn

mit

10 m

20 m

Detonation nach 5 Sek

bombe. In their place, it was possible to carry two SC-1000 or four SC-500 *Minen-bomben.* All bombload variations envisaged mounting on external suspensions. This was equally true for the *Elektron-brandbomben* for which new jettison containers had first to be evolved. For the likewise twin-engined Ju 88A-4, in its Rüstzustand (equipment condition) A, there were eleven different loading possibilities. Eight of these belonged to the overload category and required special operation mission assignment orders (contained in Luftwaffe Service Regulation L.DV T. 2088A 4/Fl., Ju 88A-4 Bedienvorschrift-Fl. of July 1941).

Opposite page:

Similar in function to the nose annulus, the Prallscheibe (nose ricochet disc) seen here on the SC-250 bomb was used for attacks on shipping, enabling the bomb to travel underwater. These impact plates were made of cast steel for use against land targets, and were of welded construction when used against ship targets. The lower illustration shows how the bomb would otherwise ricochet on striking the water without the impact plate.

This page:

A line-up of SC-500 *Minenbomben* of Güteklasse III in a Luftwaffe bomb depot.

To turn now to the use of *Brandbomben.* During raids carried out in the summer of 1940, large numbers of B-1 E and B-1.3 E bombs were dropped without, however, clearly recognisable focal points. Based on tests conducted in the mid 1930s, it was known to the Luftwaffe with what bombload mixture, made up of *Spreng-* (high-explosive) and *Brand-* (incendiary) *bomben,* particularly widespread destruction of towns could be achieved. The proportion of the latter type of bomb was kept low, since the aim initially was not the destruction of towns, but the pinpointing of installations and buildings of the British military apparatus and those of the armaments industry. As related earlier, in areas consisting of domestic houses that had been cleared of junk in the topmost floors, it had been shown that the Electron incendiary bombs had had only a minor effect. In order to stimulate fires in such cases, a higher degree of penetration was necessary, so that the *Brandbomben* had to be made heavier. A longer combustion time could be achieved using a mixture of petrol mixed with crude oil, but did not bring about satisfactory results. A new method of solving this problem was demonstrated by the British themselves when the Royal Air Force dropped over domestic housing areas in the Rheinland, Inc 50 l (50-litre incendiary canisters) containing a mixture of congealed petrol and benzene with a

trace of phosphor. The containers were fuzeless; they shattered on impact and the splash of incendiary mixture was ignited on contact with the air by the phosphor.

In Germany, liquid incendiary bombs were now developed for release on specific targets on which destruction and damage through fire was to be expected. There now appeared the Brand C-50A having the ballistics and penetration power of the SC-50 J *Minenbombe* and the Brand C-250 that was comparable with the SC-250 K *Minenbombe* of Güteklasse III. The latter had an incendiary filling of 65kg (143 lb), to which phials of phosphorus formed part of the composition. Like the British incendiary containers, these ensured ignition of the sticky, easily inflammable incendiary filling. Prior to this stage, a 190gm (6.7oz) Granat-füllung 88 explosive charge shattered the bomb and distributed the mixture over an area of 30-40m (100-140ft) in diameter. Combustion time lay between 10 and 20 minutes. A disadvantage of the larger *Brandbomben* was their lower concentration in the target area and thus insufficient to create a firestorm. This could also not be basically altered by the low-level release of combined high-explosive incendiaries – the *Spreng-Brand* C-50 bombs. These contained 6kg (13.2 lb) of explosive and 30 Electron incendiary pellets of total weight 10.1kg (22.3 lb) that were ejected prior to the bomb's impact and disintegration. The

Streubrandbombe C-500 incendiary scatter bomb containing 1,200 incendiary pellets functioned in a similar manner. All of these complicated designs signify the efforts to combine the effects of high-explosives and incendiaries. Considerably simpler to evolve was the problem of simultaneously jettisoning Brand C-50 incendiary bombs and thick-walled SD-50 multi-purpose bombs. These brought the greatest success. Not only that, experience gained in the 'Battle of Britain' showed that the optimum size for *Brandbomben* lay between 4kg (8.8 lb) and 15kg (33 lb). Such incendiaries (the Brand 10) were developed until 1943.

We shall now turn our attention to a further sphere of *Abwurfmunition* – to the *Splitterbomben*. When the 'Battle of Britain' commenced in 1940, there were two such models available:

(1) The thick-walled SC-10 *Minenbombe* (also designated as the SD-10) that was equipped with the less reliable AZ (3) impact fuze (also known as the C-10 h.u.t. fuze) and enjoyed little recognition. This became modified into the SD-10 A *Splitterbombe*.

With an explosive content of 9%, the SC-10 produced 500 splinters and was effectively dropped primarily against unprotected targets as an anti-personnel bomb. Against personnel who had sought cover in a protective trench or enclosure and found themselves beneath the point of explosion of the bomb, the rapidly-spreading splinters that raced over the surface had no destructive effect.

An SC-500 *Minenbombe* of Güteklasse III with an additional annular ring at the extremity of the tailfins.

An example of captured weapons used by the Luftwaffe. Shown here is the 12F *Splitterbombe* taken over from Italian stocks in September 1943. When dropped from German air-dropped containers, these 12.2kg (26.9 lb) bombs were equipped with the super-quick eAZ (66)A impact fuze.

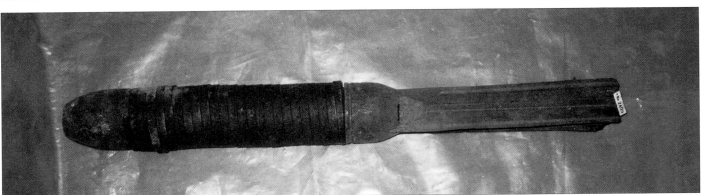

Right: **The PC-500 RS** *Panzerdurchschlags-bombe* **was a thick-walled torpedo-shaped bomb with a multiple-nozzle solid propellant propellant charge at the rear. It first made its appearance in 1940 in the Western Campaign and was produced in only small numbers.**

Below and bottom: **Successor to the PC-500 RS was the PC-1000 RS. In both these photos the tailfins are not attached. The rocket unit was ignited 2.7 seconds after release and had a burning time of 3 seconds.**

Of interest is a comparison of the minimum jettison heights that were given for the SC-10 in a 'secret' classified tabulation of 1st April 1940 (Supplement to Gen.z.b.V.b. Gen.Insp./L. Insp. 2 Nr. 640/40 geh. A). For a high-level attack it was 120m (394ft) when the Zünder (3) fuze was set without time-delay, and 20m (66ft) for low-level attack for the SC-10 without tailfins and the Zünder (3) fuze used with the safety ignition-delay setting. Concerning the problems existing with release at low level and the efficiency of the splinter effectiveness, details have already been provided in the foregoing text. This had the result that use of the SC-10 was temporarily abandoned.

(2) The SD-50 that had been introduced at the beginning of 1939 was termed a *Mehrzweckbombe* (multi-purpose bomb) but was in fact a *Splitterbombe*. Its weight of explosive (30% or 16kg = 35.2 lb), was insufficient to develop an adequately significant pressure-wave destructive effect to destroy buildings. The splinter effectiveness on the other hand, was sufficient to render troops, aircraft and trucks unusable. Minimum jettison height for the SD-50 and SBe-50 equipped with the El.AZ (55), (15) or (25) electrical impact fuzes without delayed-action was given as 500m (1,640ft) when dropped in a high-level attack. For the low-level case, and with the El.AZ (55)

set for a safety time-delay, the height was 20m (66ft). With the El.AZ (15) fuze set for an ignition time-delay, 50m (165ft) was the acceptable figure.

Both bombs did not represent a final solution. In many instances, the release height and compactness of the splinters over the target did not satisfy tactical requirements. Lack of availability, particularly of the SC-10, was known ever since the Spanish Civil War. Already at the beginning of 1939, a completely new design of *Splitterbombe* was under development: the SD-2. Work on this was prolonged because of a few setbacks suffered until 1940. Mass-production of it commenced in the autumn of that year. In a ready-to-drop state, it weighed 2kg (4.4 lb) and consisted of a bomb body made of steel or a special casting, the fuze, and the braking airscrews and their connecting shaft. Explosive used for filling was Fp 60/40 powder of 225gm (0.55 lb) weight. When the bomb shattered, there were on average 50 splinters each of 5gm weight and a further 200 splinters that were lighter. That the SD-2 from the tactical and technical aspect represented a completely new quality, was shown by details of possible jettison heights and a wide range of usage possibilities. To quote from the Luftwaffe Regulation L.DV D (Luft) 4001 'Schlachtfliegerbombe SD-2 (mit Zünder (41) Beschreibung und Wirkungsweise'

A size comparison with the PC-1400 *Panzersprengbombe*. It had a length of 2,836mm (111.65in) and diameter 562mm (22.13in). The PC-1400 was fabricated of alloy steel (Güteklasse I) of penetration capability 110mm (4.33in) armoured steel at a minimum impact angle of 60°, or else of non-alloyed steel or cast steel.

1941 covering the recognition and destruction of SD-2 'duds'.

The SD-2 bombs were at first jettisoned with the aid of Abwurfrüstsätze (air-drop equipment sets) vertical magazine Vemag 90 or Rost 24 racks. *Abwurfbehälter* (jettison containers) that had previously only been filled with *Elektronbrandbomben* gained in importance. They were able to accommodate 22 or 96 SD-2 bombs. The AB-70-5 *Abwurfbehälter* could be filled with 23 SD-2 Stör bombs. For attacking airborne targets during the war using SD-2 bombs set to explode in the air, the AB-250-2 and AB-250-3 air-dropped containers appeared that could hold 144 and 108 SD-2 bombs respectively.

The SDS-2 *Splitterbomben* were first used in action on 29th October 1940 in Operation *Opernball* (Opera Ball). A Rotte (pair) of Do 17s of 8./KG 76 on that day attacked parked twin-engined Bristol Blenheim bombers on the airfield at Wattisham. Oberst i.G. Boenicke, Chief of Staff in the Generalkommando I. Fliegerkorps, reported on 23rd November 1940 on the subject in document reference Abt. Ia Br.B.Nr. 5812/40 geh. that: *'The effectiveness of the SD-2 against aircraft is excellent. Due to the close succession of bombs dropped, the effectiveness is thorough ...'* It further continues: *'The capability of being able to jettison the SD-2 from low heights offers improved possibilities of surprise ... and considerably impedes answering-fire by the enemy defences.'*

In contrast to the previously available *Splitterbomben*, the SD-2 bomb was seen as a significantly progressive step – experiences that were initially only recognised one year later during the campaign in Russia. Of greater importance for the partially unsatisfactory effectiveness of air-dropped weapons, besides the false choice of bombs – *Mehrzweckbomben* or *Minenbomben* of Güteklasse I, II or III, were the fuzes used. The Chef des Ausbildungswesens (Chief of the Training Division) at the Office of the Reichsminister for Aviation and C-in-C of the Luftwaffe, announced in relation to this on 10th August 1940 in the document entitled Az. Nr. 2097/40 geh. (L.In.2 (D)): *'Evaluation of previous wartime experiences and on-the-spot determination of bomb effectiveness has time and again revealed the following mistakes:*

that is 'SD-2 Ground-attack Air-dropped Bomb with Fuze (41) Description and Effectiveness' of February 1941: *'The SD-2 can be released in a low-level attack from any desired height. It first detonates in every instance when the launching aircraft has distanced itself sufficiently far from the jettisoned bomb. The most useful release height lies between 5m (16ft 4⅞in) and and 50m (165ft). In order to achieve a detonation height of up to 10m (33ft) above the ground, using the fuze set at the 'time' setting, the release height must be between 25m (82ft) and 40m (131ft).'*

The *Splitterbombe* was used as an antipersonnel bomb against transport columns, unarmoured vehicles, aircraft, and other easily damageable targets. Used in conjunction with the mechanical long-duration

LZtZ (67) time fuze, the interference-resistant Störzünder (70)B equipped with a chemical time-delay from 4 to 30 hours, mixed with the mechanical Doppelzünder (41) or (41)A duplex fuze, the SD-2 also served to mine hinterland roadways and airfields. These numerous possibilities of application forced the British, particularly in the North African theatre of war, to pay considerable attention to 'mine-clearance'. Especially dangerous was the Störzünder (70) fuze which was primed by the rotation of the brake airscrews, but did not explode upon impact. Detonation was caused by the most minute vibration such as a passing vehicle or an aircraft taking-off. This sensitivity often endangered one's own troops, for which reason a Luftwaffe Service Regulation had to be issued in May

1. The bombs are dropped too low,
2. The wrong choice of fuze,
3. The wrong type of fuzing...'

In horizontal low-level drops in particular, up to 50% of the bombs did not explode, attributable to the low jettison altitude and the use of time-delay fuzes. Particular value was placed by the Chef des Ausbildungswesens on the timely acquisition of correct types of bombs and fuzes. A distinct advantage for the supply of German air-dropped bombs was that in the Luftwaffe munitions centres in the home war theatre, that they should be to some extent ready for use complete with fuzes when delivered to the frontline. In the air forces of other nations, this was not so. The bombs were dismembered into their component parts, delivered without fuzes and fuze installations, and had to be put together at the forward airfields. This required numerous ground personnel with corresponding specialist training which also cost time – a decisive factor in wartime. During the course of the 'Blitzkrieg' campaigns in Poland, Belgium, France and in the Balkans, the advantage of the electrical fuze was demonstrated for the speed and readiness of its use in frontline operations. Careless handling of the *Abwurfmunition* also played its part, as well as long months of storage in rain and snow.

The electrical fuzes were sensitive to moisture penetration, and in this connection, a British report on German unexploded bombs is of interest. During the course of large-scale bombing raids in the autumn of 1940, the proportion of unexploded bombs was less than 5%. This figure increased noticeably in the winter, and in spring 1941, rose to more than 10%.

Viewed as a whole, the electrical instantaneous and time-delay impact fuzes, like all German bomb fuzes, represented a very high state of technical development. Their handling and functional safety lay above those of the mechanical ignition system fuze, and had a low proportion of 'duds'. During the air war against Great Britain, a contest developed on the scientific and technical potential of both opponents in the realm of fuzes. This particularly involved the long delay-time *Störzünder* (harassment fuze) with which the effectiveness time of bombing attacks exceeding that of the raid itself could be extended. The aim here was to aggravate the opponent who

had to tie-up his manpower resources and reaction time to cope with the task of rendering them harmless.

The simplest form of *Störzünder* fuze was the electrical Sonderzünder (50) special fuze that was used in the SC-50 and SC-250 *Minenbomben* of Güteklasse I and II, the SC-500 of Güteklasse I, and all *Stachelbomben* (spike-nosed bombs). In the Luftwaffe Regulation for Abwurfmunition, Part 20 of October 1941, it was described as a 'highly-sensitive electrical fuze' which was certainly not activated in less than 120 seconds after bomb release. Its action time could be delayed for up to 48 hours and

even after four weeks, was still capable of functioning. The electrical *Sonderzünder* possessed no dismantling barrier, and could, for this reason, as long as sufficient quantities of the Zusatzzünder (40) auxiliary fuze were available, be installed together with it. This became activated upon impact of the bomb and in any attempt to remove the *Sonderzünder* fuze, led to detonation of the bomb.

The Storzünder (50) were also used in the so-called *Stachelbomben*. These comprised 50kg (110 lb) and 250kg (551 lb) *Minenbomben* fitted with a long cylindrical spike extension as shown in the accompa-

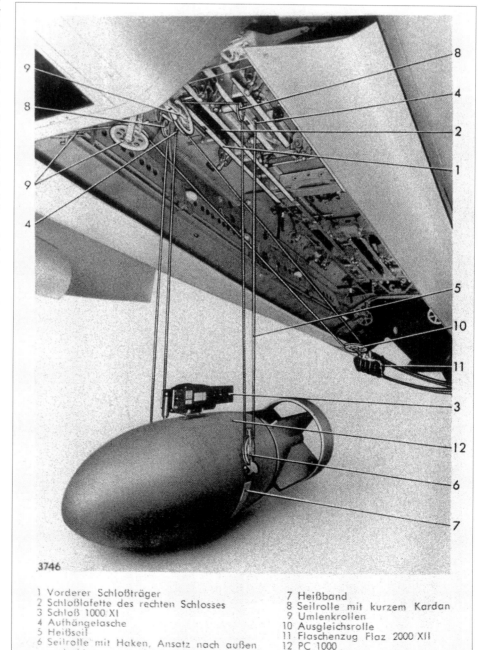

3746

1 Vorderer Schloßträger	7 Heißband
2 Schloßlafette des rechten Schlosses	8 Seilrolle mit kurzem Kardan
3 Schloß 1000 XI	9 Umlenkrollen
4 Aufhängelasche	10 Ausgleichsrolle
5 Heißseil	11 Flaschenzug Flaz 2000 XII
6 Seilrolle mit Haken, Ansatz nach außen gedreht	12 PC 1000

Loading a Dornier Do 217E-2 or E-4 with a PC-1000 *Panzersprengbombe,* the bomb itself retouched by the wartime censor. Suspension equipment consisted of the bomb Schloss 1000/XI and the Flaz 2000/XII Flaschenzug (pulley).

nying illustrations. The Luftwaffe dropped these along open stretches of railway track where they remained embedded by their spikes. Vibrations from passing trains led to their detonation. Attempts by de-fuzing detachments to neutralize the fuze condensers by means of a connecting plug, caused a short circuit that led equally to detonation of the bomb.

Another *Störzünder* was the 0.7kg (1.54lb) electrical-mechanical long delay LZtZ (17) time fuze. The delay time of the A model was from 2 to 72 hours, and that of the B model from 5 to 120 minutes, this fuze being used with the SC-250 *Minenbombe*. This harassment fuze could also be combined with the auxiliary Zusatzzünder (40) fuze, in order to hinder attempts at removal. The latter was often deliberately used in the course of the war with whatever happened to be the currently available fuzes in various types of bombs, so that when German unexploded bombs were discovered that possessed the facility to have these built-in, the possibility always had to be reckoned with that the Zusatzzünder (40) was present. Its successor was the Zusatzzünder (42) auxiliary fuze.

Opposite page:

Preparing to load a PC-1000 *Panzersprengbombe* mounted on a special transport dolly.

Hoisting a PC-1600 *Panzersprengbombe* from the special loading dolly. The PC-1600 replaced the PC-1400. Used against armoured targets, it was dropped from altitudes up to 6,000m (19,685ft). Clearly visible is the annular tail ring.

This page:

A line-up of PC-1400 *Panzersprengbomben* on a combat airfield, photographed in 1943.

The British government was very soon to realise what dangers threatened the armaments industry, communications vehicles and traffic routes, as well as the populace by the presence of German bombs fitted with the removal-harassment *Störzünder* fuzes. The British Prime Minister Winston Churchill commented after the war on this subject: *'In the middle of September, the enemy introduced a new, enormously destructive means of attack. Large numbers of time-bombs rained down on us over a wide perimeter and faced us with difficult problems. Long stretches of railways, important junctions which led to the entrances of factory complexes, airfields, and main roads had to be cordoned-off dozens of times and were thus made unusable, where we of course, needed them so badly. These bombs had to be dug out and exploded or rendered safe. This was an extraordinarily dangerous task, especially at the beginning, when all means and methods had to be tried out in a systematic series of decisive experiments.'*

Scientific committees developed all conceivable methods for disposing of unexploded bombs. In order to restrain the electro-mechanical Langzeitzünder (17) long-delay time fuze, a large electromagnet was placed on top of it. The electrical Sonderzünder (59) was brought into contact with a weakly-conductive fluid which discharged the condensers. On the German side again, everything was undertaken to cut-across these measures. The result was the non-explosive electrically primed chemical Langzeitzünder (17) fuze having an anti-dismantling and shatter-proof feature. The delay-time lay between 1 and 100 hours. It was divided into three delay-time groupings which could be achieved by the variable concentration strength of the acetone solvent. This chemical delay fuze was used in the SC-50, SC-250 and SC-500

Minenbomben of Güteklasse I. The British bomb disposal squads also found a way here of de-fuzing such bombs. They opened the fuze head and pumped out the air in order to rapidly fill the gap with compressed synthetic rubber. The already-begun dissolving process of the celluloid discs by the acetone was able to be stopped by the sub-cooling of the cylinder head. Countermeasures were soon found by the Germans. Precisely with this method of extraction, they caused detonation to take place for example, whereby the electrical spools which had been stimulated into activity by the superimposed electromagnets, closed the electrical circuit. A further possibility was offered by the use of bi-metallic springs which reconnected the electrical circuit that had been interrupted by the sub-cooling or heating and caused the bomb to detonate. It also became a practice to use various types of *Störzünder* in an air attack or, in opposition to the British knowledge of German 'orderliness', to use fuzes with confusing designations. Thus, the little-known electrical Zünder (60) fuze was stamped as 'Nummer (25)'. It was, however, made recognisable with the letter **Y** behind the manufacturer's code. A few hundred of these fuzes were dropped over Great Britain where this ruse was soon recognised and the effectiveness of such fuzes were nullified by freezing them to a temperature of −30°C.

Despite the fact that ways and means were being found for de-fuzing German bombs equipped with *Störzünder*, they still served their purpose, causing losses, disruption to public and economic life in Great Britain, and kept numerous specialists occupied. The efforts that had to be exercised for the task stood in no relation to that expended in the development of the fuzes themselves. So much for a little-known chapter of the 'Battle of Britain'.

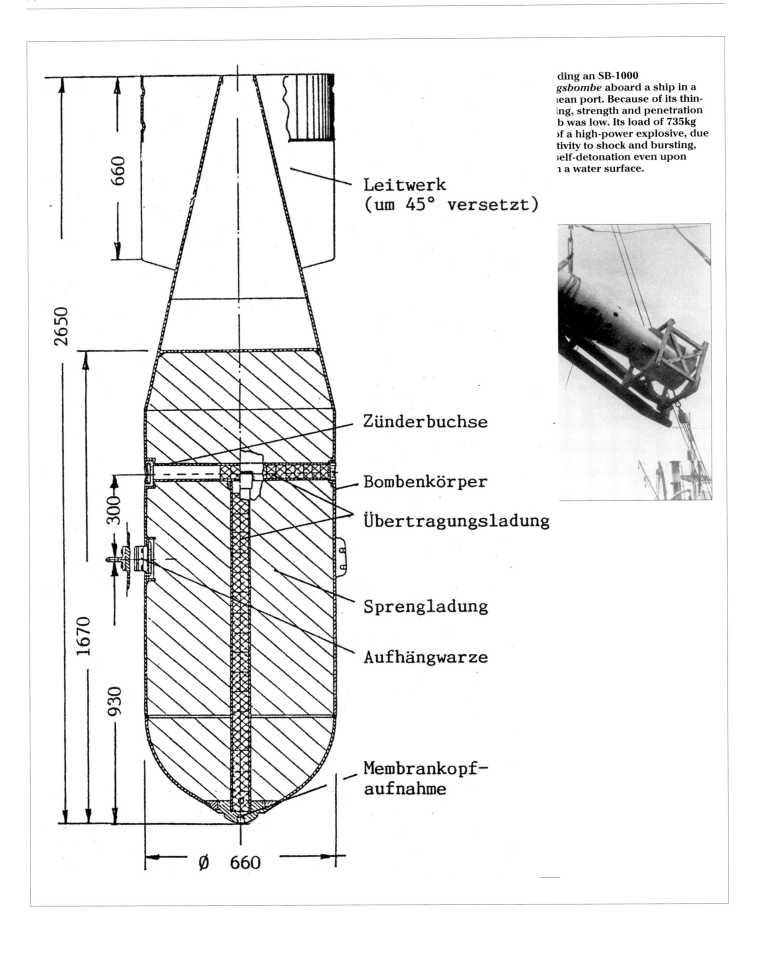

Leitwerk
(um 45° versetzt)

Zünderbuchse

Bombenkörper

Übertragungsladung

Sprengladung

Aufhängwarze

Membrankopf-
aufnahme

660

2650

300

1670

930

Ø   660

...ding an SB-1000
...gsbombe aboard a ship in a
...ean port. Because of its thin-
...ing, strength and penetration
...b was low. Its load of 735kg
...of a high-power explosive, due
...tivity to shock and bursting,
...self-detonation even upon
...n a water surface.

Above: **An SC-1000 *Minenbombe* on its transport cradle. Weighing a maximum of 1,050kg (2,315 lb), the bomb contained between 530kg (1,168 lb) and 590kg (1,30l lb) of explosive and was used with the El.AZ (25) B, El.AZ (28) B-2 with intermediate fuze setting III and El.AZ (55) fuzes. When filled with Trialen, the SC-1000 L was intended solely for use against shipping. [Note that this particular example bears the affectionate inscription 'Für W.C.' (for Winston Churchill) – Translator.]**

Below left: **Loading a Dornier Do 217E-2 or E-4 with an SC-1000 *Minenbombe* mounted on the TG-3 Transportgestell (transport cradle) of 140kg (309 lb) weight beneath the bomb. Hoist was the Flaz 2000/XII, the bomb supported on Schloss 1000/X**

Below right: **The Lotfe 7C-2 bombsight in the Dornier Do 217E-2.**

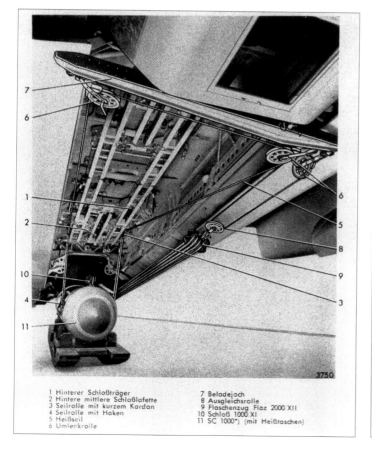

```
1 Hinterer Schloßträger        7 Beladejoch
2 Hintere mittlere Schloßlafette  8 Ausgleichsrolle
3 Seilrolle mit kurzem Kardan   9 Flaschenzug Flaz 2000 XII
4 Seilrolle mit Haken          10 Schloß 1000 XI
5 Heißseil                     11 SC 1000*) (mit Heißtaschen)
6 Umlenkrolle
```

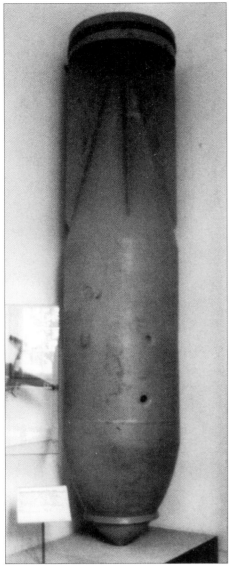

3747

1 Vorderer Schloßträger	7 Beladejoch
2 Heißrollenträger mit Seilrollen	8 Ausgleichsrolle
3 Heißseil	9 Flaschenzug Floz 2000 XII
4 Seilrolle mit Haken	10 Schloß 1000 XI
5 Heißband	11 SC 1700
6 Umlenkrollen	

Above left: **This multipurpose SD-1700** *Splitterbombe* seen on permanent display in the Militärhistorisches Museum in Dresden on the Königstein Festung was originally filled with 720kg (1,587 lb) of explosive.

Above: **Loading a multi-purpose SD-1700** *Splitterbombe* on a Dornier Do 217E-2 or E-4. It is resting on a Flaz 2000/XII and was hoisted up to the Schloss 1000/X.

Left: **The SC-1800** *Minenbombe* was used against building complexes and large merchant ships, causing extremely destructive effects by virtue of its pressure waves. It was filled with 1,000kg (2,205 lb) to 1,100kg (2,425 lb) of high-explosives, detonated by the El.AZ (25) B and C as also by the El.AZ (28) B/0.7 electrical impact fuze.

Above: **For loading training exercises the practice ZC-1800 *Zementbombe* was used, like this one found in Bavaria after 1945.**

Above right: **An SD-1700 bomb packed on its TG-4 transport cradle which had an empty weight of 215 kg (474 lb).**

Below: **A formation of Junkers Ju 87B-series Stukas of SKG 2 'Immelmann'.**

Above: **A bomb crew in process of loading an SC-250 *Minenbombe* beneath a Ju 87.**

Below: **Visible in this frontal view are the extension arms that lowered the bomb to clear the propeller disc when it was released by the Ju 87 in a dive.**

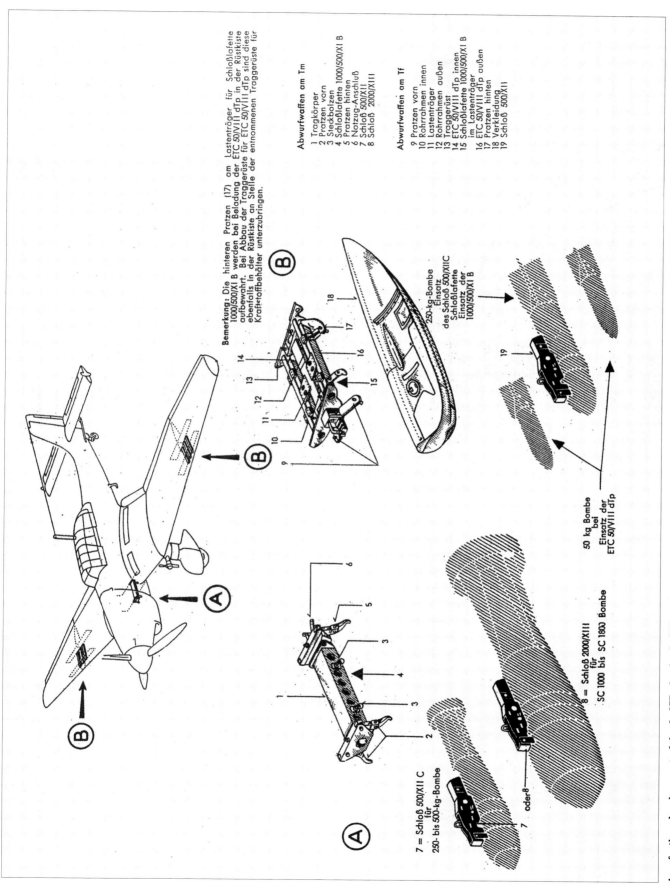

Bemerkung: Die hinteren Pratzen (17) am Lastenträger für Schloßlafette
1000/500/XI B werden bei Beladung der ETC 50/VIII dTp in der Rüstkiste
aufbewahrt. Bei Abbau der Traggerüste für ETC 50/VIII dTp sind diese
ebenfalls in der Rüstkiste an Stelle der entnommenen Traggerüste für
Kraftstoffbehälter unterzubringen.

Abwurfwaffen am Tm

1 Tragkörper
2 Pratzen vorn
3 Steckbolzen
4 Schloßlafette 1000/500/XI B
5 Pratzen hinten
6 Notzug-Anschluß
7 Schloß 500/XII
8 Schloß 2000/XIII

Abwurfwaffen am Tf

9 Pratzen vorn
10 Rohrrahmen innen
11 Lastenträger
12 Rohrrahmen außen
13 Traggerüst
14 ETC 50/VIII dTp innen
15 Schloßlafette 1000/500/XI B
   im Lastenträger
16 ETC 50/VIII dTp außen
17 Pratzen hinten
18 Verkleidung
19 Schloß 500/XII

250-kg-Bombe
Einsatz
des Schloß 500/XIIC
Schloßlafette
Einsatz der
1000/500/XI B

50 kg Bombe
bei
Einsatz der
ETC 50/VIII dTp

8 = Schloß 2000/XIII
für
SC 1000 bis SC 1800 Bombe

7 oder 8

7 = Schloß 500/XII C
für
250- bis 500-kg-Bombe

As a further development of the Ju 87B, the the Ju 87D-series appeared in 1940,
intended to carry bombloads up to 1,800kg (3,968 lb). Illustrated above are the various
Rüstsätze (field equipment sets) and possible bombloads for each of them.

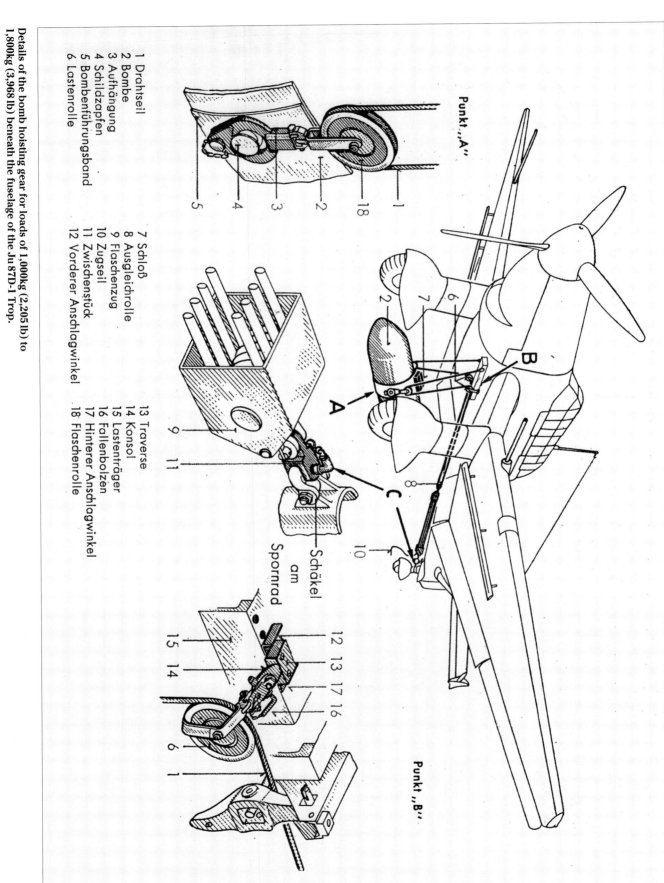

Details of the bomb hoisting gear for loads of 1,000kg (2,205 lb) to 1,800kg (3,968 lb) beneath the fuselage of the Ju 87D-1 Trop.

1 Drahtseil
2 Bombe
3 Aufhängung
4 Schildzapfen
5 Bombenführungsband
6 Lastenrolle

7 Schloß
8 Ausgleichrolle
9 Flaschenzug
10 Zugseil
11 Zwischenstück
12 Vorderer Anschlagwinkel

13 Traverse
14 Konsol
15 Lastenträger
16 Fallenbolzen
17 Hinterer Anschlagwinkel
18 Flaschenrolle

Punkt „A"

Punkt „B"

Schäkel am Spornrad

Towing a succession of 500kg (1,102 lb) bombs on a combat airfield in France. The eight coupled bomb transport trailers are being towed by a captured French Unic-Kegresse P-107 tracked vehicle which bore the Captured Equipment designation U-307(f).

The 500kg (1,102 lb) *Minenbomben* seen here were conveyed on combat airfields on the Transportkästen (crate) 500 or on a TG-1 Transportgestell (cradle).

During the air war against Great Britain, this type of bomb was mainly dropped against resilient industrial installations, and fitted with a nose ring, against shipping targets. It had become customary to decorate the bombs with caricatures and messages, as seen on this example.

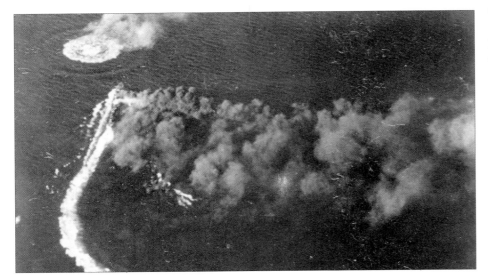

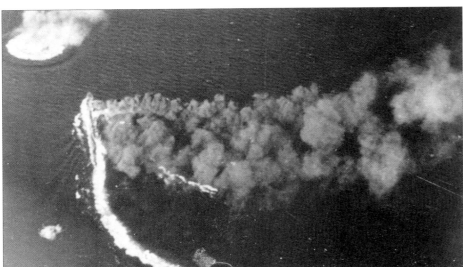

This page:

A sequence of photos showing the attack with 500kg (1,102 lb) *Minenbomben* on a warship that attempts by continually changing course to make itself a more difficult target for the bomber crew.

Opposite page:

The most important bomber during the 'Battle of Britain' was the He 111, pictured here after an emergency landing in France in the late summer of 1940.

Inside the empty bomb-bay of a Heinkel He 111.

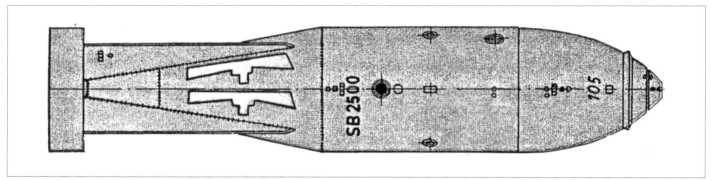

This page:

Top left: **The bomb-aimer's position in the He 111H. The sliding upholstery pads are in the closed position.**

Top right: **Here, the padding has been slid back to reveal the bombsight in the He 111H.**

Above: **There were two models of the SB-2500 *Großladungsbombe*. The SB-2500 (Al) was made in one piece out of cast aluminium or of welded aluminium sheet and held 1,950kg (4,300 lb) of explosive. The other variant was of thin sheet steel with a cast-steel warhead nose and held 1,710kg (3,770 lb) of explosive. So that the SB-2500 could be carried by the newer Do 217 and He 177 aircraft, an SC-2500 with reduced dimensions was brought out during the war. [The '105' indicates it was filled with Trialen 105 explosive – Translator]**

Opposite page:

The Junkers Ju 88 was capable of being fitted with various Rüstsätze (field equipment sets) for bombs. Beneath the starboard wing is an SC-1000 and beneath the port wing, an SC-500 *Minenbombe*.

The SC-1000 *Minenbombe* was used in conjunction with the Schloss 2000 or ETC-2000, PVC-1006 and (strengthened) ETC-500 attachment gear.

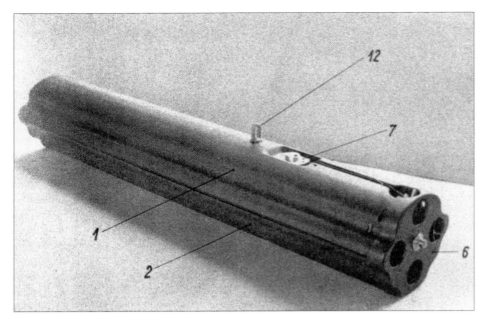

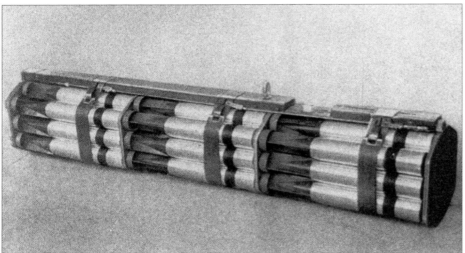

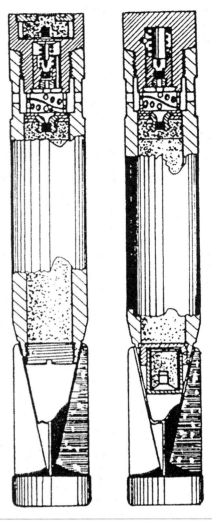

Above: **Sectional views of (left) the B-1 E and (right) the B-1 EZ *Brandbomben*.**

Top left: **The AB-36 *Abwürfbehälter* (air-dropped container) was used to house B-1 E incendiary bombs in the horizontal suspension mode. It could accommodate 36 B-1 E bombs and was jettisoned as a closed container which opened flight shortly after release and freed the bombs to fall individually. In Rüstzustand A (Equipment Condition A), a Ju 88 was able to carry a maximum of 28 AB-36 containers, whilst a Ju 87 could carry four AB-36 containers suspended from the ETC-50/VIII racks beneath the wings.**

Centre left and bottom left: **The AB-42 *Abwürfbehälter* was able to hold 42 x l kg (2.2 lb) and 1.3kg (2.87 lb) *Brandbomben* and could be suspended from all horizontal bomb fittings intended for 50kg (110 lb) *Minenbomben*. Made mainly of wood, it weighed 43.5kg (95.9 lb) or alternatively 59kg (130 lb), according to the bombs carried.**

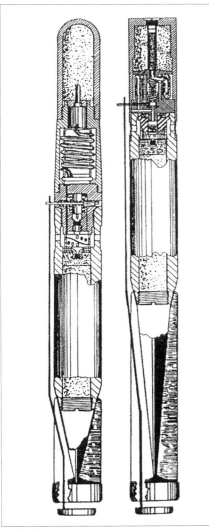

Left: **Sectional views of the B-2 E and B-2 EZ *Brandbomben*.** These Electron incendiaries of 2kg (4.4 lb) weight were ejected in clusters from the BSK-36 cluster container.

Right: **The SD-2, also known as the *Schlachtfliegerbombe* (Ground-attack bomb) consisted of:** a 2kg (4.4 lb) bomb equipped with the non-explosive mechanical Uhrwerkzünder (41) clockwork fuze – the SD-2 B had the Zünder (41) A fuze – the small Zündladung 34 fuze charge capsule of compressed synthetics, the two concave braking surfaces, and the connecting suspension cable. The brake mechanism first opened during the bomb's descent.

Below: **For conveying bombs to the bomber aircraft, various types of transport and loading dollies were used. In this scene, SC-50 bombs are being loaded aboard.**

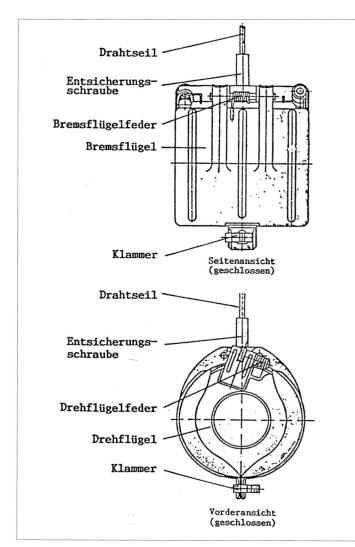

Drahtseil

Entsicherungs-
schraube

Bremsflügelfeder

Bremsflügel

Klammer

Seitenansicht
(geschlossen)

Drahtseil

Entsicherungs-
schraube

Drehflügelfeder

Drehflügel

Klammer

Vorderansicht
(geschlossen)

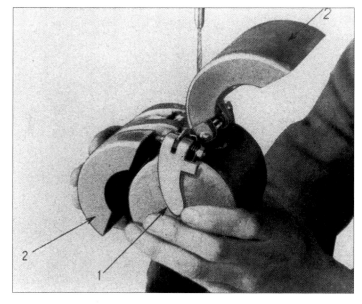

This page:

Above: **The two airbrake surfaces on the SD-2 shown being closed at left and open at right.**

Left: **Side and head-on sectional views of the SD-2 bomb.**

Below: **Junkers Ju 87 dive-bombers on a combat airfield. In the foreground are SC 500 *Minenbomben* on their transport sleds. The wooden crate weighed about 70kg (154 lb) and could be towed.**

Opposite page:

The electro-mechanical Langzeitzünder (17) long-delay time fuze came in versions A and B that differed in their time settings. Bombs that contained this fuze were denoted with the fuze time duration inscribed on them.

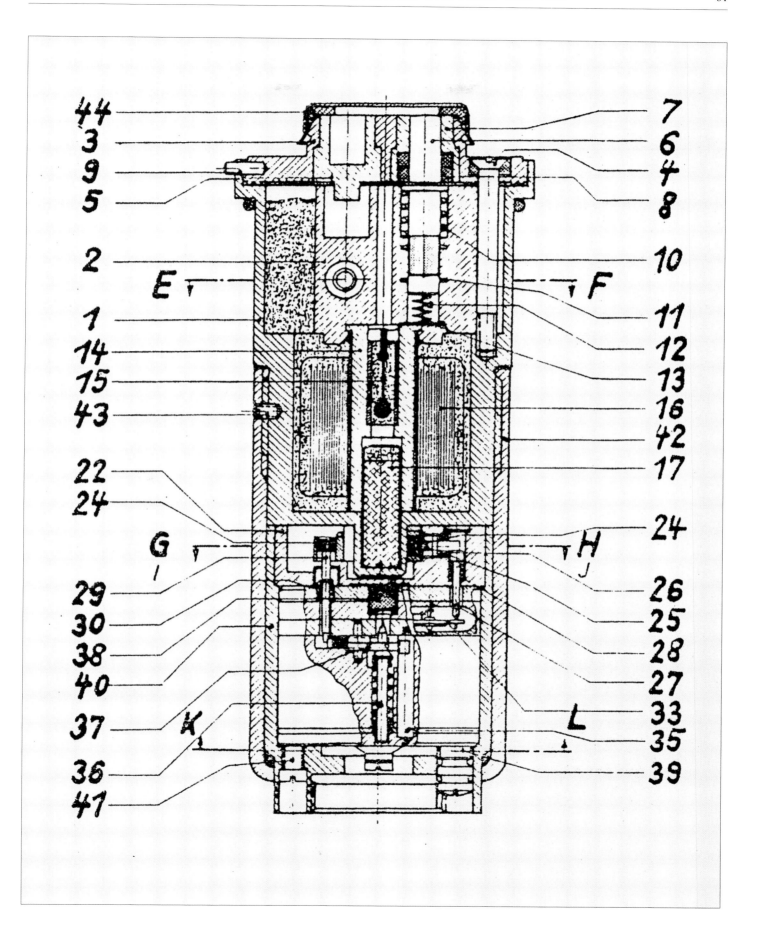

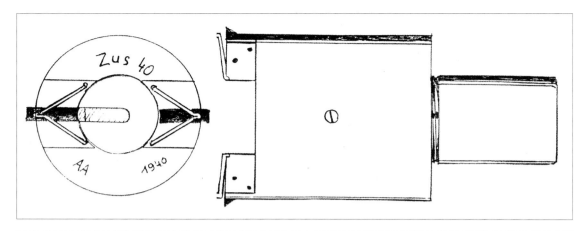

Left: **The Zusatzzünder (40) auxiliary fuze came as an anti-removal safety extension together with the Langzeitzünder (17) A or B in the SC-250 and SC-500 *Minenbomben*, both of Güteklasse I. It was primed on impact and shattered the bomb if any attempt was made to remove the time-delay fuze.**

Centre left: **The El.AZ (55) electrical impact fuze was primarily used in the SD bombs.**

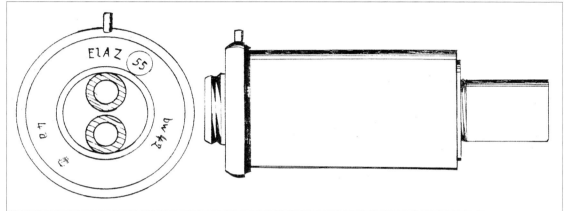

Below: **The Stabo SC-50, SC-70 and SC-250 Stachelbomben (spiked-nosed bombs) used principally for the destruction of roads, and railways. It was dropped at low-level at a minimum height of 100m (328ft) at 450km/h (280mph). In a glide, penetration shots could still be achieved from as low as 60m (198ft). The spike buried itself in the target preventing it from bouncing away.**

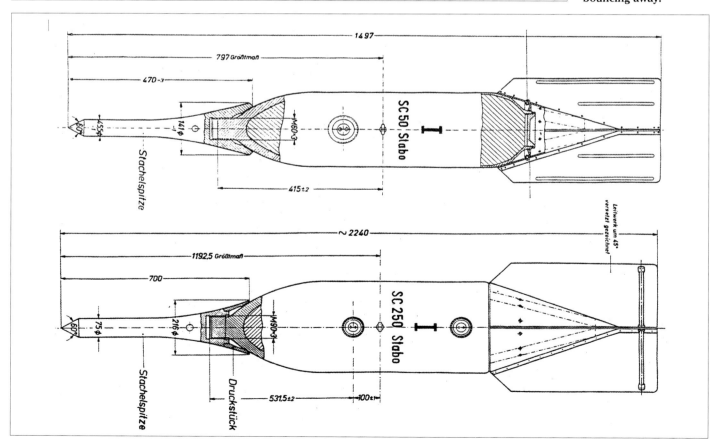

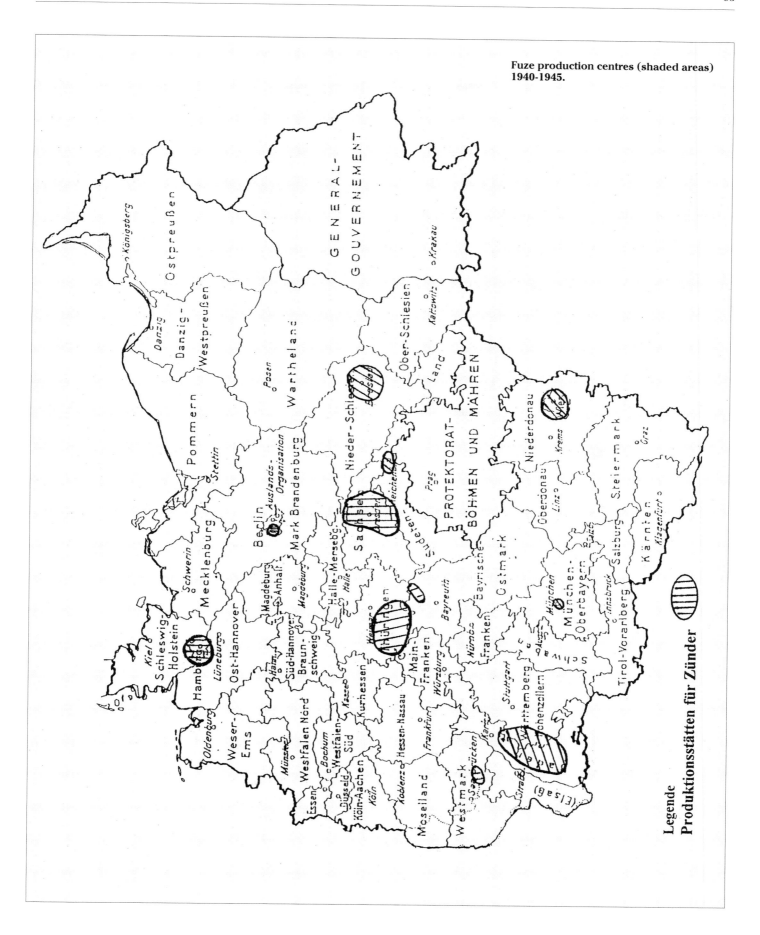

Fuze production centres (shaded areas) 1940-1945.

Explosives Used in Air-dropped Bombs, Mines, Torpedoes and Anti-Aircraft Shells

Generalluftzeugmeister document Az 74 g LC 7 Nr. 330/41 gKdos (IIF) of 4th March 1941.
Explosive fillings based on the tri-allocations in the 1941 2nd Quarter for all Flak and Air-dropped Munitions

Number	Bomb Type	Explosive Filling*
Bombs, Mines and Torpedoes		
1	SD-1	Fp 60/40
2	SC-50	Fp 50/50 or Amatol 39
3	SD-50	Fp 60/40 or Amatol 39
4	SC-250 J/A and L	Fp 60/40 or Amatol 39
5	SD-250	Fp 60/40 or Amatol 39
6	SC-500	Fp 50/50 or Amatol 30 or PH-Salz mixture
7	SD-500	Fp 60/40 or Amatol 39
8	PC-500	Fp 02 or Hexogen (phlegmatised)
9	SC-1000	Fp 60/40 + Amatol DJ, or Fp 50/40/10 (Al = 10%) + Amatol DJ
10	SD-1000	Fp 60/40 (phlegmatised)
11	PC-1000	Fp 02 or Hexogen (phlegmatised)
12	SD-1400	Fp 60/40 (phlegmatised)
13	SD-1700	Fp 60/40 Spitze (phlegmatised)
14	PC-1700	not yet determined
15	SC-1800	Trialen 105; exceptionally Fp 60/40 or Fp 50/40/10 (Al = 10%)
16	SC-2500	Trialen 105
17	BM-1000	SW 36
18	LM A	SW 36
19	LM B	SW 36
20	F5 Torpedo	SW 36
Anti-Aircraft Shells		
21	Flak 8.8cm	Fp 60/40
22	Flak 10.5cm	Fp 60/40
23	Flak 12.8cm	Fp 60/40

*For the chemical composition of the explosives mentioned, see Appendix 2 compiled by Translator.

A special fuze used for parachute-dropped flares, flash-bombs and chemical bombs was the electrical Zeitzünder (9) time fuze. It is shown here fitted with the screw-on Zundladung C/98 fuze charge. The delay time of 8 to 20 seconds could be set in flight.

A Messerschmitt Bf 110E equipped with the electrical ETC-500/IXb for 500kg (1,102 lb) bombs. Zerstörer aircraft so equipped were used as dive-bombers with the Revi 12d Reflexvisier (reflex gunsight). The electrical ZSK 244A ignition device served to prime the fuze in the bombs. Photo is of a Zerstörergeschwader 1 aircraft taken in 1941.

Use of Sprengbomben (High-explosive Bombs)

The following is a transcript of the original Luftwaffe table on the use of the individual types of Sprengbomben.

Supplement to Gen. z.B.V.b. Gen.Insp./L.Insp.2 Nr. 640/40 geh. (A) of 1st April 1940. Secret ! Use of Sprengbomben.

Target Type	Attack Method	Bomb Type	Fuze Type	Ignition	Minimum Altitude
Normal buildings up to two floors (houses)	high-level	SC-50	25 (15)	m.V	250m
		SD-50	55 (15, 25)	o.V	500m
Normal buildings of over three floors (industrial)	high-level	SC-250	25 (15)	m.V.	500m
		SC-500	25 (15)	m.V.	500m
As above, with below-ground installations (gas/water/electricity)	high-level	SC-50 II	25 (15)	V.Z.	1,000m
		SC-1000	55	V.Z.	1,000m
High-rise buildings, underground installations to 8m (26.3ft) depth	high-level	SC-500 II	25 (15)	V.Z.	2,000m
		SC-1000	55	V.Z.	2,000m
Concrete roofs up to 0.2m (8in) thick (MG-Stands)	high-level	SC-50 I	25 (15)	m.V.	1,000m
Concrete roofs up to 0.5m (20in) thick	high-level	SC-250 I	25 (15)	m.V.	1,000m
Concrete roofs up to 1.0m (3.28ft) thick	high-level & dive	SD-500	35 (28)A	m.V.	500m
Concrete roofs over 1.0m (3.28ft) thick	high-level & dive	SD-1000	35	m.V.	500m
Concrete roofs over 2m (6.56ft) thick; fixed fortifications	high-level & dive	SD-1400	35	m.V.	1,000m
Light and medium bridges	high-level	SC-50	25 (15)	o.V.	250m
		SC-250	25 (15)	o.V.	500m
Iron bridges	high-level	SD-1000	55	o.V.	1,000m
		SC-1800	55	o.V.	1,000m
Stone- and concrete bridges	high-level & dive	SD-500	35 (28)A	m.V.	1,000m
		PC-1000	35 (28)A	m.V.	1,000m
Open ammunition depots	high-level	SD-50	55 (15, 25)	o.V.	500m
		SC-50	25 (15)	o.V.	250m
		SC-250	25 (15)	o.V.	500m
Fixed railway installations; signals, overhead- and below-ground passages	high-level only	SC-50	25 (15)	m.V.	250m
		SD-50	55 (25, 15)	o.V.	500m
		SD-50	55 (15, 25)	o.V.	500m
		SC-250	25 (15)	m.V.	500m
		SC-500	25 (15)	m.V.	500m
High railway embankments	low-level	SC-500	25	V.Z.	20m
	90° to embankment	SC-500	15	V.Z	50m
		SC-1000	55	V.Z.	20m
		SC-1800	55	V.Z.	20m
Railway rolling stock, rail tracks, troop transports	high-level	SD-50	55 (15, 25)	o.V.	500m
		SBe-50	55 (15, 25)	o.V.	250m
		SBe-250	55 (15, 25)	o.V.	500m
	low-level	SD-50	55 (25)	V.Z.	20m
		SD-50	15	V.Z.	50m
Hangars/assembly halls, large airfield complexes	high-level only	SC-50	25 (15)	m.V.	250m
		SD-50	55 (15, 25)	o.V.	500m
		SC-250	25 (15)	m.V.	500m
Especially large hangars		SC-500	25	m.V.	500m
		SC-1000	28 B	m.V.	1,000m
Parked aircraft	high-level	SD-50	55 (15, 25)	o.V.	500m
		SBe-50	55 (15, 25)	o.V.	250m
Easily inflammable material		SBe-250	55 (15, 25)	o.V.	500m
	low-level	SD-50	55 (25)	V.Z.	20m
		SD-50	15	V.Z.	50m
Anti-personnel (living targets)	high-level	SC-10	3	o.V.	120m
	low-level	SC-10t	3	V.Z.	30m
Troop columns	high-level	Bü C-10	3	o.V.	120m
		SD-50	55 (15, 25)	o.V.	500m
		SBe-50	55 (15,25)	o.V.	250m
		SBe-250	55 (15,25)	o.V.	500m
	low-level	SD-50	55 (25)	V.Z.	20m
		SD-50	15	V.Z.	50m

1. Minimum altitude = highest point of the target, to be carefully noted in low-level attacks, for example hangar roofs. The minimum heights are safe jettison heights;
2. The most favourable bomb calibre is emphasised in each case; 3. This data sheet is not to be taken aboard an aircraft under any circumstances;
4. Bomb designation abbreviations used are as follows:

SC-10	10kg Splitterbombe (t = without tail surfaces)	SBe-250	250kg Splitterbombe of Beton (concrete) with scrap-iron inlay	SC-1700	1,700kg Minenbombe with increased structural penetration strength
Bü C-10	Bündel (cluster) of C-10 for jettison from Ju 87				
SC-50	50kg Minenbombe	SC-500	500kg Minenbombe	PC-1700	1,700kg Panzerdurchschlagsbombe
SD-50	50kg Minenbombe mit Splitter (splinter) effect	SD-500	500kg Panzersprengbombe	SC-1800	1,800kg Minenbombe
SBe-50	50kg Splitterbombe of Beton (concrete) with scrap-iron inlay	PC-500 RS	500kg Panzerdurchschlagsbombe	I and II	Güteklasse (Quality Classification or Grade) I and II
		SC 1000	1,000kg Minenbombe		
SC-250	250kg Minenbombe	PC-1000	1,000kg Panzersprengbombe	Fuze Type	m.V. = with delay-time
SD-250	250kg Minenbombe with Splitter (splinter) effect	PC-1000 RS	1,000kg Panzerdurchschlagsbombe		o.V. = without delay-time
		PC-1400	1,400kg Panzersprengbombe		V.Z. = safety delay-time.

Chapter Nine

The Focal Point in the East: Air-Dropped Weapons in the War Years 1941-1945

In Hitler's War Directive No 21, document OKW/WFSt/Abt. L (I) Nr. 33 408/40 g.K.Chefs dated 18th December 1940 for Operation *Barbarossa* – the attack on the Soviet Union, it was required of the Wehrmacht (Armed Forces) that: *'The German Wehrmacht must be prepared, even before the cessation of the war against England, to suppress Soviet Russia in a rapid military campaign.*

'For this purpose, the Army will engage all available forces with the limitation that the occupied territories shall be secured against surprises.

'The Luftwaffe will have the task of making available such strong forces in support of the Army for the Eastern Campaign that a rapid discharge of the final thrust in ground operations can be reckoned with, and that damage to the East German region due to enemy air attacks will be kept as low as possible.'

On the subject of the operational conduct of the Luftwaffe, the directive stated in

Section III B.) Luftwaffe: *'Its task shall be to exercise its power on the Russian Air Force as much as possible to paralyse and destroy it, as well as to provide adequate support for the Army at their focal points; specifically, the concentration of Army Group Centre and on the main focal area of Army Group South. According to their importance, the Russian railways are to be interrupted or alternatively, their most important objects within reach (river crossings!) are to be taken possession of through the audacious use of paratroops and airborne landing troops.*

'In order to be able to concentrate all forces against the enemy Air Force and provide immediate support to the Army, the armaments industry shall not be attacked during the main offensive. Only after the conclusion of advancement operations shall such types of attack, primarily in the Ural region, be considered.'

The tasks assigned to the Luftwaffe mirrors its previous experiences in the conduct

of air warfare. The most important objective at the beginning of an indigenous offensive operation was the acquisition of air superiority. It was dependent upon the bomber forces performing surprise attacks on the enemy's air warfare potential and destroying it on the ground. Only when air superiority had first been achieved in this way, would it then become possible to employ multi-engined bombers for the close support of the Army.

For Operation *Barbarossa* there were in all four Luftflotten (Air Fleets) with 3,055

This page below: **In the early morning hours of 22nd June 1941, the Luftwaffe participated with all available forces in the attack against the Soviet Union. [Seen here is a damaged Tupolev ANT 6 (TB-3) four-engined bomber – Translator]**

Opposite page: **The initial heavy onslaughts were aimed at aircraft of the Red Air Force...**

...after which road and rail networks were attacked...

bombers, reconnaissance, transport, and communications aircraft made available. In this connection, however, Luftflotte 5 was only partially involved with its complement of aircraft. Of the total, 865 were bombers, 341 dive-bombers and 87 Zerstörer (twin-engined heavy fighters). On 22nd June 1941, starting at 0315 hours, groups of 4 to 15 bombers flying at low level attacked the Red Army forward airfields in the Western Special Military Region. Generaloberst Franz Halder, Chief of the Army General Staff, on 22nd June already noted in the early afternoon in his War Diary that: '*Luftwaffe reports 800 enemy aircraft destroyed. ... Own losses up to now ten aircraft.*' Two days later, he wrote: '*The enemy Air Force, after very heavy losses (supposedly 2,000) has been completely thrashed.*'

In fact, on the very first day alone, the Red Air Force lost 47% of their aircraft on hand in the Western Special Military Region. The total losses involved 1,200 aircraft, of which almost 900 were destroyed on the ground. A high proportion of the Luftwaffe's success was attributable to the air-dropped SD-2 *Splitterbomben* – also called the SD-2 *Schlachtflieger-bombe* (ground-attack bomb) that had been dropped en masse on this day. In preparing for mission capability and upon the directive of the

...and finally, the tanks and tracked vehicle units were destroyed.

A sequence of various steps in the manufacture of SC-250 *Minenbomben* of Quality Class I (Güteklasse I). After being extruded, the raw bomb casings were furnace-cooled in measured stages.

The wall thickness of the bomb body was measured again after the rear end had been formed.

Uneven areas were then smoothed out.

Luftwaffe High Command, the aircraft of several Bombengeschwader equipped their Heinkel He 111H-3 bombers with exchangeable fittings for this type of air-dropped bomb.

Characteristic of further development in the sphere of air-dropped weapons were the tactical and technical requirements up to 1942 that had been contained in the GL Procurement Programme dating from 1940. At this time, however, another development trend became noticeable that had already appeared during the 'Battle of Britain' and which by means of a flexible reaction to the demands of the flying units was of significance. As an example in the foregoing chapter from page [103] onwards, the SB-2500 *Großladungsbombe* should be mentioned. As a general rule, the Luftwaffe High Command approved such proposals retroactively. Long-term effective concepts and plans for air-dropped weapons no longer existed. This was understandable on the one hand since the Luftwaffe had available a wide-ranging arsenal of effective weapons that had already been tested in wartime as well as having the corresponding devices and equipment. They had, nevertheless, to respond to newer demands. These were the result of changing operational conditions which forced the bombers within their tactical and operational scope that were strongly influenced by armament and economic factors as also the overall deteriorating war situation from 1942/43. Echeloned timewise, this resulted in new tactical and technical demands on the Luftwaffe's air-dropped weapons which for the period up to the end of 1944 were consolidated and could be portrayed as follows:

1. The development of simple, small-calibre *Splitterbomben* for anti-personnel use. From the beginning of 1942, the need for these increased continuously during the war in the North African theatre. The availability of such *Abwurfmunition*, however, became more and more a demand by frontline flying formations on the Eastern Front that were confronted with the task of supporting the Army to defend themselves from the massive attacks by Russian infantry.

2. Almost simultaneously, the development of small, armour-piercing bombs became necessary to combat tanks from the air.

3. Further development of armour-piercing bombs to destroy warships whose appearance was to be expected during the course of Allied amphibious landing operations against 'Fortress Europe'.

4. Due to the low impact accuracy of only 6% obtained with classical bomb releases on ships from altitudes of 6,000-7,000m (19,685-22,965ft), the RLM asked for a guided *Panzer-sprengbombe* in 1939 – a development that became of increasing significance in 1942.

5. The development of *Schrapnellbomben* for defence against enemy bombers.

Air-dropped weapons that were already available were further developed and adapted, armament and economic necessities being taken into consideration. Already in 1941, the manufacture of a monthly average of 51,959 tonnes of bombs absorbed 50% of the Luftwaffe's iron and steel allocation. For the year 1942, a monthly requirement of 56,770 tonnes was required. Of the planned 9,500 tonnes of explosives, the lion's share of 7,726 tonnes was intended for bombs. Bomb fuzes were ordered in batches of between 10,000 and 120,000 examples and in 1942, had cost between Reichsmarks RM 5.27 each for the super-quick eAZ (55) fuze, RM 11.37 each for the electro-mechanical ZtZ (17) long-delay time fuze, and RM 16.80 for the El.AZ (25) A and C electrical impact fuze, as extracted from the H Mende Radio & Co firm's Dresden Industrial Production Centre records.

Air-dropped bomb consumption rose steadily, and during the war on the Eastern Front, attained new peak figures in summer 1941. Between 22nd June 1941 and 30th November 1941, the following are the monthly average consumption figures:

288,783	2kg Splitterbomben (SD-2)
190,368	50kg Minen- and Mehrzweckbomben
31,813	250kg Minen- and Mehrzweckbomben
8,100	500kg Mehrzweckbomben
774	1,000kg Panzersprengbomben
56	1,400kg and 1,600kg Panzersprengbomben

After the tail surfaces had been attached to the bomb body, the overall dimensions were checked once more.

The completed bombs were then sprayed on their way to the drying furnaces. Colour originally applied was dark grey. Bombs intended for the tropics were coated bright blue (initial delivery was in an aluminium tone). From July 1942, beige-grey (RAL 2027) was applied to all bombs.

47	1,800kg Minenbomben
9	2,500kg Großladungsbomben
479,679	Brandbomben
1,250	Flammenbomben

In the winter of 1941/42 and in the following spring, consumption was considerably less. For the period 1st December 1941 to 30th April 1942, the following figures were able to be established:

34,200	2kg Splitterbomben (SD-2)
96,26	50kg Minen- and Mehrzweckbomben
22,160	250kg Minen- and Mehrzweckbomben
5,797	500kg Minenbomben
602	1,000kg Panzersprengbomben
14	1,400kg and 1,600kg Panzersprengbomben
54	1,800kg Minenbomben
0	2,500kg Minenbomben
27,840	Brandbomben
44	Flammenbomben

The low consumption in the winter and spring months enabled a stockpile of air-dropped weapons for the expected battles in the summer of 1942 to be amassed. At the beginning of 1942, during the course of an advisory meeting with Albert Speer, the Reichsminister for Armaments and War Production, Adolf Hitler expressed his satisfaction over bomb production figures by the armaments industry. From Albert Speer's records concerning the meetings on 28th and 29th June 1942, it is mentioned that this planning level would be maintained despite the high stocks of completed bombs. The continual supply of bombs to the flying units could thus be upheld, but this also caused increasing problems. Material shortages, raw materials and workforce deficiencies promoted rivalry between the three branches of the armed forces amongst one another as well as with the Waffen-SS. The Luftwaffe in particular, campaigned against the planning and dis-

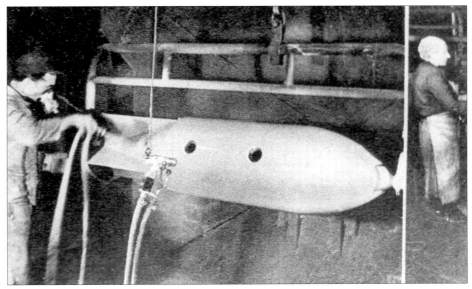

tribution system steered by committees and production rings. They did not have the desired influence on the regulation of the entire war economy, nor on the quantities of bombs produced either. For this purpose, there existed in the RfRuK, Hauptausschüsse (Main Committees) for Munition (Munitions) as well as for Pulver (Powder) and Sprengstoff (Explosives) and the Sonderausschüsse (Special Committees) for Bomben (Bombs), Bombenzünder (Bomb Fuzes) and Sprengstoff (Explosives). Edmund Geilenberg of the Reichswerke Hermann Göring, who led the Hauptausschüss Munition, had exerted his efforts massively on the side of the Luftwaffe and was responsible for the high level of bomb production.

The Luftwaffe retained the new and further development of Abwurfmunition as well as the necessary fittings and equipment for them. The Bombenreferat (LC 7) specialists received, in view of tactical and operational uncertainties pertaining to the further employment of bomber aircraft, a close feeling for the aircrews. On the one hand, the goal was to be able to conduct a rapid evaluation of operational experiences, and on the other, to timely ascertain the needs of the field. The sinking significance of level bombers and dive-bombers was recognised. In the Air Armament Programme 223/1 that was valid from 15th April 1944, it was intended that production of single-engined fighters would for the first time exceed and rapidly increase over that of bomber aircraft. A significant proportion of this was to have been achieved by the single-engined Focke-Wulf Fw 190 fighter which, initially in the A-2/U3 variant, was used in the ground-attack role and would generally replace the Junkers Ju 87 dive-bomber and the Henschel Hs 129 ground-attack aircraft. From 1942 onwards, the 'Stuka-tactic' found itself in a dilemma. Twin- and four-engined dive-bombers, from the tactical and technical aspect, had proved to have been a mistaken concept.

General (Ing.) Dipl.-Ing. Ernst Marquardt of the RLM Technisches Amt had estimated that: *'The most important bomb calibres in the Eastern campaign were the trusty SD-50 and SC-250 bombs, and only on industrial installations were the SC-500 bombs necessary; all other larger calibres were a waste.*

Top and centre left: **Scenes in the manufacture of the SC-250 *Minenbomben* of Güteklasse I. With this model, the cylindrical body was welded to the moulded nose cone and tail end.**

Bottom left: **PC-1400 *Panzersprengbomben* seen immediately before delivery, being fastened for transport on the TG-3 Transportgestelle (transport chassis).**

The Flammbomben that are still used effectively in the West had no particular success on the morale of the Russian soldiers; Brandbomben found little application…'

Wooden buildings, as commonly found in Russia, also burned when hit by *Sprengbomben*. When *Minenbomben* fitted with *Störzünder* (harassment fuzes) were jettisoned along traffic routes, the danger existed that the movements of one's own Army units were hindered. This also limited the use of the SD-2 *Splitterbomben* for mining purposes. Of interest in this connection is a communication dated 7th July 1941 directed to the Armeeoberkommando 2 (Army High Command Detachment 2). In this, mention was made of the *Stachel* (spike-nosed) SC-250 *Minenbomben* dropped on railway embankments east of Borisov, whose highly-sensitive electrical *Sonderzünder* (special fuzes) remained effective for up to 12 months. The troops should be warned that removing the danger was only possible by gunfire.

A Junkers Ju 87B 'Stuka' dive-bomber equipped with a siren and multi-purpose SD-50 *Splitterbomben* beneath the wings. Later variants of this aircraft had an M-2 Rüstsatz (field equipment set) beneath each wing for 2 or 4 SD-70 bombs or one 250kg (551 lb) bomb. Suspension gear for the SD-50 and SD-70 bombs were the ETC-50/VIIIe Tp.

Monthly Average Bomb Consumption 1941-1944

Bomb Weight	Bomb Type	Monthly Average in Period		
		1941/42	1942/43	1943/44
50 and 70kg	Minen- & Splitterbomben	144,684	193,824	175,523
250kg	Minen- & Splitterbomben	27,127	47,124	32,720
500kg	Minen- & Splitterbomben	6,972	7,923	5,219
500kg	Panzersprengbomben	10	5	2
1,000kg	Minenbomben	568	736	528
1,000kg	Panzersprengbomben	122	248	91
>1,000kg	Minenbomben [over 1,000kg]	65	87	69
>1,000kg	Panzersprengbomben	24	42	51
1 to 15kg	Splitterbomben in AB 70 container	13,761		
1 to 15kg	Splitterbomben in AB 250 container	3,578		
1 to 15kg	Splitterbomben in AB 500 container	1,610		
1 and 1.3kg	Brandbomben	260,412	261,270	406,080
2 to 10kg	Brandbomben	2,400	8.600	
50 to 500kg	Brandbomben	980	2,237	4,347
-	Lufttorpedos (air-dropped torpedoes)	35	104	146
-	Minen (air-dropped mines)	1,269	430	399

In the spring of 1942, the Red Army attacked on the southern sector of the Eastern Front. Typical for its method of combat were mass attacks by infantry supported by tanks, which made it necessary for the Luftwaffe to lend support to the Army. Suddenly, there was a great need for *Splitterbomben*. The SD-10 *Splitterbombe* that had formerly been underestimated gained prominent attention, but its production had unfortunately been already terminated. Stocks still available were converted

with the AZ (3) alias AZ C-10 (h.u.t) impact fuze into the SD-10 A. These were fitted with an intermediate component and the superfast eAZ (66) fuze. Its method of functioning was based on the principle of magnetic ignition.

A resumption of SD-10 production out of cast steel was no longer possible. Production capacity that had formerly been utilised for for this purpose had been meanwhile converted for the manufacture of artillery ammunition. In addition, there was

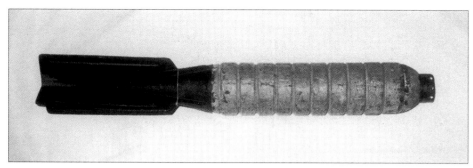

An SD-10C *Splitterbombe*. Characteristic of this bomb were the ten milled bands at which points the bomb would break apart upon bursting. Due to its favourable external form and the high sensitivity of its impact fuze, the SD-10C achieved an extraordinarily good splinter effect.

The splinter (upper) and effectiveness (lower) pattern of the SD-10 bomb.

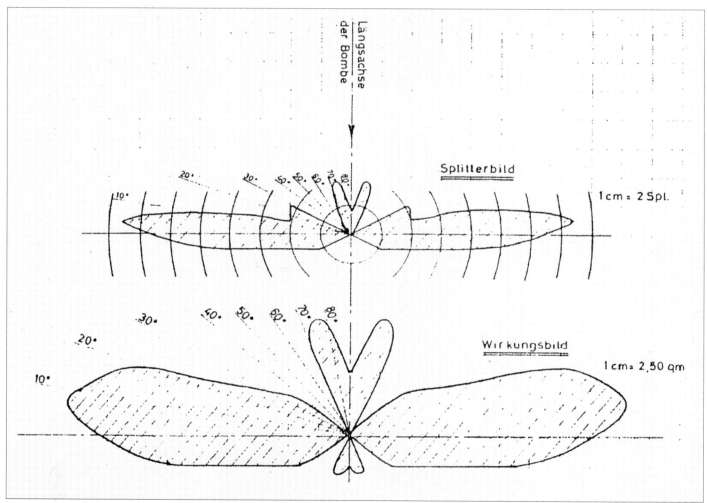

a lack of high-grade steel for the *Splitterbomben*. A substitute design appeared in the form of the SD-10 dw (doppel-wändig = double-walled) with an intermediate space intended to house several hundred 5gm weight iron chippings. A further interim solution was the SD-10 B that could be delivered made of the same quality steel as the Wurfgranaten (projectiles) for the Army Granatwerfer (trench mortar). The SD-10 C appeared with a cast steel body of 40mm (1.575in) wall thickness that featured ten characteristic intentional bursting points. This model existed in several variants: of Preßstahl (Pr) = moulded steel; cylinder

with pre-formed grooves (L), Temperguss (Te) = malleable iron casting, Sonderguss (Sge) = special casting, and Perlitguss (Pe) = cast Pearlite. Production continued to the end of the war. The SD-10 did not basically lose any of its splinter effect. Its use against parked aircraft and troop concentrations in high-altitude drops was from jettison containers. For low-level and dive-bombing attacks with the Ju 87 that had no release mechanisms for the SD-10, four bombs were fastened together as a bundle in a Bündel Bd 4 C-10 which were mounted on the bomb-release fittings for 50kg (110lb) bombs. The impact of the

bundled bombs was comparable with an artillery salvo of four mortars that exploded at a distance of 20 to 30m (65 to 98ft). Some 2,000 splinters covered the target. From 1943 onwards, the AB-500-1 *Abwurfbehälter* containing 37 x SD-10 A *Splitterbomben* came into use.

To relieve the deficit in *Splitterbomben*, those of 9.3kg (20.5 lb) weight of French origin were used, designated as the SD-10 frz. These were fitted with the original Mle. 21/31 H 21 nose fuze or the super-fast eAZ (66)A fuze. These were jettisoned in bundles of four as the Bd. frz. 10, or in bundles of 37 from the AB-500-1B container.

A further fully-developed *Splitterbombe* readily available was the SD-2, mentioned earlier on. Consumption increased from almost 289,000 examples on a monthly average in the summer of 1941 to 436,000 in July and to 520,000 in August 1943. The quantities required by the Luftwaffe General Staff lay considerably above these numbers, so that newer ways had to be found for the procurement of smaller *Splitterbomben*. The qualitative characteristic of this type of bomb, determined by the number of splinters, their density, the optimum pattern and the average weight of the splinters, all had to be taken into account. The average weight of the splinters in an SD-10 bomb was 8gm (0.28oz), and in an SD-50 17gm (0.6oz). The smaller *Splitterbomben* produced several but lighter splinters whose effects were nevertheless sufficient to at lesser distances to put a living target out of action. The desired distance was easily attained when a large and concentrated number of *Splitterbomben* were dropped. In order to achieve the desired production volume, the economical aspects had to be considered from the very outset. Assistance in this regard was obtained by the Luftwaffe through the meanwhile evaluated captured French and Russian air-dropped bombs. Of particular interest was a small, merely 0.52kg (1.15 lb) drop-shaped *Splitterbombe* that formed part of the captured French stocks. It brought recollections of the German bombs used in World War One used by 'infantry' pilots. Available in large numbers, this French bomb was incorporated into the arsenal of German air-dropped weapons under the designation SD-1 frz (for französisch = French).

When evaluating captured Russian air-dropped weapons, it was noted that the majority of the roughly 20 types of *Splitterbomben* ranging in weight from 2.5kg (5.5 lb) to 50kg (110 lb), were of calibres 45mm (1.77in) to 152.4mm (6.0in). The *Panzersprengbombe* BRAB-220 also stemmed from a naval artillery Panzersprenggranate (high-explosive armour-piercing mortar shell). It appeared advisable to adopt this weapon. Mortar

shells that were already in the course of production and which upon acceptance by the HWA did not satisfy the close tolerances in terms of dimensions and material quality, were also able to be reworked in Germany without any problems into *Splitterbomben*. For the SD-1, projectile bodies of the 5cm Wurfgranate 36 of the lightweight Granatwerfer 36 were taken over. In addition, a large proportion of the several million rounds of munitions stocks for this weapon were converted after they fell into disuse by the HWA into SD-1 bombs. These were fitted with a ring tail surface and the non-explosive mechanical AZ (73) A-2 membrane or diaphragm impact fuze whose design was traceable back to a French forbear. The complete bomb weighed 0.76kg (1.68 lb), of which the Fp 20/80 explosive filling weighed 60gm (2.12oz). It disintegrated with an average of 120 splinters weighing 1gm, plus five larger splinters. To obtain a better splinter distribution, later SD-1 bombs manufactured featured internal corrugations. These were dropped from various air-dropped containers where the AB-50 could accommodate 49 x SD-1 which covered a surface area of 100 x 100m (328 x 328ft) with 6,150 splinters much better than did the release of a bundle of 4 x SD-10 A bombs. The use of the SD-1 outlined in the Luftwaffe Service Regulation L.DV 4200 'Die deutsche Abwurfmunition' June 1943 edition, is described as follows: *'Used in high-level attack,* [is] *released from air-dropped containers against living targets and easily injurable non-living targets.* [Used] *for combating field positions and similar emplacements, since the number of bombs inside an Abwurfbehälter provides good coverage and direct hit possibilities.'*

The SD-1 was used for the first time in summer 1941. From then on, monthly consumption rose continuously from over 5,100 examples to 1,633,750 in August 1943. In a similar manner to the SD-1, the following *Splitterbomben* appeared:
- SD-3 – a modified 8cm (3⅛in) Wurfgranate 34 (mortar shell)
- SD-9 – a modified 8.8cm (3½in) Sprenggranate (high-explosive shell)
- SD-15 – a modified 10.5cm (4⅛in) Sprenggranate (high-explosive shell)

These were also jettisoned in large numbers from air-dropped containers and first came into frontline use during 1943. The 15kg (33 lb) weight SD-15 in particular, produced an average of 660 splinters varying in weight from 8.3gm (0.29oz) to 12.5gm (0.44oz) and proved to be an excellent *Splitterbombe*. The bomb body necessary for its manufacture, however, was urgently required for fulfilling Army needs, and for this reason did not attain the production levels of the SD-1.

Operational use of the small-calibre *Splitterbomben* required the use of *Abwurfbehälter*, as already adopted for the *Brandbomben* of 1kg (2.2 lb) and 1.3kg (2.87 lb) weight that were already available in the form of the AB-36, AB-42, ABB-500 and others. The ABB-500 – to name but one as an example, was able to accommodate 140 x B-1 E incendiaries and could be attached to every fitting for 500kg (1,102 lb) bombs. It was opened during the descent by a small explosive charge in accordance with the time-delay setting of between 2.5 secs to 33 secs, whereupon the incendiaries fell individually to earth. Based on this model, air-dropped containers appeared in 1942/43 for *Splitterbomben* with weights of

The AB-23 *Abwurfbehälter* (air-dropped container) housing 23 x SD-2 *Splitterbomben* had already been introduced in spring 1942. Empty weight was about 14kg (30.86 lb) and loaded weight 60kg (132 lb) with 23 x SD-2 bombs. Fuzes used were the electro-pyrotechnic Zeitzünder (79)A or B time fuzes with which it could be dropped from heights of 1,000m (3,280ft) to 2,000m (6,560ft) against area targets. Its ballistic free-fall path differed considerably from that of the high-explosives bombs themselves.

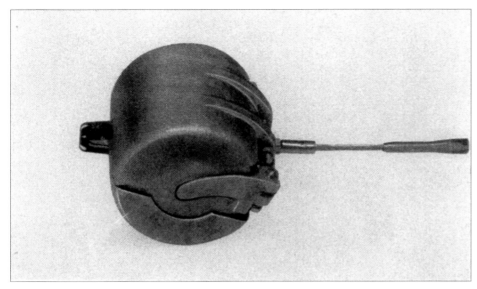

An SD-2 *Splitterbombe* with its two braking surfaces or vanes in the closed position.

The SD-1 *Splitterbombe* in comparison with the Wurfgranate (mortar shell) for the light 5cm Granatwerfer 36 trench mortar used by the German Army.

Two variants of the SD-1 *Splitterbombe*. The earlier modified Werfergranate (mortar shell) is at right, with the later model at left.

Opposite page:

Cross-sectional and overall views of the SD-1 *Splitterbombe* with the non-explosive mechanical membrane AZ (73) impact fuze for one-sided impact that was manufactured until the end of the war in several variants.

1kg (2.2 lb) to 15kg (33 lb). They were made to contain bombs of 50kg, 70kg, 250kg, 500kg and 1,000kg weight *Minenbomben* or *Mehrzweckbomben* that could be suspended from mountings on bombers as either internal or external loads. In an Amtschefbesprechung (meeting of department heads) on 12th February 1943, it was reported in this connection that, other than the AB-70-4 (for fighter-bomber use), the AB-70-5 (equipped with SD-2 *Störbomben* dropped from high altitudes), the AB-250-2 (ballistic flight-path in low-level releases), the AB-500 and AB-1000 were expected were expected to become available for operational use as soon as possible. Development of the AB-1000 was not yet completed as of January 1943.

All containers were made of sheet iron and had two outward opening half-shells. Like the air-dropped containers for *Brandbomben*, depending on the ignition time-delay setting selected beforehand, these were electrically opened by a powder charge, releasing the *Splitterbomben* which spread out on impact over the target area. Fuzes used were the electrical ZtZ (79) A, (89) B and (69) D time fuzes.

The contents of the *Abwurfbehälter* were variable. Thus, the AB-250-2 container with 224 x SD-1 bombs weighed 215kg (474 lb), but could also be filled with 144 x SD-2 bombs (280kg = 617 lb), 17 x SD-10 A (220kg = 485 lb), or 28 x SD-10 weighing 270kg (595 lb). The need for drop-containers which were also used in this form for *Seemarkierungsbomben* (sea marker-bombs) rose drastically. This spurred Albert Speer, the Reichsminister for Armaments and War Production, to commence the Special Undertaking 'Massenwurf' (Mass-drop) at the beginning of 1943, in the course of which, monthly production rose from an initial 7,000 to an intermediate 10,000 and was further increased later on. Average monthly production for 1943/44 amounted to almost 13,800 AB-70, about 3,500 AB-250, and 1,600 AB-500 containers.

At the beginning of May 1943, The Armed Forces C-in-C Adolf Hitler expressed his extreme satisfaction concerning the delivery of small bombs. His particular interest concerned the first large-scale use undertaken successfully in July and August 1943 when Allied bomber streams were attacked with air-dropped SD-2 bombs.

Until 1942, the Luftwaffe had used three different types of *Splitterbomben* – the SD-2, the SD-10, and the SD-50. The latter, like the SD-250, should be regarded as a *Mehrzweckbombe*. It was displaced during the war by the SD-70. At the suggestion of frontline units, all multi-purpose bombs were fitted with a 100cm (39⅜in) or 170cm (67in) long telescopic nose extension rod. Upon penetration of this nose spike into the ground, the bomb detonated above the surface and robbed the enemy of any possible cover, with disastrous results.

Regarding the quantity, variety, and effectiveness of *Splitterbomben*, the year 1942 was marked by an extraordinary increase that can be divided into two groups:

1. Small *Splitterbomben* of up to 5kg (11 lb) weight, having an explosive percentage of 11 to 12%. These were especially suitable for use as anti-personnel bombs and against unarmoured targets.

2. Large *Splitterbomben* of between 8kg (17.6 lb) and 15kg (33 lb) weight, with an explosive content of 9 to 10%. Used against vehicles and as anti-personnel bombs.

Splitterbomben of both groups were used by the Luftwaffe up to the end of World War Two. In ground battles, their splinter effects had to enhance army artillery and even replace them.

One of the other important tasks of the Luftwaffe in 1941/42 was the use of bombers to combat tanks. This was essentially nothing new. In the Army Service Regulation D 87 'Richtlinien für die Panzerabwehr aller Waffen' (Guidelines for all Weapons used for Anti-Tank Defence) of 2nd May 1936, it included the following:

'Direct hits scored by air-dropped bombs, depending on the calibre and jettison height, even penetrate armour plating. Pressure and splinter effects are only able to achieve hindrance effects under favourable preconditions.'

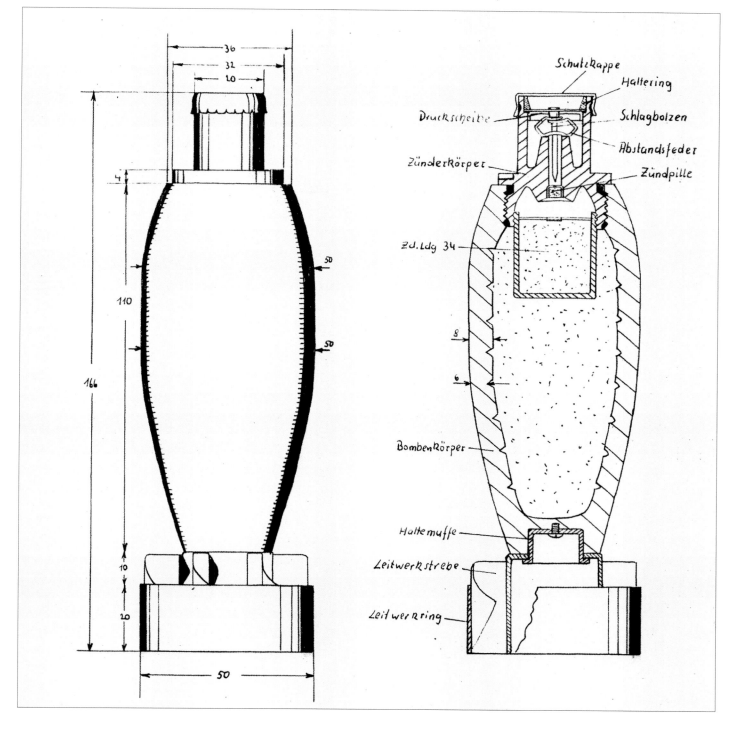

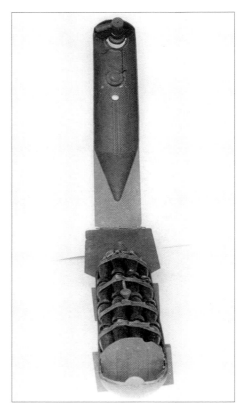

In the autumn of 1935, tests carried out by the RLM Technisches Amt in collaboration with the HWA at the Kummersdorf Artillery Proving Grounds, had revealed that by using the SC-10 and SC-50 *Minenbomben*, even the lightly-armoured Panzerkampfwagen I (MG) (Sd. Kfz 101) tank was still reliably protected from distances of 5 to 10m (16ft 4⅞in to 32ft 9¾in). In one of the first estimates of 20th December 1935, the HWA Wa Prüf came to the conclusion '... *that attacks using air-dropped bombs against tanks are not very successful.'* The best chances of obtaining success using bombs against tanks was provided when these were attacked whilst being prepared

The opened AB-70-4 *Abwurfbehälter* seen from the front.

The opened AB-70-4 container seen from the side. First used in 1943, it could hold 50 x SD-1 *Splitterbomben* and compared to the SD-70-1 container, had a better ballistic shape. Intended only for low-level release, it was equipped with the ZtZ (69) D time fuze.

Close-up of the SD-1 *Splitterbomben* inside the AB-70-4 container.

for combat. For attacking tanks from the air, the correct type of air-dropped weapons were lacking. At the new experimental Bomb Proving Grounds at Udetfeld in Upper Silesia, north of Beuthen (in Polish: Bytom), detonation tests carried out in 1942 demonstrated the comparatively low efficiency of large bombs as anti-tank weapons. On the test area was an assembly of ten Russian T-34 tanks, an American M-4 'Sherman', and three British 'Churchill' Mark IV tanks. The latter proved to have the least resilience to attack, as an SC-250 bomb going off at a distance of 5m (16ft 4⅞in) ripped apart its riveted armoured shell. The T-34 and the M-4 withstood the effects well even at a distance of only 3m (9ft 10⅛in). The pressure effects generated by the bomb, however, was sufficient to kill the guinea-pig animals inside the tanks, the diesel fuel in the T-34 being set aflame. Results of the tests clearly showed that for anti-tank warfare, small *Streubomben* (scatter bombs) were necessary to enable direct hits to be obtained, and by means of hollow-charge warheads, a sufficient penetration capability was achieved. To obtain a destructive effect similar to that of 'buckshot' slugs, a requirement was drawn up to drop such bombs from containers the size

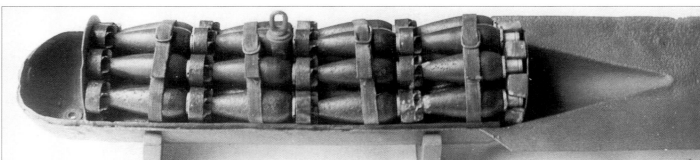

The AB-250-2 *Abwurfbehälter* **accommodating 224 x SD-1** *Splitterbomben.* **The minimum jettison height for this container weighing 215kg (474 lb) loaded was given as 150m (492ft).**

The AB-250-2 *Abwurfbehälter,* **this time with 28 x SD-10 C** *Splitterbomben.* **In a low-level attack, it was not to be dropped below a height of 300m (984ft). Weighing 270kg (595 lb) loaded, it was delivered to the Luftwaffe fully-filled from their ammunition depots.**

of an SC-250; furthermore, the ability to penetrate 100mm (3.94in) of armoured steel and at the same time achieving good splinter effects against living targets was demanded. The latter was to be achieved against Russian infantry who in numerous instances accompanied tank-led attacks. Based on these requirements, the SD-4 HL bomb was developed. Test models were fitted with a very short ring tail that had to be lengthened during the course of development and resulted in improved scatter. The number of such bombs was thus reduced inside an AB-250-2 air-dropped container from 50 to 40.

Trials with the SD-4 HL occupied almost a year. The aim had been that out of four tanks positioned within an area measuring 18 x 24m (59 x 79ft), to destroy two of them. Therefore it was necessary to achieve a scatter pattern whereby each tank was hit by at least two SD-4 HL bombs. An advantage was offered here by the AB-500-1 *Abwurfbehälter* containing 74 x SD-4 HL bombs of total weight c400kg (882 lb) whose use in this form became the norm. The SD-4 HL itself weighed only 4kg (8.8 lb) and held 0.31kg (0.68 lb) of TNT and Hexo-

gen explosive. Detonation was effected by the supper-quick eAZ (66) and (66) A impact fuze. These bombs also existed in a number of variants, identified by the suffix letters Pr = Preßstahl (moulded steel), Rohr (one-piece tubular shellcase), Stg = Stahlguss (cast steel), Te = Temperguss (tempered steel), Grauguss (cast iron with graphite layer), Perlitguss (Pearlite cast), and Ge = Sonderguss (special cast) bomb bodies. Penetration strength was given as 130mm (5.1in) armoured steel at a 60° angle of impact, to which was added 300 to 400 bomb splinters.

On 5th March 1944, Adolf Hitler approved the operational use of the SD-4 HL for the

first time, after Generalfeldmarschall Erhard Milch had reported on the large-scale use of the PAB 1.5kg (3.3 lb) hollow-charge bomb by Russian ground-attack aircraft. The SD-4 HL was judged favourably by frontline troops. The only cause for complaint was the folding-door jettison container that was not particularly suitable for the desired wide-scatter 'buckshot' effect. As well as the SD-4 HL, an SD-5 HL and SD-10 HL were being developed, but did not pass the experimental stage.

As it transpired, bombs with hollow-charge warheads or *Hohlladungsbomben,* were not only suitable for use against armoured vehicles. At the end of the 1930s,

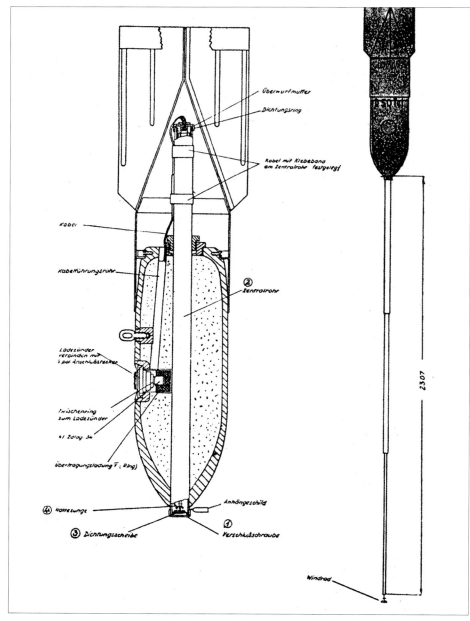

they appeared to present a highly promising alternative to the *Panzersprengbomben* and *Panzerdurchschlagsbomben* for attacking bunkers and especially for use against armour-plated warships. In this connection, the Luftwaffe had already taken up the subject with the Rheinmetall-Borsig AG in Düsseldorf, but had been restrained in this activity since further development of hollow-charge munitions was tied to the HWA. Even so, usable results were obtained up to the spring of 1942 in the realm of large-calibre air-dropped weapons. In January that year, a report on the application of the hollow-charge warhead principle was laid before Erhard Milch that stated: '*Based on preliminary tests carried out with the SC-50 and SC-250 that had been modified to incorporate explosives in the hollow-charge arrangement, the GL/C herewith submits a proposal for a Hohlladungssprengbombe under the designation SH-250 which, instead of the formerly-used purpose, is able to exceed it and represents a simple and purpose-designed use of the hollow-charge principle.*' It continued further: '*The SH-250 is derived from the SD-250 through the provision of a special hollow space in the explosive charge at the nose of the bomb and through displacement of the side fuze as an electrical base contact fuze.*'

Usage possibilities of the SH-250 were foreseen to combat fortified installations by which means the ability to penetrate 300cm (118in) of steel-reinforced concrete or 300mm (11.8in) of armoured steel was to be expected. The fragmentation (splinter) effects against living targets was comparable to that of the SD-250 bomb. By using time-delay fuzes, the bomb could be basically used against all seaborne targets. In direct hits on all merchant vessels and warships, the degree of penetration was sufficient to burst through the upper deck of ships up to the size of a 10,000 tonne cruiser, detonating in the innards of the vessel. At this time, preliminary trials had already been under way to employ the hollow-charge principle in the SC-1000 and SC-1800 *Minenbomben*. Extensive tests were also conducted against shipping targets with another *Hohlladungsbombe*, the SC-500 HL. In the summer of 1942, an old

Two 500kg (1,102 lb) bombs with annular tail ring beneath camouflage foliage. Note the hoisting lug between the cruciform fins.

The SD-50 Tel had a 2,307mm (90.83in) long telescopic extension rod. It was only made in small numbers and required particularly careful storage. It was mainly used on the Eastern Front during the months when snow or muddy conditions prevailed.

French cruiser was used that was run aground at the mouth of the Gironde.

For the further development of *Hohlladungsbomben*, the Luftwaffe freed itself from the size limitations of air-dropped weapons that had been introduced up until then and demanded in particular, the design of hollow-charge bombs of larger diameters that resulted in the SHL-500 and the SHL-800. Since this development did not lie in the special priority category, the manufacture of experimental models and their testing dragged on for over one year. The SHL-500 was able to penetrate through 700mm (27.6in) of armoured steel and 3,500mm (137.8in) of steel-reinforced concrete; with the SHL-800, the figures rose to 1,000mm (39.4in) and 5,000mm (196.85in) respectively. Both, however, did not attain operational status. On 30th May 1943, Armaments Minister Albert Speer noted in his daily War Diary: *'The Führer does not wish that the SHL-500 bomb be used operationally, we should expect to be faced with significantly greater disadvantages in attacks with these types of bomb on our installations. In comparison, the enemy possesses absolutely no targets that are sufficiently thickly concreted ! The Führer therefore orders further trials to be conducted with the bomb ...'*

The bombs were not to be put into production; neither were they to become used in the form of solitary examples at the Front.

An interim solution was offered by the use of the so-called *Bombenvorsatzkörper* or projecting casings from the nose of the bomb body which housed a quantity of hollow-charge explosive that would penetrate armour-plating. These were tested in conjunction with 70kg (154lb) BVK-70 and 250kg (551lb) BVK-250 bombs, but were not employed in live air-drops.

During the course of 1943, the development of a so-called *Weitschuss-Hohlladungsbombe* (increased-range hollow-charge bomb) was taken up. It was given the designation SHL-4000 and was intended for use preferably against ship targets. At that time, however, there was not only a lack of an experimental target whose design and construction was made up of several armoured layers, there was also a lack of suitable bombs and an appropriate method of attack to avert the danger from its being counter-attacked by the anti-aircraft weapons of all calibres that protected the Allied warships. A suitable means of transporting such a hollow-charge bomb-load appeared to be the so-called 'Hückepack-Flugzeuge' (piggy-back aircraft) combination that was also known as the 'Vater und Sohn' (Father and Son) or 'Mistel' (Mistletoe) project designation. This satisfied the desire of executing a method

of attack that would overcome the strong enemy anti-aircraft defences. The thoughts behind this 'Mistel' development was based on the experience gained by Ju 88 pilots in shallow diving attacks they had made from long distances. By maintaining their attack course, they had made use of the well-functioning 3-axis autopilot steering. The idea was thus originated of employing a proportion of these numerously available aircraft combined with a superimposed guidance aircraft such as the Bf 109 or Fw 190 fighter, and used as an unmanned explosives carrier. This method

Sectional arrangement of the SD-4 HL *Splitterbombe*. This experimental model is distinguished by its shorter ring tail.

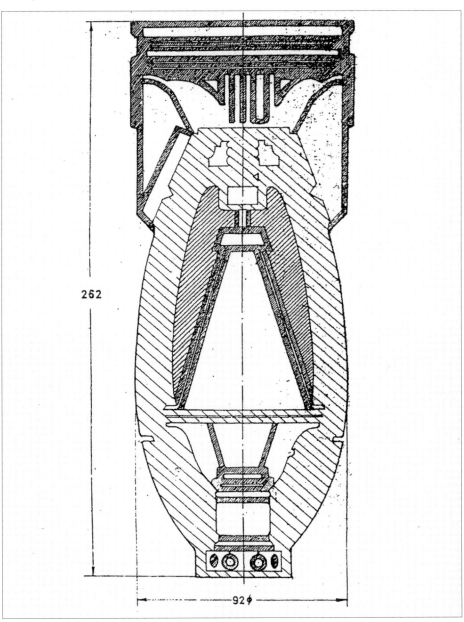

of attack had already been tested at the beginning of 1943. The pilot of the upper guidance aircraft brought the combination within visible reach of the target, put it into a shallow dive from a distance of 10-12km (6.2-7.5 miles) away from the target and checked the correct approach course and diving angle. At around 3,000-4,000m (3,280-4,375 yds) distance from the target, the pilot released his aircraft from the explosive-laden unmanned lower component and turned away whilst the latter continued its preset approach course until it impacted. The chances of a strike on large warships such as battleships or aircraft carriers were considered good. The Luftwaffe envisaged suitable targets among the British Home Fleet in Scapa Flow. Because of its high resistance, this method of attack

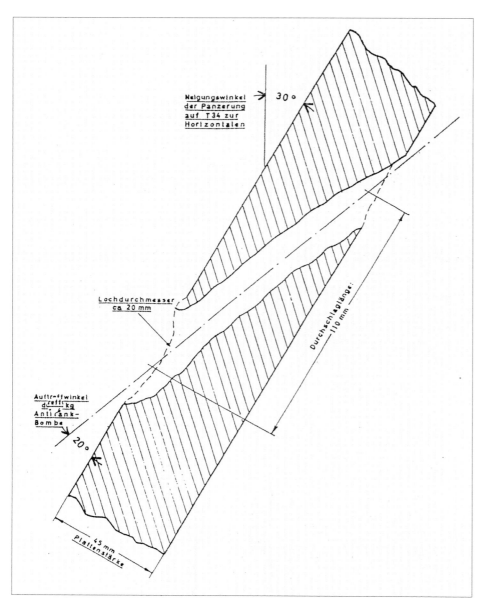

The penetration path of an SD-4 HL *Splitterbombe* through the front 45mm (l.77in) thick armour-plating of a Russian T-34 tank.

an angled impact where the aircraft's wing was the first to graze the target.

A total of some 300 examples of the SHL-4000 were ordered. A few of them were used with minor success in June 1944 against the Allied landing fleet before the Normandy coast. Others were used in the spring of 1945 against the Oder river bridges of the Red Army on the eastern approach to the Reich capital of Berlin. One further development was the SHL-6000, whose installation was planned in the larger 'Mistel' combination consisting of the Heinkel He 177 and Fw 190. Plans also existed to use the SHL-6000 in Operation *Eisenhammer* (Iron Hammer) – the attack on power stations serving the Russian armaments industry.

The already well-known and highly-decorated Stuka-pilot Oberleutnant Hans-Ulrich Rudel, was serving in September 1941 in Sturzkampfgeschwader 2 'Immelmann', based at the wartime port of Kronstadt (Kotlin Island, west of Leningrad). In his daily war diary, he described how difficult it was to score effective hits with dive-bombers on the Russian battleships *Marat* and *October Revolution*. The numerically superior strong anti-aircraft defences around the Bay of Kronstadt and the warships' own flak defences – the *Marat* alone had 6 x 7.6cm (3in) and 16 x 4cm (1.575in) flak and lighter guns, and as Rudel wrote, laid with their time-fuzes 'entire cloudbanks of explosive clouds' between the attacking German aircraft and the warships. Despite this, Rudel was able to sink the 23,606-ton *Marat* with a direct hit on the forecastle. The 23,256-ton *October Revolution* received several hits which put it out of action for a long time.

These spectacular successes, nevertheless, were not able to detract from the fact that the dive-bombing assault tactics were facing a difficult phase. How could the well-protected ship targets continue to be attacked by airborne artillery with good prospects of success? The chances of scoring hits in level flight from high altitudes were much too low. The Greifswald Lehrgeschwader (Instructional Wing), in attacks from 6,000-7,000m (19,685-22,965ft) with air-dropped weapons on the 13,200-ton target battleship *Hessen*, presenting a target of 126 x 22.2m (413 x 74ft) in area, achieved only 6% hits. An improvement in this figure was to be expected if it were possible to control the path of the bombs after release, that is to guide them onto the target.

was deemed best suited to be carried out with the SHL-4000, which occupied the crew space in the forward fuselage of the twin-engined bomber. In place of the crew compartment, the hollow-charge warhead of almost 4,000kg (8,818 lb) weight was installed, consisting of a 2,800kg (6,170 lb) weight of powerful explosive (70% Hexogen and 30% TNT) enclosed in a 1,000kg (2,205 lb) heavy iron casing. Diameter of the hollow-charge load was 2.0m (6.56ft), its projecting 'elephant's trunk' nose equipped with six highly-sensitive eAZ (66) impact fuzes.

Trials of the weapon took place in various stages. Available for this purpose was the 25,000 tonne French battleship *Océan* that lay at anchor at Toulouse. At first, detonation tests against the forward gun turrets were carried out. The 423mm (16.65in) armour-plating and turret mounts were

completely penetrated. The detonation energy, however, was first discharged after a penetration depth of 25m (82ft), at which point a further 200cm (78¾in) of iron and steel structure could be penetrated. At the beginning, the diameter of the penetration opening was 400mm (15.75in), and as Navy specialists confirmed, an intact battleship would have been completely destroyed and sunk.

In mid-March 1944, a few months before the commencement of Operation *Overlord* – the Allied landings in Normandy, a complete 'Mistel' composite was used against the *Océan* battleship. Further live trials were conducted from the Luftwaffe E-Stelle Peenemünde-West against the chalk cliffs of the Danish island of Moen. Here, the opportunity was also taken to examine the behaviour of the unmanned explosive-laden component in the event of

As early as 1939, the RLM had formulated such a requirement. In the DVL in Berlin-Adlershof, work was begun under the leadership of Dr Max Kramer to investigate remote-control methods on free-falling bombs. Trials involved, among others, the use of 250kg (551 lb) bombs fitted with cruciform tapered wings in X-form. These were carried out in Brackwede, Westphalia, and resulted in the appearance of the radio-guided free-falling PC-1400 X alias 'Fritz X' bomb – the X denoting the flattened X-shaped configuration of its stub wings. In the initial series of tests, the SD-1400 bomb was used, succeeded later by the PC-1400 containing a 350kg (772 lb) warhead. The optical and electronic guidance system came from the firm of Carl Zeiss in Jena. In a test-drop conducted on 8th August 1942, a 'Fritz X' was able to penetrate a 120mm (4.7in) thick armoured bulkhead. The accuracy was also good; with a target area measuring 10m (32ft 9¾in) in diameter, 60% hits were able to be obtained at a release height of 5,000m (16,400ft) at a distance of 10km (6.2 miles) away. The free-fall velocity was 280m/sec (918.6ft/sec = 626mph). Further trials conducted at the E-Stelle Süd (South) in Foggia, Italy. The first examples of 'Fritz X' were received at the frontline at the beginning of 1943; its greatest success was the sinking of the 35,000-ton Italian battleship *Roma* on 9th September 1943. Production of the bomb was cancelled at the end of 1944 since the possibilities of using it as well as operational conditions had drastically altered.

A parallel development to the 'Fritz X' was the Henschel Hs 293 glide-bomb. Its development had likewise commenced in 1939, based on a requirement issued by the RLM that called for a bomb that could be used to combat merchant vessels and lightly-armoured warships, without the attacking aircraft being endangered by the enemy's defensive anti-aircraft fire. The missile that resulted weighed 970kg (2,138 lb), of which 259kg (571 lb) consisted of explosive. It featured tapered mid-mounted wings, a constant-chord tailplane and a ventral stabilising fin surface, and was powered by an underslung Walter 109-507 rocket motor which enabled it to reach gliding speeds of between 160m/sec (525ft/sec = 358mph) and 265m/sec (870ft/sec = 593mph). Command guidance was by means of radio signals transmitted to the bomb by its guidance operator in the launching aircraft. The explosive warhead was detonated by an all-ways El.AZ (38) B electrical impact fuze. When dropped from an altitude of 8,000m (26,250ft), it could reach targets up to a maximum of 16km (10 miles) distant.

The Hs 293 glide-bombs were chiefly carried by the four-engined Heinkel He 177A-3 bomber specially fitted with two ETC-2000/XII racks with Schloss 2000/XIIIB and the FuG 203d transmitter and used against ships in the Bay of Biscay and in the Mediterranean. Some 12,000 examples had been manufactured, but its significance waned after the Allies had succeeded in cracking the transmission codes. Further developments in the sphere of *Gleitbomben* (glide-bombs) were the powered Henschel Hs 294 and the unpowered Blohm & Voss Bv 246. But despite some setbacks, the command-guided free-falling or controlled glide-bombs marked the end of the classical activities of naval forces on the high seas. Their most devastating weapon, regarded until then as undefeatable – the battleship, largely lost its importance by virtue of the introduction of this new combat weapon. Control of the world's waters had been taken over by airpower.

In addition to the 'Fritz X and Hs 293 for combating ship targets, there was a ricochet bomb known as the *Rollbombe* (rolling bomb). The initiative for its development was the successful use by the Royal Air Force of 4,000kg (8,818 lb) heavy bouncing bombs that destroyed the Möhne and Eder dams on the outskirts of the Ruhr industrial areas. The Luftwaffe wanted to

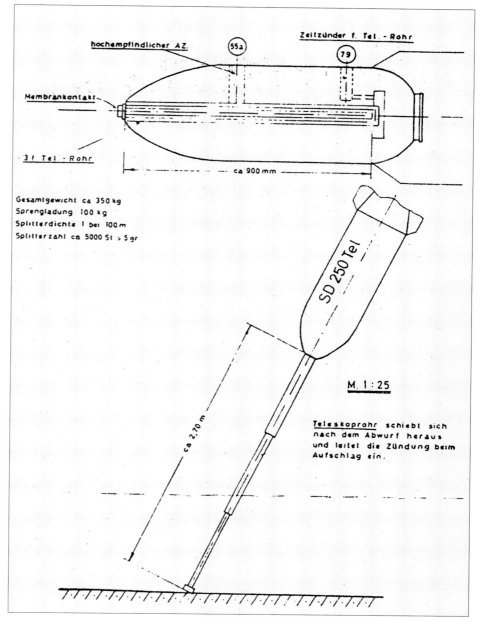

The effectivity of an SD-250 Tel multipurpose *Splitterbombe* with its 2.70m (8ft 10¼in) long telescopic extension. It was used against targets hidden in trenches or beneath a high layer of snow. Total weight was 350kg (772 lb), of which 100kg (220 lb) was the explosive content.

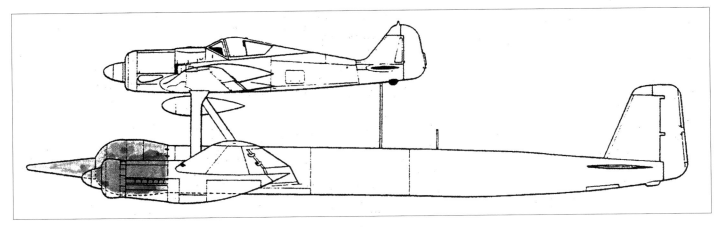

3,2 m

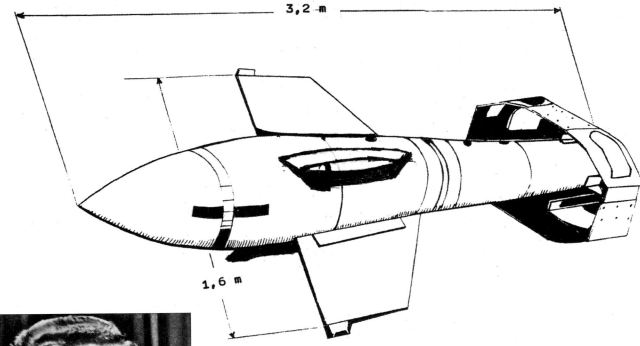

1,6 m

The 'Mistel' (Mistletoe) 3C composite consisting of the Ju 88 lower, and Fw 190A-8 upper component. The hollow-charge SHL-4000 warhead is shown shaded.

The remotely-guided 'Fritz X' free-fall bomb. With the wing, tail and remote-control additions, it weighed 1,600kg (3,527 lb).

The most-decorated airman in World War Two, 'Stuka'-Oberst Hans Ulrich Rudel (1916-1982) gained fame as the 'Tank destroyer from the air'. He and his air-gunner destroyed no less than 519 Russian tanks, most of them with the two 3.7cm (1½in) Bordkanone equipped with steel-core ammunition mounted beneath the wings of his Ju 87D-3 dive-bomber. Among his total of targets destroyed were 800 vehicles, 150 field howitzers, 4 armoured trains, 70 landing craft, 1 destroyer, 1 cruiser, the Russian battleship *Marat*, as well as numerous bridges and supply columns. Rudel was five times wounded and shot down 30 times.

The external configuration of the 'Fritz X' differed fundamentally from the other large-calibre bombs that had been used until its appearance. Its principal distinguishing features were the four stub wings and unique tail surfaces housing the remote-control guidance system. The 'Fritz X' was reliably effective in being able to penetrate the armoured layers of large warships to explode deep inside the ship, causing the severest of damage and destruction. Its most famous victim was the sinking of the 35,000-ton Italian battleship *Roma* on 9th September 1943.

The thick-walled shellcase of the 'Fritz X' bomb was filled with 350kg (772 lb) of the highly-powerful Hexogen or Trialen explosive.

The Henschel Hs 293 remote-controlled missile consisted of the 970kg (2,133 lb) weight bomb body to which was attached the tapered mid-wings, tail surfaces and the guidance system. Beneath it was the Walter HWK 109-507B liquid-propellant rocket motor of 78kg (172 lb) weight, containing 66kg (145.5 lb) of T-Stoff and Z-Stoff. The rocket provided a thrust of 600kg (1,323 lb) for 10 seconds, enabling a speed of up to 265m/sec (869ft/sec = 593mph).

have comparable special bombs for use against dams in Eastern and Southern Europe. The Rheinmetall-Borsig plant in Berlin-Marienfelde was assigned the task of development, the project known under the codename 'Kurt' 2000, the later improved model known as the 'Kurt I'.

Initial trials involved the use of explosive-filled drums or casks which, due to their being thrown off course by the water-surface wave crests, proved to be unsuitable. The next step was to experiment with explosive-filled spheres which, after impact with the water surface, steered a straight-line course for the next 500-600m (550-660 yds). The target, located 1,000m (1,090 yds) away, however, could not be reached. New military requirements envisaged such operations against ship targets, for which reason further development was directed towards a *Lufttorpedo* (air-launched torpedo) with rocket propulsion. The target distance now lay at 10,000m (10,940 yds) where, because of imprecise estimation of the distance to the target, some 2,000m (2,190 yds) formed a ricochet stretch. After it had reached the target, the *Rollbombe* sank, and at a depth of 6 to 8m (20 to 26ft), the two hydrostatic fuzes were activated and detonated the bomb. A third fuze with a delay-time of 25 seconds also went into action.

On the German side, the remote-controlled air-dropped weapons developed during World War Two for use against ship targets were highly promising weapons

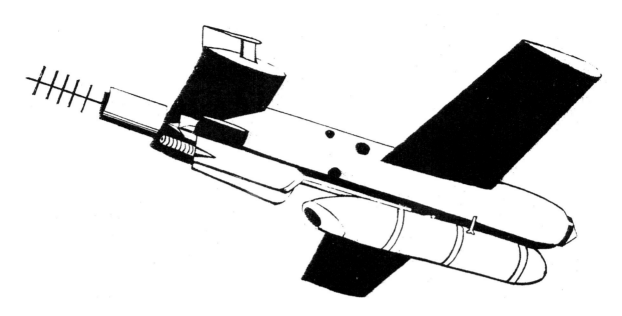

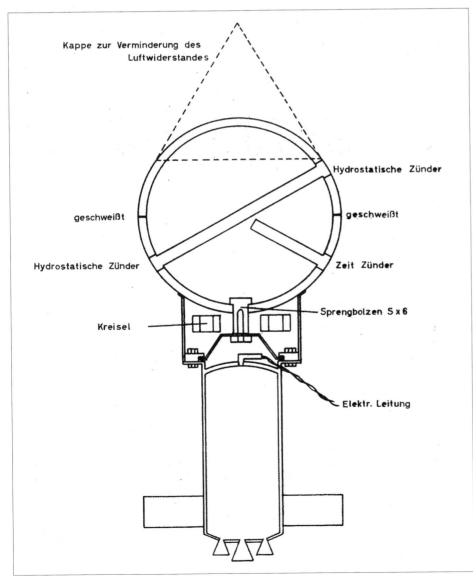

Kappe zur Verminderung des
Luftwiderstandes

Hydrostatische Zünder

geschweißt   geschweißt

Hydrostatische Zünder   Zeit Zünder

Sprengbolzen S x 6

Kreisel

Elektr. Leitung

Schematic arrangement of the Henschel
Hs 293 in flight.

The 'Kurt I' *Rollbombe*. At the top is a
conical ballistic hood and beneath the
spherical rolling and bouncing bomb, the
solid-propellant rocket motor. Dimensions
were quoted as 1,500mm (59in) length,
diameter 600mm (23.6in) and tailspan
800mm (31.5in). [The similar 'Kurt 2000' of
c1,500mm (59in) wingspan and 2,100mm
(82.7in) overall length, was powered by two
solid-propellant rocket motors, one on each
side of the fuselage – Translator]

Opposite page:

Of the total weight of 1,000kg (2,205 lb), the
BM-1000 *Bombenmine* (air-dropped mine)
consisted of some 680kg (1,500 lb) of
explosive. There were several versions.
The tail surfaces were made of Kunstharz
(synthetic resin).

Bombs with Assigned Names

(Expanded by the Author from the RLM LC VII C list, Berlin, 27.09.1941).

Bomb Type	Name	Remarks
SD-50	Dora	SD-50 (Pr, L, StG)
SC-50	Ida	SC-50 (J/A, L)
SD-250	Dolly	SD-250 (J/B, L, Stg)
SC-250	Irma	SC-250 (J/A, L)*
SD-500	Dagmar	-
SD-500 A	Diana	SD-500 (StG)
SD-500 II	Erna	-
SD-500 J	Lisa	SD-500 (L)
SC-1000 L2	Hermann	(formerly SC-1000)
PC-1000	Esau	(formerly SD-1000)
PC-1000 A	Esau new type	(new development)
PC-1400	Fritz	(formerly SD-1400)
PC-1400 II X	Fritz X	-
SD-1700	Dietrich	(formerly: Siegfried, Sigismund, SC-1700)
SC-1800	Satan	-
SC-2500	Max	-
SC-2500	Stahl-Max	SC-2500 (St)
PC-500 RS	Pauline	(formerly PC-500)
PC-1000 RS	Paul	(formerly PC-1000)
PC-1800 RS	Pirat	(formerly PC-1700)
SA-4000	Satan	-
BM-1000	Monika	-
Kugelbombe	Kurt I	-

* In BIOS Final Report 476, Item 3 & 31, are mentioned SC-250 No 24 and No 62 'Alto' and 1,000kg billet 'Pandora'. In Fritz Hahn's *Deutsche Geheimwaffen 1939-45* is mentioned SB-800 RS 'Kurt', SD-1400 'Esau', the 'Peter X' replacement for 'Fritz X', and PC-1800 RS 'Panther'. – Translator.

systems that pointed the way to the future, but no overwhelming success was achieved with them up to the end of the war.

Likewise developed for use against ship targets were *Seeminen* (air-dropped sea mines). The German Navy's Sperr-Versuchskommando (Blockade Test Detachment) in Kiel, developed for the Luftwaffe the LM A *Grundmine* (seabed-mine) of 500kg (1,102 lb) weight with remote detonation, the LM B of 1,000kg (2,205 lb) weight, and the LM C of 1,000kg weight equipped with an anchor cable and remote detonation. Only the LM B entered series-production.

In order to release sea mines from high altitudes and for mining harbour entrances and waterway channels, the Luftwaffe right from the beginning of the war supported development of the BM-1000 *Bombenmine* (mine-bomb). From a jettison height of 2,000m (6,560ft), the minimum water depth was 8m (26ft). The tailplane of the BM-1000 was made of Kunstharz (synthetic resin) that broke off on contact with the water. The variants H and M with an unlimited release altitude, had no braking parachute. Other differences were in the ignition apparatus and related ignition installations. In the event that the *Bombenminen* fell on land, they exploded immediately.

Less well known is that conventional *Minenbomben* were also used by the Luftwaffe as sea mines. Following the Allied landings in Normandy in the summer of 1944 the SC-250 *Minenbomben* was equipped with the AD-103 ignition apparatus. It was jettisoned with the aid of the targeting and release mechanisms for bombs that had meanwhile been fitted to fighter aircraft. Equally unproblematic was the arming of the *Seemine*, now designated as the BM-250. As in the case of electrical bomb fuzes, this was effected via a special nose charge. This was important since, due to the overwhelming Allied air superiority by day, only fighters were able to operate with any chance of success in the enemy airspace. With their help, it became possible to destroy the supply convoys in the English Channel, in shallow coastal waters, rivers, and canals.

Designed to serve the very similar purpose of hindering the enemy's supply lines was the *Treibminen* (drifting mines) which, however, had only been first demanded by the Luftwaffe General Staff in 1944. Like the 'Mistel' project, the underlying idea was to destroy the Russian hydro-electric power stations whose waterway entrances were protected by torpedo nets.

To overcome these barriers, the idea of dropping specially modified bombs was pursued, to utilise the weak current of 0.1m/sec (0.33ft/sec) in a typical artificial reservoir where the bomb would be carried along by the weak current towards the dam wall or the power station respectively. This led to development of the air-dropped devices known as the *Wasserballon* (Water Balloon) and *Winterballon* (Winter Balloon). The former consisted of an

SC-1000 *Minenbombe* equipped with plastic tail surfaces taken from the BM-1000 *Bombenmine* that broke off on contact with the water. As the illustration [p.149] shows, the bomb then sank to the bottom of the reservoir. At the tail end of the bomb, the built-in folded rubber balloon was then inflated by a compressed-air bottle in the bomb to its maximum diameter of 1,400mm (55in). The SC-1000 bomb then erected itself as shown, without surfacing, and drifted below the protective torpedo nets towards the power station entrance to the turbines. Appropriate testing that had been undertaken in the Walchensee in Upper Bavaria, confirmed the feasibility of the project. Not so successful, however, was the development of a fuze activated by the water current, so that the vibration-sensitive electrical Sonderzünder (50) special fuze was eventually used. A number of the *Treibminen* were equipped with the electro-mechanical LZtZ (17) long-duration time fuze. These were to have detonated the other drifting mines that had meanwhile gathered at the dam wall or power station turbine entrance. The plan had called for a typical operation in which some 100 SC-1000 bombs would be dropped, giving a total explosive weight of 60 tonnes that would be detonated all at once.

In order to be safely able to use such *Treibminen* during the winter months as well, the *Winterballon* was developed. This consisted of an SC-1000 L with a 30°-angled Prallscheibe (anti-ricochet disc) filled with 450-500kg (992-1,102 lb) of Trialen explosive. Special equip-ment carried included a Leitschirm 08 parachute, a carbon dioxide bottle filled with 3kg (6.6 lb) of liquid car-

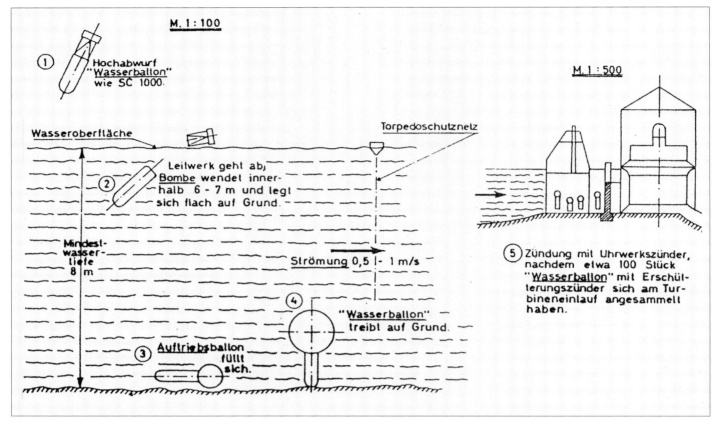

bon dioxide and the suspension balloon of 700 litres volume. Ignition was by means of the electro-mechanical LZtZ (17) A long-delay time fuze. A preliminary report describing the *Winterballon* was put together by the Luftwaffe E-Stelle Trave-münde. Its use is described therein as: *'The Winterballon is intended for use against hydro-electric power stations, preferably with the onset of ice conditions. After penetrating the surface ice layer, the bomb would be raised by the balloon so as to drift with the aid of the current beneath the ice layer towards the intended object.'* The angled *Prallscheibe* served to rapidly turn the nose of the bomb in shallow water. In all, some 1,000 examples of the *Wasserballon* and *Winterballon* were produced, intended to be dropped during the course of Operation *Eisenhammer* (Iron Hammer) by Kampfgeschwader KG 100, but never got to this stage. The only thing known is of *Sommerballon* (Summer Balloon) operations on the Western Front. At the beginning of 1945, the Luftwaffe dropped such drifting mines over the Maas river and the Lower Rhine. These were of the BM-1000 H model, which could be detonated by a passive (short-wave transmission) fuze, and were intended for bridge destruction to prevent the unhindered flow of supplies of all kinds, since the war by this time had already advanced to within the German borders.

A further *Treibmine* that was based on the design of a bomb that was used by the Luftwaffe was the air-dropped TM-50 drifting mine. It was made out of the empty bomb bodies of standard SC-50 *Minen-bomben* minus their tailfins, the 1,100mm (43.3in) long bomb body being sealed by a welded cap. It thus formed a lift-generating body that enabled the mine to drift in a vertical position. Its 7 to 8kg (15.4 to 17.6lb) explosive content was sufficient to cause such heavy damage to a 250-ton landing ship that it sank. Using their jettison mechanisms for 250kg and 500kg bombs, fighter-bombers could carry bundles of four TM-50 mines. In the water, these were connected to each other by floating cables 50m (165ft) long and connected by a drift anchor which provided a blockade zone 150m or nearly 500ft wide. The *Treibminen* were detonated by the vibration-sensitive *Sonderzün-der* (50) special fuze. Details concerning the use of this interesting development on the Normandy landing front are unfortunately not available.

The Luftwaffe's participation on measures to combat warships, whose massive presence in connection with amphibious landing operations was to be reckoned with, led to a whole range of interesting developments in the sphere of air-dropped weapons. The efforts expended stood in no relation to the usage attained, especially since a whole series of important precondi-

The sequential phases when the *Wasserballon* (Water Balloon) drifting mine was air-dropped with the aim of destroying a turbine-driven hydro- electric power station.

tions for their successful employment were lacking. As a rule, it was lack of air superiority over the operational area, and very often, the targets lay outside the range of the bombers.

The attention of the Luftwaffe leadership was tied to another sphere of activity – to their original characteristic realm, namely: that of conducting air warfare against the numerically superior Allied bomber formations. These were active day and night over Reich territory, destroying housing areas, the armaments industry, and the infrastructure. It became obvious that existing stocks of air-dropped weapons should also be modified or newly developed to combat the menace. As already related elsewhere in this narrative, a large-scale test had been conducted in July 1943 in the course of which, SD-2 bombs had been dropped en masse against the streams of enemy bombers. In addition, trials took place using SC-500 *Minenbomben* and SD-500 *Mehrzweckbomben* that lasted for a year. The question that needed to be answered was whether it was the pressure or the frag-

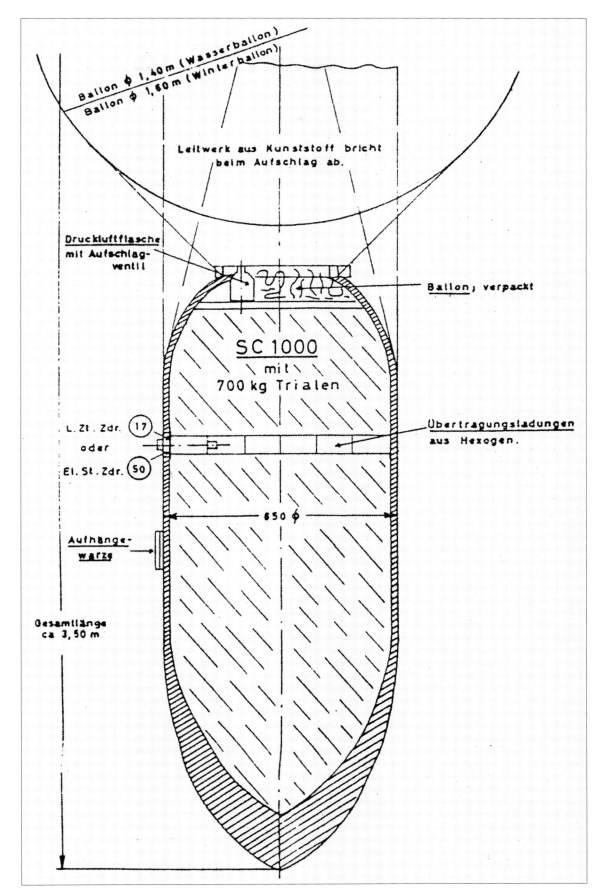

Cross-section of a *Wasserballon* (Water Balloon) filled with 700kg (1,543 lb) of Trialen explosive as in the SC-1000 *Minenbombe*. Balloon diameter was 1.40m (55in) for the *Wasserballon* and 1.60m (63in) for the *Winterballon* (Winter Balloon).

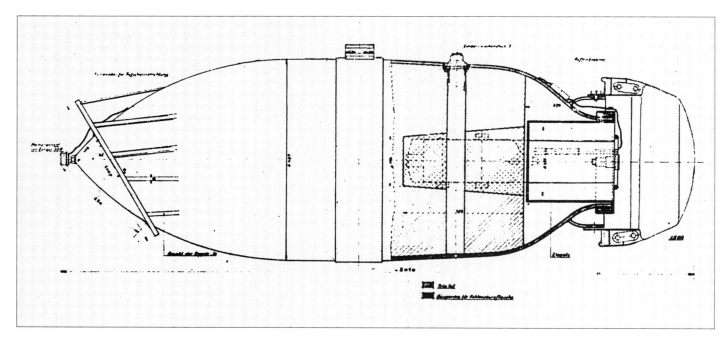

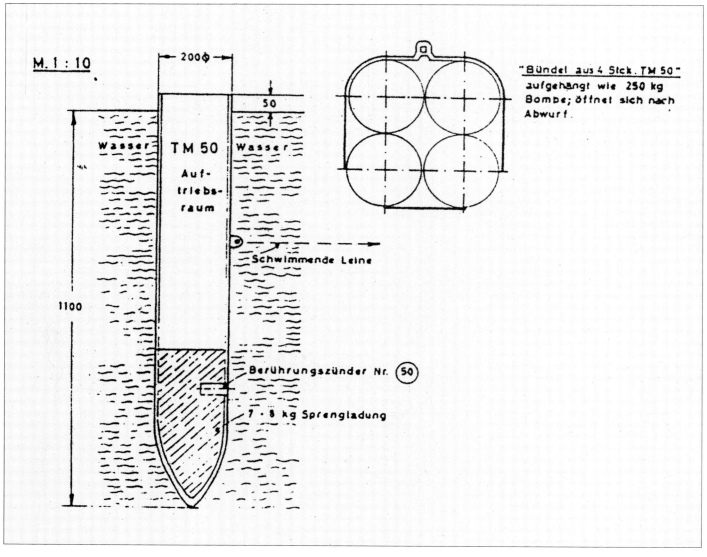

M. 1 : 10

200ϕ

50

Wasser TM 50 Wasser
Auf-
triebs-
raum

1100

Schwimmende Leine

Berührungszünder Nr. (50)

7 · 8 kg Sprengladung

"Bündel aus 4 Stck. TM 50"
aufgehängt wie 250 kg
Bombe; öffnet sich nach
Abwurf.

mentation effect that was responsible for the destruction of essential components that led to the certain crash of four-engined bombers. The viewpoint upheld that it was due to the gas pressure of large bombs, was strengthened in tests of explosives directed at the wings of the He 111. An SC-500 bomb detonated at a distance of 20m (66ft) led to breakage of the wing, whereas the damage resulting from the splinter effects through an SD-500 bomb indicated no quick prospects of success. In frontline trials carried out under the leadership of General der Jagdflieger Adolf Galland, both types of bombs were therefore used. Fuzes employed were the non-explosive pyrotechnic ZtZ (69) and ZtZ (79) time fuzes that had already proved themselves reliable in the *Abwurfbehälter* for *Splitterbomben*, and demonstrated that the fragmentation effects when combating air targets with bombs, made the greater impact. As a result, a special *Splitterbombe* designated Shr-500 was ordered. This consisted of a conventional SC-250 *Minenbombe* containing an explosive in an inner cylindrical column on its longitudinal axis. The intermediate space up to the surrounding bomb casing was filled with a few thousand sharp-pointed, heavy 100gm (3.6oz)-weight splinters. Also termed a *Schrapnellbombe* (shrapnel bomb), successful results could above all be achieved in instances where the Allied bomber formations enjoyed very weak or almost no fighter protection. In the last phase of the air war, however, and especially on the Western Front, this was seldom the case.

To turn our attention now to other, special types of bombs. Heading the list are the *Kampfstoffbomben* (toxic chemical or biological bacteria bombs) of which the Luftwaffe had built up quite a store during the war, but never used any operationally. In the spring of 1944, the following numbers of filled and unfilled *Kampfstoffbomben* were on hand:

49,391	KC-250	Weißkreuz
16,186	KC-500	Weißkreuz
347	KC-1800	Weißkreuz
47,314	KC-50 II	Buntkreuz
121,105	KC-250	Grünkreuz
16,125	KC-500	Grünkreuz
786	KC-1800	Grünkreuz
189,730	KC-250	Gelbkreuz
120,445	KC-500	Gelbkreuz
95,191	KC-250 III Gr.	Tabun
120,445	KC-250	Zäh- and Mischlost
2,333	KC-500	Zäh- and Mischlost
779,398	Kampfstoffbomben*	

* For their chemical contents, see Appendix 1.

In his unpublished work on German *Abwurfmunition*, General (Ing.) Dipl-Ing. Ernst Marquardt mentions around 100,000 filled *Kampfstoffbomben* which, because of their pervious thin-walled bomb bodies, required considerable expenditure. Replacement orders amounted to almost 10% annually. Concerning additional work that was required for storage of these *Kampfstoffbomben*, the following is contained in a Report on the Luftwaffe Munitionsanstalt (Munitions Institute) Burgwald: *'From mid 1942, only bombs filled with toxic chemical materials were stored. Light volatile Kampfstoffe came came already filled inside the bombs for storage in the*

Opposite page:

The *Winterballon* as shown in a technical drawing of December 1944.

The TM-50 *Treibmine* (drifting mine) air-dropped in bundles of four, was intended specially for use against troop landing ships.

This page:

Cross-section of a *Sommerballon* (Summer Balloon) filled with 750kg (1,653 lb) of Trialen as in the BM-1000 and equipped with passive ignition with the aid of photocells.

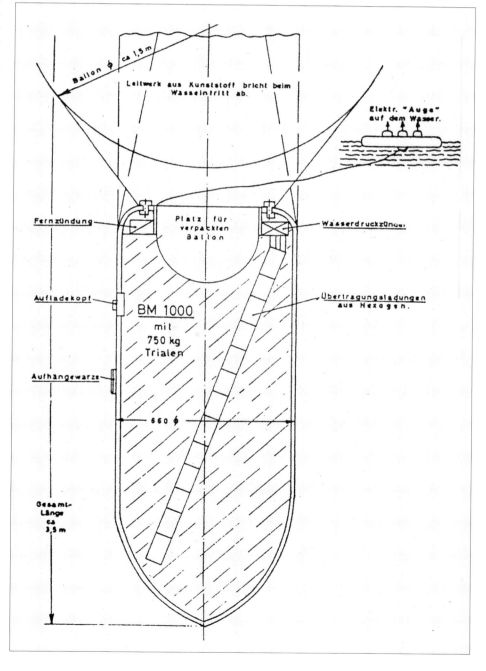

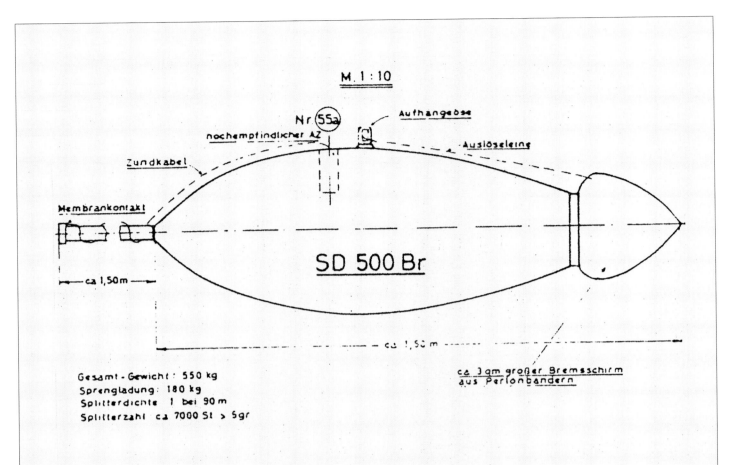

M. 1:10

Nr. 55a

Authangeöse

nochempfindlicher AZ

Auslöseleine

Zundkabel

Membrankontakt

SD 500 Br

ca 1,50 m

ca 1,50 m

ca 3 qm großer Bremsschirm
aus Perlonbändern

Gesamt-Gewicht: 550 kg
Sprengladung: 180 kg
Splitterdichte: 1 bei 90 m
Splitterzahl ca 7000 St > 5gr

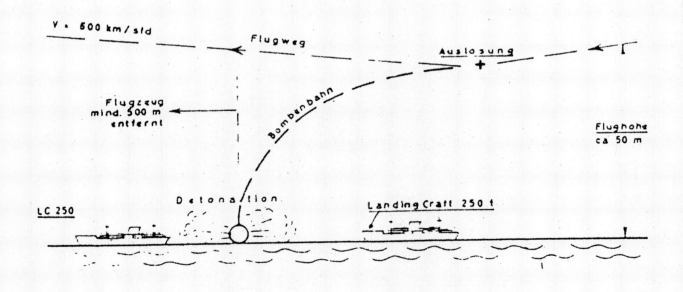

M. 1:1000

V = 500 km/std

Flugweg

Auslösung

Flugzeug
mind. 500 m
entfernt

Bombenbahn

Flughohe
ca 50 m

Detonation

LC 250

Landing Craft 250 t

depot, heavy volatile (sedentary) Kampf-stoffe were also delivered in large containers which were then decanted in the storage facility …

'There were a large number of empty bomb bodies stored on the grounds, for the purpose of being able to re-fill defective bombs with heavy volatile Kampfstoffen.'

'For damaged bombs filled with light volatile Kampfstoffen (mainly Phosgene), there was a neutralisation basin at Fritzbach. The bombs were suspended on a gallows and then fired at. The exuding Kampfstoff mixing together with the basin water formed Salzsäure (hydrochloric acid) which was then neutralised with Chlorkalk [chloride of lime].'

On 28th March 1945, the Chef OKW made known his decision telegraphically that upon the approach of the enemy, bombs filled with *Kampfstoffen* (for example Tabun), were to be definitely removed for transportation and that their destruction through sinking in the Edertalsperre (Eder reservoir) was rejected. Bombs with older *Kampfstoffen* that were already familiar to the enemy were to remain unmarked in the Munitions Institute.

Opposite page:
A further bomb developed to combat landing craft of 250 tons weight was the 550kg (1,218 lb) weight SD-500 Br *Bremsschirmbombe* **(brake-parachute bomb) which detonated on the water surface, but was not used operationally.**

This page:
The SD-500 A (Stg) cast-steel multi-purpose *Splitterbombe* **that was also manufactured by other processes such as Preßstahl (moulded steel) or Röhren (cylinders). On detonation, it generated some 6,800 splinters with an average weight varying from 5gm to 40gm each.**

In an undated instructional document for Luftwaffe artificers, a Blaukreuz (Blue Cross) KC-10 *Kampfstoffbombe* was mentioned, whose *Kampfstoff* was effective in still-air conditions in a circle of 20m (66ft) radius and was said to have produced good splinter effects within a 25m (82ft) radius. Far more effective was the Gelbkreuz (Yellow Cross) KC-250 *Kampfstoffbombe* that weighed 150kg (331 lb) filled with 70 litres of *Kampfstoff*. It was equipped with the Zünder (15) all-ways impact fuze and a time-delay that could be selected in flight, as well as a self-detonating safety fuze. Upon bursting, a surface area of 5,000m² (53,820ft²) up to a height of 100m (328ft) was poisoned. A further example named was the Grünkreuz (Green Cross) KC-250 bomb that weighed 130kg (287 lb) containing 60 litres of Phosgene. Already in the autumn of 1942, practical air-drop tests were conducted on an island in the bay of Riga with bacteriological *Kampfstoffen*, namely Milzbrandbakterien (anthrax bacteria). This liquid, emanating from the Insel Riem, was sprayed from two Nebelgeräte (fog-dispensers) mounted on a Ju 88. It was later able to be confirmed that the test brought about positive results, but no further details are available.

On 9th April 1943, in the presence of Hermann Göring's deputy, Erhard Milch, a demonstration by the Luftwaffe of chemical *Kampfstoffen* took place in Berlin. From the S-200 Nebelgerät, liquid *Lost* was was sprayed. In low-level flight at 70m (230ft), KC-250 bombs also filled with liquid *Lost* were jettisoned in order to contaminate areas of ground. High-level attacks with *Kampfstoffbomben* likewise formed a part of the demonstration.

The chances of success of chemical warfare were once more discussed among the German leadership heads on the 19th and 20th February 1945. The Reichsminister für

Volkserklärung (Peoples' Enlightenment) and Propaganda, Josef Goebbels, in retaliation for the destruction of Dresden, had demanded the dropping of bombs filled with Tabun on British cities. The Navy C-in-C Großadmiral Karl Dönitz, however, was of the opinion that the disadvantages of such action outweighed the advantages, and thus found himself in agreement with the WFSt Chef Generaloberst Alfred Jodl. Chemical air warfare over the British Isles never took place. The production of *Kampfstoffen* and their filling in bombs, however, was only finally terminated in March 1945.

Further types of bombs used by the Luftwaffe were *Nebelbomben* (smokescreen bombs) for blinding the enemy, *Blitzlichtbomben* (flash-bombs) to provide illumination for night photography, *Fallschirmleuchtbomben* (parachute-dropped flares), *Bodenmarkierungsbomben* (ground marker-bombs) and *Luftmarkierungsbomben* (aerial marker-bombs) or -*körper* (bodies). For training purposes, *Zementbomben* (cement bombs) were used, containing smoke cartridges of various colours. These were made in almost all calibres of air-dropped weapons. To supply indigenous ground troops that were at the spearhead of one's own fighting units engaged in combat or who were surrounded by the enemy, *Mischlastabwurfbehälter* (mixed-load air-dropped containers) or 'Versorgungsbomben' (victuals bombs) were used. During the war, their importance grew steadily.

Hardly any details on the subject of *Flugblattbomben* (air-dropped leaflet bombs) alias 'Propagandabomben' worth mentioning could be unearthed. Leaflets – one of the weapons that were aimed at the soul of the enemy, were dropped from the usual jettison altitudes over a wide area and for their occasional use, the AB-50 and AB-70 air-dropped containers were modified for this form of warfare.

Opposite page:

The SD-500 E was made of Preßstahl (moulded steel) and including the 75kg (165 lb) Fp 60/40 explosive, weighed between 457kg (1,008 lb) and 503 lg (1,109 lb). Its length also differed from the other *Mehrzweckbomben* (multi-purpose bombs) of this calibre. SD-500 A length was 2,020mm (79.5in), whilst the SD-500 E was only 1,744mm (68.7in).

Being prepared for loading here on a Ju 88 are SD-500 *Minen-bomben*. The loading personnel are inserting the electrical impact fuzes in the rear fuze housing slot. Photograph taken in 1943.

This page:

The 1,000kg (2,205 lb) *Mischlast-Abwurfbehälter* (mixed-load air-dropped container) 'emergency-solution' model. Externally, it resembled the LM B mine, and was intended to provide frontline troops with air-dropped heavy and cumbersome articles. Maximum payload was 750kg (1,653 lb).

Up to the spring of 1944, the Luftwaffe had introduced two models of the *Mischlast-Abwurfbehälter* 250 air-dropped containers – a *Flussigkeits-Abwurf-behälter* 250 for liquids, and a *Waffen-Abwurfbehälter* 250 for weapons, intended only for paratroops.

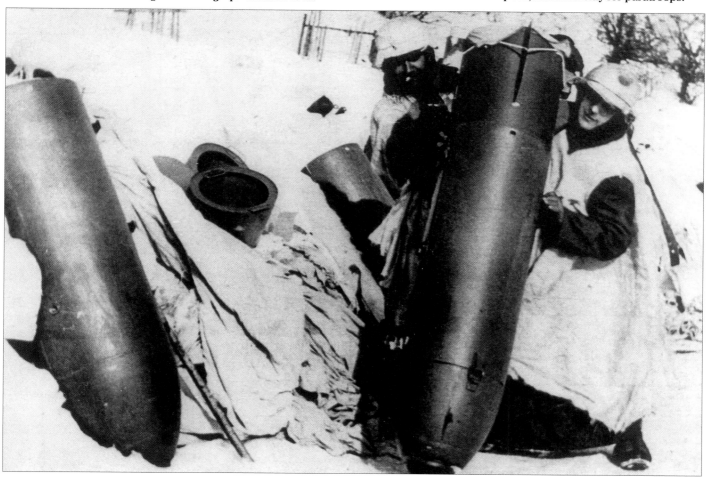

Scenes showing the use of *'Versorgungsbomben'* (provisions bombs) during the 1943/44 winter. The first models of the *Mischlast-* (mixed load) and *Flussigkeits-Abwurfbehälter* (air-dropped containers for liquids) were already in use in 1940 when supplies to hard-pressed tank spearheads were of prime importance. From the winter of 1941/42, these containers increased in significance to furnish hemmed-in units of the Army and Waffen-SS with provisions, as in Cholm, Demyansk, or Stalingrad.

Chapter Ten

Development Trends up to the End of World War Two

In 1944, the Luftwaffe leadership was forced to adapt the basic operating principles of their bomber units to strategic defensive measures needed on land and in the air. It thus pursued the goal of organizing much closer co-operation between the Army and the Luftwaffe, for which purpose planning centres staffed with Luftwaffe liai-

This page and the following page:
A Messerschmitt Bf 109E-3 fighter experimentally equipped with the underfuselage ETC-500/XIb (electrically-operated carrier for cylindrical bombs) carrying an SC-250 *Minenbombe*. With this special fitting, the Bf 109E-7 and E-8 were capable of carrying bombs of up to 500kg (1,102 lb) weight or a 300 litre auxiliary fuel tank.

son officers coordinated with various Army Groups, Corps, and even individual Army Divisions. They evaluated the requirements set by the army filed units and determined how their airborne resources would best be used. Pivoted at the centre were the Schlachtflieger (ground-attack units) where a distinction at this time was made into three categories:
- Night ground-attack units
- Day ground-attack units
- Anti-tank ground-attack units

The most important Schlachtflugzeug (ground-attack aircraft) was the Focke-Wulf Fw 190, that existed in many variants converted to the fighter-bomber role. Besides these, there were several Junkers Ju 87 'Stuka' dive-bombers and the Hen-

schel Hs 129 – the sole aircraft that had been conceived on the German side as an armour-plated ground-attack aircraft that were still operational. As a contrast, the importance of pure bomber forces waned significantly during the last year of the war, which in turn reflected the consumption figures for air-dropped weapons that formed a part of the monthly evaluation of the losses, consumption, and stock figures established by the OKW Org Vb branch on behalf of the Wehrmacht including the Waffen-SS. Clearly recognisable was the increasing number of air-dropped weapons whose use was a typical characteristic of the ground-attack formations. These included the SD-50 and SD-70 multi-purpose bombs as well as all air-dropped containers for *Splitterbomben* up to 15kg

(33 lb) weight. In July 1944, the consumption figure for 50kg (110 lb) and 70kg (154 lb) bombs alone was 169,960 and for all those dropped in AB-70 containers, 22,319 bombs. Replenishments for the 70kg multi-purpose bombs in particular, gave cause for anxiety, and with the air-dropped containers, because of the complete deficit in AB-70 production as well as the persistently high consumption at the frontline, a noticeable deterioration had occurred. In August 1944, the corresponding consumption figures were 310,170 for the SD-50 and SD-70 *Mehrzweckbomben* and 31,316 for the AB-70 *Abwurfbehälter*. In the report previously cited, it states: *'The very high consumption of air-dropped containers with small-calibre bombs continues unabated due to increased sorties by the ground-attack units. The expansion in production meanwhile instituted will compensate for consumption only in two to three months' time.'*

Experiments to equip the Messerschmitt Bf 109 fighter for use as a dive- and fighter-bomber with a bomb suspension rack dated back to 1939. Here, another view of the Bf 109E-3 (CA+NK) with a multi-purpose SD-500 Splitterbombe. For carrying 50kg (110 lb) bombs, a rack with four ETC-50/VIII could be attached.

Through a fall in consumption and a stepping-up of deliveries by industry, a slight relief in the supply situation was brought about in September 1944. With the remaining types of air-dropped weapons, the Report continued, no replenishment and supply difficulties were to be expected for the following three months. The September 1944 consumption of 17,380 SC-250 *Minenbomben* and SD-250 *Mehrzweckbomben*, as well as 2,883 SC-500 and SD-500 bombs of these types lay considerably below the monthly average of the previous year. Added to that, not a single PC-500 *Panzersprengbombe*, and only 156 SC-1000 *Minenbomben* plus 165 PC-1000 *Panzersprengbomben* had to be taken into account – an indication of reduced-scale activity of the bomber units.

In October 1944, a renewed increase in consumption figures of almost all types and calibres of air-dropped weapons was registered. Presumably only a small quantity of the bombs were actually dropped. A further portion was released to the Army engineers so as to be able, within the scope of the general withdrawal of German forces, to blow up bridges, buildings and industrial installations. Earlier in the late summer of 1942, engineers of the Afrikakorps had buried Luftwaffe air-dropped bombs near El Alamein to serve as *Großladungsminen*

(mines of high explosive content). At the end of April 1945, during the course of the final defence of the Reich capital of Berlin, a large number of bridges over the Spree and Havel rivers as well as important canals running through the city were destroyed with the help of Luftwaffe bombs due to the scarcity of explosives normally used by the Army engineer units.

The majority of the air-dropped weapons were lost during the retreats, since available transport capacity proved insufficient or else the traffic routes had already been dismembered. For the return transport of a munitions depot stocked with 2,000 250kg (551 lb) bombs alone, 35 railway freight cars of the Deutsche Reichsbahn were necessary. The OKW Report of 21st November 1944 remarked laconically that: *'Replenishment situation* [for *Abwurfmunition* – Author] *satisfactory. The high consumption is due to the large number of munitions destroyed or else fallen into enemy hands.'* During the terminal phase of the war, the Russian Air Force made good use of most of the captured German weapons, partly to compensate for lack of availability of their own weapons. The 250kg and 500kg bombs especially, were suitably modified. They were provided with all-ways impact fuzes – the so-called *Kompressions-* or *Luftpump-Zünder* (compression or air-pump

fuzes) which by the simplest means such as explosion rings, etc, fuzes were inserted and fixed into the laterally-placed fuze compartments in the bombs. As simple as these conversions were, they produced an equally high number of 'duds', confirmed at least by the numerous unexploded bombs of this type found in the provinces of Brandenburg and East Saxony.

In the spring of 1945, the fighting power of the Luftwaffe sank not only because of their continually high personnel and materiel losses. The main reason was the lack of fuel that had hindered combat operations in no small measure. From mid-February, the entire programme of flying training had to be discontinued step by step, and existing bomber units were disbanded. The massive engagement of Luftwaffe strengths, primarily those of the fighter-bombers and ground-attack units against the Red Army along the Oder front, had only become possible by concentration and availability at focal points with the very last reserves. The still appreciable quantities of existing *Abwurfmunition*, above all the large-calibre bombs, were of no use on the German side in the final phase of the war.

At the end of 1944, the Luftwaffe Quartermaster-General reported the following quantities of bombs in stock:

Qty	Weight	Type
335,530	250kg	Minen- & Mehrzweckbomben
52,019	500kg	Minen- & Mehrzweckbomben
297	500kg	Panzersprengbomben
4,907	1,000kg	Minenbomben
5,706	1,000kg	Panzersprengbomben
5,525	>1,000kg	Minenbomben
4,622	>1,000kg	Panzersprengbomben

The stock of *Brandbomben* (incendiaries) lay at over 14 million bombs. The stores of individual types of bombs, based on the average consumption figures of 1943/44, would have been sufficient right up to October 1945 and beyond. Heinrich Himmler, Reichsführer SS and simultaneously from the end of July 1944 Befehlshaber des Ersatzheeres (Commander of the Replacement Army) and Chef der Heeresrüstung (Chief of Army Munitions) therefore proposed at the beginning of 1945 that the quantities of explosives available in the numerous bombs that were no longer required, be used for mine fillings.

Side and plan views of the ETC-500/IXb (Fl. Nr. 50 570) mounted on a Messerschmitt Bf 109F-4 fighter-bomber.

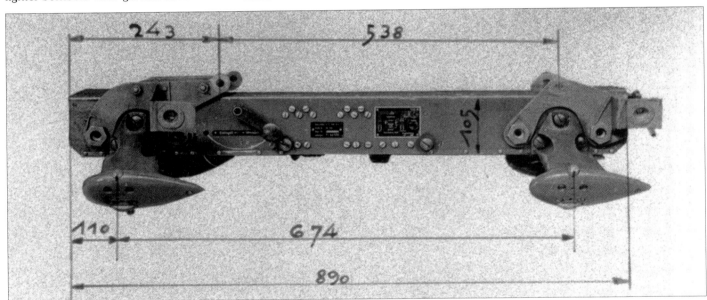

A Focke-Wulf Fw 190A-4/U3 with an ETC-500 and 4 x SC-50 *Minenbomben*.

In this hopeless situation, the suggestion made on 22 nd March 1945 during one of the Führer Conferences that the twin-jet Arado Ar 234 high-performance aircraft be equipped with either one 1,000kg (2,205 lb) or two 500kg (1,102 lb) bombs and sent on frontline missions appeared almost grotesque, as only several dozen aircraft and a few test prototypes existed.

The reduced need for large-calibre *Abwurfmunition* stood in opposition to the undiminished interest in small *Splitterbomben* and *Mehrzweckbomben* of up to 70kg (154 lb) weight. In the Luftwaffe Munitionsanstalt Lübberstedt where among others, SD-1 and SD-4 *Splitterbomben* were filled with explosives, the emergence of the SD-10 C *Splitterbombe* gained in significance at the beginning of 1945. On 30th January 1945, the head of this plant noted in his war diary: *'Because of the increased demand for explosives-filled SD-10 C by other Service Centres, the Filling Section*

from today onwards will be working a nightshift.' At this location in February 1945, a total of 94,441 SD-10 C bombs were filled, and 108,948 such bombs were packed into 3,891 AB-250-2 *Abwurfbehälter*. In the following month, 29,632 SD-10 C bombs were filled, and 37,346 examples stood ready for packing into 1,337 AB-250-2 *Abwurfbehälter*. Other bombs, among them the SB-3 as well as containers, were examined by the establishment's personnel and again made ready for use. Because of a lack of sufficient quantities of explosives, production of the SD-10 C bombs and their insertion in the air-dropped containers continued with interruptions and was finally terminated only at the beginning of May 1945.

In the last weeks of the war, destroyed traffic routes presented enormous difficulties for the delivery of air-dropped weapons. The connections between the manufacturers of the bomb casings, the fuzes and other component parts to be delivered to the Luftwaffe Munitions Centres were often cut off. The scarcity of explosives meant that the filling centres could no longer function. Only in this way is it possible to explain that the thick-walled

SD-70 *Mehrzweckbomben* came to be prepared for delivery filled with incendiary materials and phosphor additives.

The solitary new *Splitterbombe* that made its appearance towards the end of the war was the SD-0.5. Its design was encouraged by the Russian RG-2 *Splitterbombe* of 1.8kg (3.97 lb) weight, in which the bomb body of merely 400gm (14oz) weight and 5mm wall thickness had space to accommodate 100gm (3.5oz) of explosive. The bomb was fitted with a super-quick impact fuze and jettisoned with a parachute from the *Abwurfbehälter*. Additionally, there was also a small bomb of only 3kg (6.6 lb) weight that produced the equivalent effects of a mine, but of which no details are available.

Extensive trials were undertaken with rocket-propelled bombs intended for various applications where the following lines of development were pursued:

1. Further development of already-introduced *Minenbomben* and *Sprengbomben* combined with a solid-propellant rocket propulsion charge.
2. Designs for new rocket-propelled bombs.

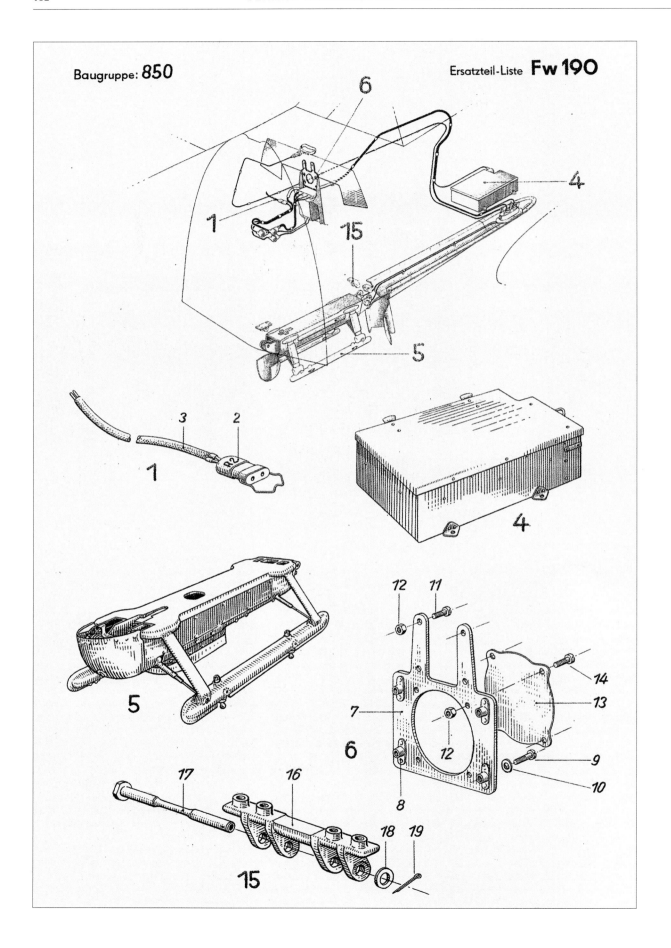

Baugruppe: **850**

Ersatzteil-Liste **Fw 190**

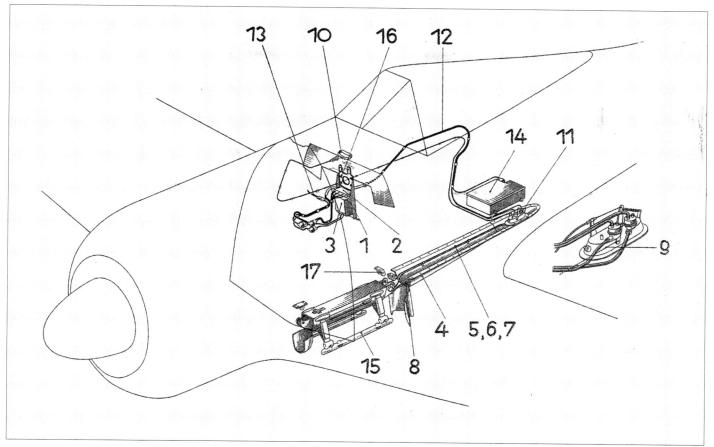

The first group included the SC-50 RS, SC-250 RS and SC-500 RS. For the last named, the rocket unit used was also intended for the PC-500 RS. Out of the SD-70, two rocket-powered bombs were developed – the RD-50 and the RD-100. With a thrust of 2,500kg (5,512 lb), speeds between 400m/sec (1,312ft/sec = 815mph) and 500m/sec (1,640ft/sec = 1,118mph) were attained. Among the smaller rocket-powered bombs for use against ground targets, the SD-4 RS is worthy of mention.

Almost ready for immediate introduction were the SC-20 RS and PC-20 bombs of the second group. The PC-20 weighed 20kg (44 lb), had a diameter of 200mm (7.87in) and length 946mm (37.24in). Its solid-fuel rocket charge consisted of two diglycol cylinders.

Foe combating airborne targets, the SD-6 rocket-bomb with a hollow-charge explosive warhead was envisaged. It was expected to have good chances of success against large, compact bomber formations, for which reason its development priority had been accorded a particularly high urgency. Likewise to be employed against airborne targets was the R-100 BS, whose hollow-charge warhead consisted of 20kg (44 lb) of explosive and 33 small cylindrical incendiary bodies made of Electron housing a mixture of magnesium powder and

Opposite page and above: The bomb jettison installation as used on the Focke-Wulf Fw 190A-1, A-2, A-5 and A-6 variants. The ETC-501 for bombs up to 500kg (1,102 lb) weight could support four SC-50 or SD-50 bombs beneath the ETC-50/VIII rack.

Right: **A typical example of captured German bombs used by the Red Air Force. This SC-250 *Minenbombe* adapted to use the Russian AW-1 fuze, had to be rendered safe in Zittau on 18th August 2000. The fuze was anchored in the fuze slot by wooden wedges.**

barium nitrate. Its operating range was quoted as 2,200m (2,406 yds). The Messerschmitt Me 262 jet fighter was to have carried four R-100 BS projectiles, but work on the project had not been finalised at the end of the war.

The above thus concludes the development of German *Abwurfmunition* during the Second World War. It is obviously valid in relation to what Generalfeldmarschall (retd) Albert Kesselring had recorded in his book: *Bilanz des Zweiten Weltkrieges* (Balance-Sheet of the Second World War) published in 1953, in a reference to the Luftwaffe: 'The more the war neared its end, the more had German aircraft disappeared from the skies. The Allies had

gained unlimited air superiority with dreadful results for the German populace and armaments. All technical and tactical measures adopted that clearly indicated the will not to be defeated by any means whatsoever, bore the stamp of sudden inspiration and momentary action. Enduring success was denied them. Additionally, mobile warfare with its considerable possibilities of success, due to lack of sufficiently strong close-combat air strength in its desired form, was condemned to defeat. A resuscitation of the operative air war under the circumstances described, was absolutely unthinkable any more ...the Luftwaffe was destroyed on the ground.'

During the course of planned withdrawals of Army and Luftwaffe personnel and equipment, these SC-1000 *Minenbomben* were prepared for transport and eventual demolition.

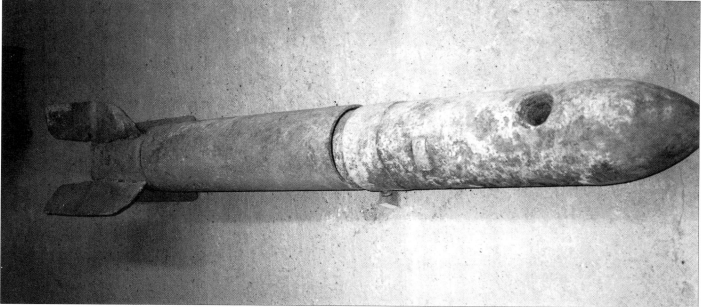

The strong anti-aircraft defences that were available to the Allied ground forces compelled the Luftwaffe to seek new solutions in the further development of air-dropped weapons. The development of rocket-propelled bombs and air-dropped containers was begun in the second half of 1944. These included the 15cm (6in) calibre Wurfkörper SD-4 HL/30 (ejecting 14 SD-4 HL) and the SD-1/30 (ejecting 60 SD-1) bombs, as well as the 19cm (7½in) calibre Wurfkörper SD-70 seen in these photographs.

Left: **Left-over bombs. After the war, the numerous bombs presented a considerable disposal problem. Shown here are samples of 50kg (110 lb) bombs that needed appropriate attention by the Baden-Württemberg Bomb Disposal Service.**

Below and bottom: **Bomb detonation performed by the Bomb Disposal Service of the Freistaat Sachsen (Free State of Saxony) and the crater left after the explosion.**

Weapon Detail Part One

Abwurfmunition
(Air-Dropped Weapons)

Glossary (lists only those bomb types mentioned in this Section)

Blitzlichtbombe	flash-bomb (for night photography)	Nebelbombe	fog or smoke-cover bomb (non-explosive)
Brandbombe	incendiary bomb (inflammable liquid filling)	Panzerbrandbombe	armoured-nose incendiary bomb (Italian)
Elektron Brandbombe	Electron incendiary bomb	Panzersprengbombe	armour-piercing high-explosive bomb
Flammenbombe	inflammable oil-filled incendiary bomb	Panzerdurchschlagsbombe	armour-piercing HE penetration bomb
Gleitbombe	glide-bomb (winged, remote-controlled)	Schrapnellbombe	shrapnel bomb (against airborne targets)
Großladungsbombe	high explosive-content high-explosive bomb	Splitterbombe	splinter or fragmentation bomb
Hohlladungssprengbombe	hollow-charge high-explosive bomb	Spreng- and Brandbombe	combined HE and incendiary bomb
Mehrzweckbombe	multi-purpose high-explosive bomb	Streubrandbombe	scattered incendiary-fire bomb
Minenbombe	standard high-explosive demolition or anti-personnel bomb	Übungsbombe	practice bomb (cement bomb with coloured smoke trail)

Splitterbombe SD-0.5

Bomb weight:	0.498kg (1.098 lb)	Body diameter:	36.5mm (1.44in)
Explosive weight:	0.031kg (0.068 lb)	Use:	Against living and unarmoured targets
Fuze type:	Mechanical impact fuze		
Bomb dimensions:	108 x 36.5mm (4.25 x 1.44in)	Remarks:	Jettisoned on parachute.

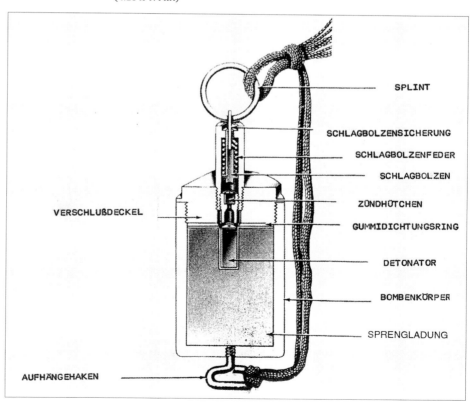

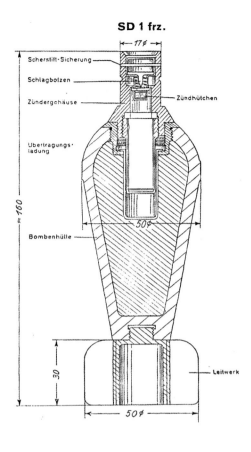

SD 1 frz.

Splitterbombe SD-1 frz

Bomb weight:	0.52kg (1.15 lb)
Explosive weight:	0.06kg (0.13 lb)
Explosive filling:	Fp 20/80
Fuze type:	Mechanical AZ (73) diaphragm impact fuze
Bomb dimensions:	160 x 50mm (6.30 x 1.97in)
Body diameter: maximum	50mm (1.97in)
Use:	Against living and unarmoured targets
Remarks:	Jettisoned from air-dropped containers Captured french bomb.

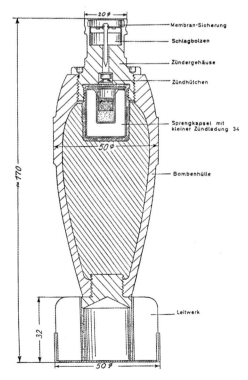

SD 1

Splitterbombe SD-1

Bomb weight:	0.76kg (1.63 lb)
Explosive weight:	0.11kg (0.24 lb)
Explosive filling:	Fp 60/40
Fuze type:	Mechanical diaphragm impact fuze AZ (73), (73)A, (73)A2 or (73)A3
Bomb dimensions:	170 x 50mm (6.69 x 1.97in)
Body diameter: maximum	50mm (1.97in)
Use:	In high-level attack against living and unarmoured targets
Remarks:	Jettisoned from air-dropped containers.

Splitterbombe SD-1 (Ex)

Bomb weight: 0.76kg (1.68 lb)

Explosive weight: None

Fuze type: Replica

Bomb dimensions: 170 x 50mm
(6.69 x 1.97in)

Body diameter: 50mm (1.97in)
maximum

Use: As SD-1

Remarks: Jettisoned from
air-dropped containers.
Concrete bomb body
with steel splinters.

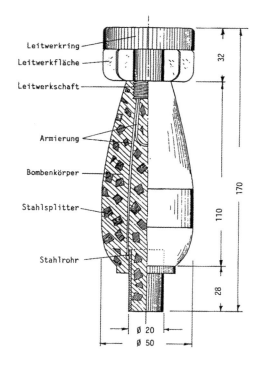

Elektronbrandbombe
B-1 & B-1.3 E

Bomb weight: 1.0 and 1.3kg
(2.2 and 2.87 lb)

Explosive weight: None

Fuze type: AZ 8312 impact fuze
with safety plug;
also designated as
Zünder (13)A fuze

Bomb dimensions: 350 x 50mm
(13.8 x 1.97in)

Body diameter: 50mm (1.97in)

Use: As incendiary, dropped
in clusters against towns
and industrial complexes

Remarks: Jettisoned from
air-dropped containers.
Bomb consists of
Electron casing with
680gm (1.3 lb) Thermite
filling. B-1.3 with steel
nosecap.

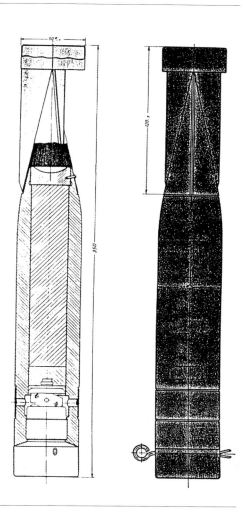

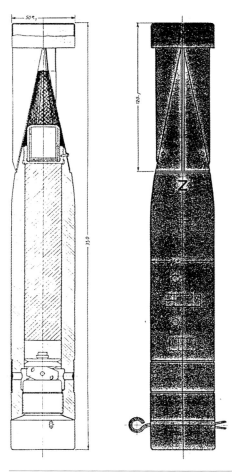

Elektronbrandbombe B-1 EZ & B-1.3 EZB; B-1.3 EZ with self-destruction shell

Bomb weight:	1.0 and 1.3kg (2.2 and 2.87 lb)
Explosive weight:	8-15gm (0.28-0.53oz)
Explosive filling:	Nitropenta
Fuze type:	AZ 8312 impact fuze with safety plug; also designated as Zünder (13) fuze
Dimensions:	350 x 50mm (13.78 x 1.97in)
Body diameter:	50mm (1.97in)
Use:	As incendiary against towns and industrial installations.

Remarks:
Jettisoned from air-dropped containers. In the latter, percentage of incendiaries with self-destruction charge may not exceed 5%. When dropped from 2,000m (6,560ft), B-1 E and B-1 EZ penetrated 5cm iron-concrete, and B-1.3 E and B-1.3 EZ 7cm.

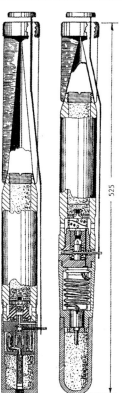

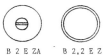

B 2 E ZA   B 2,2 E Z

Elektronbrandbombe B-2 EZ & B-2 EZ with explosive head

Bomb weight:	2.0 and 2.2kg (4.4 and 4.85 lb)
Explosive weight:	60gm (0.13 lb)
Explosive filling:	Nitropenta
Dimensions:	525 x 50mm (20.67 x 1.97in)
Body diameter:	50mm (1.97in)
Fuze type:	AZ (63) impact fuze with skew impact
Use:	As incendiary against towns and industrial installations.
Remarks:	Jettisoned from the BSK-36 in bundles or from air-dropped containers. When dropped from 2,000m (6,560ft), it penetrated 10cm iron-concrete roofings.

Splitterbombe SD-2 it (Bomba 2 Mtr.)

Bomb weight:	1.9kg (4.2 lb)
Explosive weight:	0.22kg (0.485kg)
Explosive filling:	Tritolo, moulded
Fuze type:	Mechanical all-ways impact fuze with swashplate unlocking safety mechanism
Bomb dimensions:	135 x 70mm (5.31 x 2.76in)
Body diameter:	70mm (2.76in)
Use:	Against living and unarmoured targets
Remarks:	Jettisoned from Italian air-dropped containers 100 sp (32 bombs) or from Schüttkästen (multi-bomb containers (42 bombs).

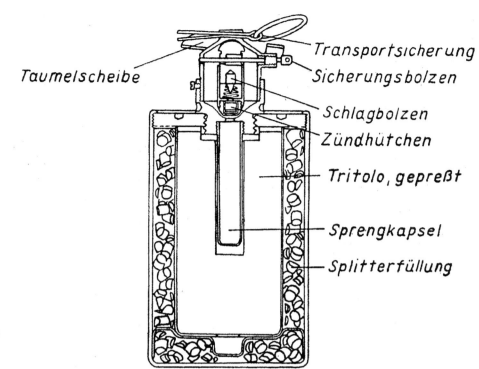

Taumelscheibe — Transportsicherung — Sicherungsbolzen — Schlagbolzen — Zündhütchen — Tritolo, gepreßt — Sprengkapsel — Splitterfüllung

Splitterbombe SD-2 & SD-2 B

Bomb weight:	2.0kg (4.4 lb)
Explosive weight:	0.225kg (0.496 lb)
Explosive filling:	Fp 60/40
Fuze type:	Mechanical (41) clockwork fuze – only in SD-2. Mechanical LZtZ (67) time fuze, or Störzünder (70) A, (70) B, (70) B1 & (70) B2 harassment fuze
Bomb dimensions:	200 x 76mm (7.87 x 2.99in) with cable attachment but without brake airscrews
Body diameter:	76mm (2.99in)
Use:	Against living and unarmoured targets and with Störzünder (deterrent fuze) as mine
Remarks:	Jettisoned from Vemag 90, Rost 24 grid or from air-dropped containers.

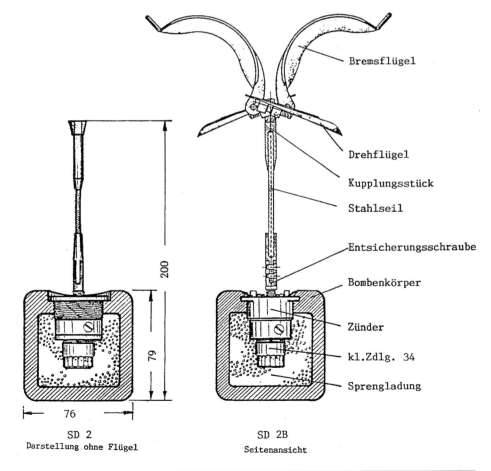

Bremsflügel — Drehflügel — Kupplungsstück — Stahlseil — Entsicherungsschraube — Bombenkörper — Zünder — kl.Zdlg. 34 — Sprengladung

SD 2
Darstellung ohne Flügel

SD 2B
Seitenansicht

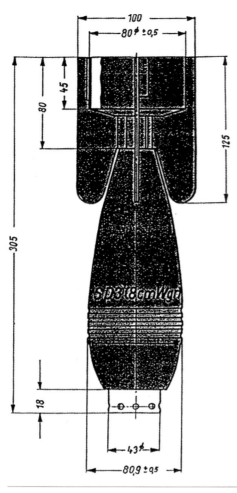

Splitterbombe SD-3

Bomb weight:	3.2kg (7.05 lb)
Explosive weight:	0.55kg (1.21 lb)
Explosive filling:	Fp 60/40
Fuze type:	Mechanical diaphragm impact fuze AZ (73) A3
Bomb dimensions:	305 x 100mm (12.0 x 3.94in)
Body diameter:	81mm (3.19in) maximum
Use:	Against living and unarmoured targets
Remarks:	Jettisoned from air-dropped containers. Modified 8cm Wurfgranate; versions made of Temperguss (malleable iron casting), Perlitguss (Pearlite casting) and Sonderguss (special casting).

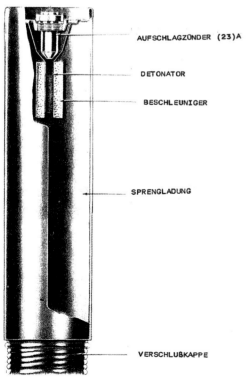

AUFSCHLAGZÜNDER (23)A

DETONATOR

BESCHLEUNIGER

SPRENGLADUNG

VERSCHLUßKAPPE

Großladungsbombe SB-3

Bomb weight:	2.43kg (5.36 lb)
Explosive weight:	1.49kg (3.28 lb)
Fuze type:	All-ways AZ (23)A impact fuze
Bomb dimensions:	346 x 81mm (13.62 x 3.19in)
Body diameter:	81mm (3.19in)
Use:	For special purposes
Remarks:	Jettisoned from AB-36 Abwurfbehälter (air-dropped containers).

Splitterbombe SD-4 HL

Bomb weight:	4kg (8.82 lb)
Explosive weight:	0.31kg (0.68 lb)
Explosive filling:	Fp 02 and Hexogen
Fuze type:	Super-fast impact fuze eAZ (66) or (66)A
Bomb dimensions:	310 x 90mm (12.2 x 3.54in)
Body diameter:	90mm (3.54in) maximum
Use:	Against tanks and tracked vehicles, also living and unarmoured targets.
Remarks:	Jettisoned from air-dropped containers. Several models: of moulded steel, tubing, cast steel, malleable iron casting, Pearlite cast and special cast.

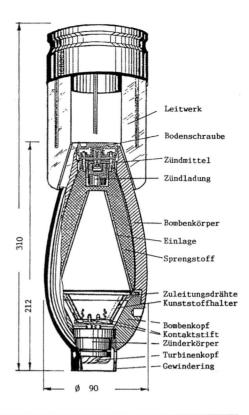

Leitwerk
Bodenschraube
Zündmittel
Zündladung
Bombenkörper
Einlage
Sprengstoff
Zuleitungsdrähte
Kunststoffhalter
Bombenkopf
Kontaktstift
Zünderkörper
Turbinenkopf
Gewindering

310
212
Ø 90

Brandbombe B-4 CH

Bomb weight:	4 to 4.5kg (8.8 to 9.9 lb)
Explosive filling:	Thermite mixture/Napthaline
Fuze type:	All-ways AZ (23)B impact fuze
Bomb dimensions:	525 x 80mm (20.67 x 3.15in)
Body diameter:	80mm (3.15in)
Use:	As incendiary against towns and industrial installations

Remarks:
Jettisoned from air-dropped containers. Several models. Also Brand 4 Chl, filled with a mixture of pitch, calcium perchlorate and ammonium nitrate. Brand D/NP 30 was filled with mixture of Diacen and Nitropenta with 30% Montanwachs. Brand 4 Na held Natrium (sodium). All were more difficult to quench or extinguish than the B-1.3 E. Dropped from 2,000m (6,560ft), they could penetrate 12cm iron-concrete, whereas the B-1.3 E only penetrated 7cm (2¾in).

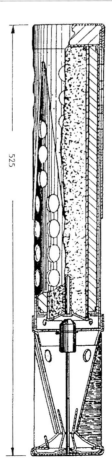

525

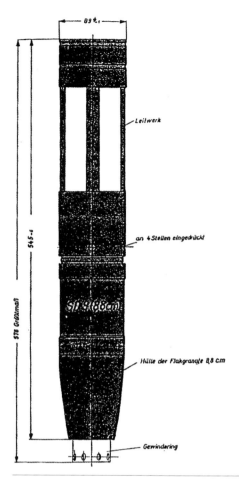

Splitterbombe SD-9

Bomb weight:	9kg (19.8lb)
Explosive weight:	0.8kg (1.76lb)
Explosive filling:	Fp 60/40
Fuze type:	Super-fast eAZ (66)A impact fuze
Bomb dimensions:	578 x 89mm (22.76 x 3.50in)
Body diameter:	88mm (3.46in)
Use:	Against living and unarmoured targets
Remarks:	Jettisoned from air-dropped containers. Modified 8.8cm Sprenggranate (HE shell).

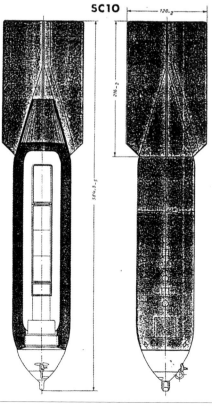

Splitterbombe SC-10

Bomb weight:	10kg (22lb)
Explosive weight:	0.9kg (1.98lb)
Explosive filling:	Fp 60/40
Fuze type:	AZ C-10 (h.u.t.) mechanical impact fuze, also designated Zünder (3)
Bomb dimensions:	584.5 x 120mm (23.0 x 4.72in)
Body diameter:	86mm (3.39in)
Use:	Against living and unarmoured targets
Remarks:	Jettisoned from 4 C-10, ESAC-250/IX inboard, and as Bd C-10 from ETC-50 outboard suspensions.

Splitterbombe SC-10 dw

Bomb weight:	c10kg (22 lb)
Explosive weight:	0.9kg (1.98 lb)
Explosive filling:	Fp 60/40
Fuze type:	AZ C-10 (h.u.t.) mechanical impact fuze, also designated Zünder (3)
Bomb dimensions:	584.5 x 120mm (23.0 x 4.72in)
Body diameter:	86mm (3.39in)
Use:	Against living and unarmoured targets
Remarks:	Jettisoned from 4 C-10, ESAC-250/IX inboard, and as Bd C-10 from ETC-50 outboard suspensions. Several models.

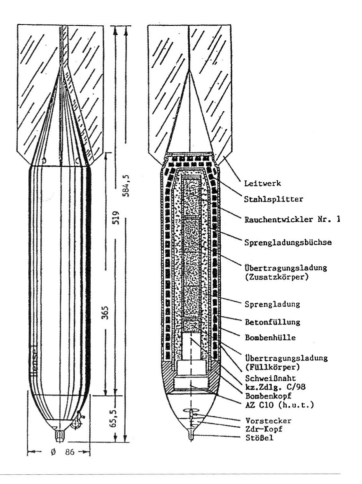

Leitwerk
Stahlsplitter
Rauchentwickler Nr. 1
Sprengladungsbüchse
Übertragungsladung (Zusatzkörper)
Sprengladung
Betonfüllung
Bombenhülle
Übertragungsladung (Füllkörper)
Schweißnaht
kz.Zdlg. C/98
Bombenkopf
AZ C10 (h.u.t.)
Vorstecker
Zdr-Kopf
Stößel

Splitterbombe SD-10 A

Bomb weight:	10kg (22 lb)
Explosive weight:	0.9kg (1.98 lb)
Explosive filling:	Fp 60/40
Fuze type:	eAZ (66) super-fast impact fuze
Bomb dimensions:	545 x 120mm (21.46 x 4.72in)
Body diameter:	86mm (3.39in)
Use:	Against living and unarmoured targets
Remarks:	Jettisoned from air-dropped containers. The SD-10 A is a modified SD-10.

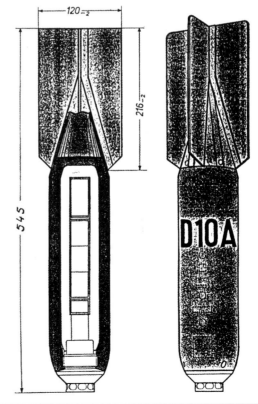

D10A

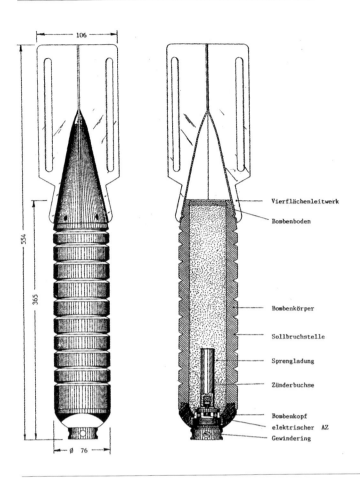

Splitterbombe SD-10 C

Bomb weight:	c8kg (17.6 lb)
Explosive weight:	0.75kg (1.65 lb)
Explosive filling:	Fp 60/40
Fuze type:	eAZ (66) super-fast impact fuze
Dimensions:	545 x 106mm (21.46 x 4.17in)
Use:	Against living and unarmoured targets
Remarks:	Various models. Jettisoned from air-dropped containers.

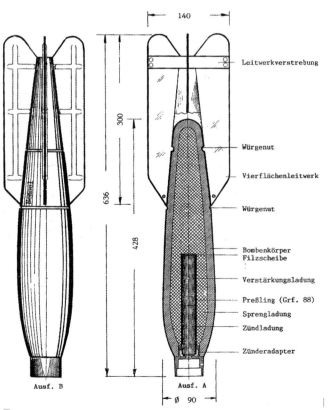

Splitterbombe SD-10 frz

Bomb weight:	9.5kg (20.9 lb)
Explosive weight:	1.25kg (2.76 lb)
Explosive filling:	MMN 70/30, Grf 88, DNAJ, and the like
Fuze type:	mle. 24/31 H 21* nose fuze (French) or super-fast eAZ (66) impact fuze
Dimensions:	636 x 140mm (25.0 x 5.51in)
Body diameter:	90mm (3.54in) maximum
Use:	Against living and unarmoured targets
Remarks:	Jettisoned in bundles (Bd. frz 10) with mle. 24/31 H 21 nose fuze, or from AB-500-1B drop-containers (28 bombs) with sensitive eAZ (66)A impact fuze.

*Also described as Type H, Model 1921, and Type H Model 1929 – Translator.

Splitterbombe SD-10 HL

Bomb weight: c10kg (22 lb)

Explosive weight: No information

Fuze type: Super-fast eAZ (66) or (66) A impact fuze

Bomb dimensions: 350 x 118mm (13.78 x 4.65in)

Body diameter: 118mm (4.65in) maximum

Use: Against tanks and tracked vehicles, also against living and unarmoured targets

Remarks: Experimental only. Capable of penetrating 130mm (5.11in) armoured steel.

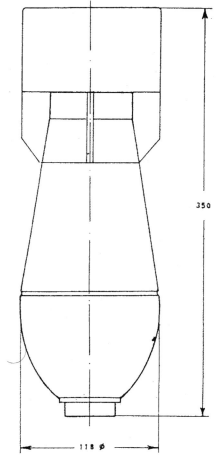

Brandbombe B-10

Bomb weight: c11kg (24.25 lb)

Explosive weight: 4kg (8.8 lb)

Incendiary filling: Effervescent synthetic material, petrol and phosphor

Fuze type: All-ways AZ (23)A impact fuze

Bomb dimensions: 1,070 x 115mm (42.1 x 4.53in)

Body diameter: 115mm (4.53in)

Use: As incendiary against towns and industrial centres

Remarks: Jettisoned from air-dropped containers. A liquid incendiary bomb. When dropped from 2,000m (6,560ft), penetrates 7cm (2.76in) of iron-concrete and burns 6-8 mins.

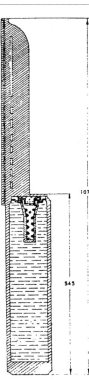

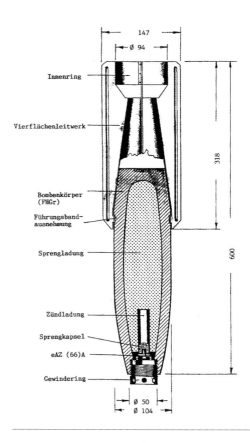

Splitterbombe SD-15

Bomb weight:	c15kg (33 lb)
Explosive weight:	1.75kg (3.86 lb)
Explosive filling:	Fp 60/40
Fuze type:	eAZ (66)A super-fast impact fuze
Bomb dimensions:	637 x 147mm (25.1 x 5.79in)
Body diameter:	104mm (4.09in) maximum
Use:	Against living and unarmoured targets
Remarks:	Jettisoned from air-dropped containers. Unmodified 10.5cm (4⅛in) army howitzer mortar shell.

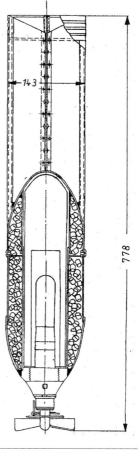

Splitterbombe Bomba 20 c V

Bomb weight:	19.9kg (43.87 lb)
Explosive weight:	2.5kg (5.5 lb)
Explosive filling:	Tritolo (TNT)
Fuze type:	Mechanical duplex fuze with eight adjustable ignition possibilities
Bomb dimensions:	778 x 143mm (30.6 x 5.63in)
Body diameter:	143mm (5.63in)
Use:	Fragmentation bomb against air targets
Remarks:	Captured Italian weapon.

Minenbombe SC-50

Bomb weight:	40-54kg (110-119 lb)
Explosive weight:	c25kg (55 lb)
Explosive filling:	Fp 02, Fp 60/40 or Fp 50/50
Fuze type:	AZ (25)B or C or AZ (55) impact fuze
Bomb dimensions:	1,090 x 280mm (42.9 x 11.0in)
Body diameter:	200mm (7.87in)
Use:	Against lightly damageable materials, hangars, railway rolling stock, ammunition depots, light bridges, and buildings up to three stories. With annular nose ring, against naval targets; also used as depth-charge.
Remarks:	Manufactured in Quality Grades Güteklasse I (SC-50 J/A and L), Güteklasse II (SC-50 J/B, J/C), and Guteklasse III (SC-50 B and K).

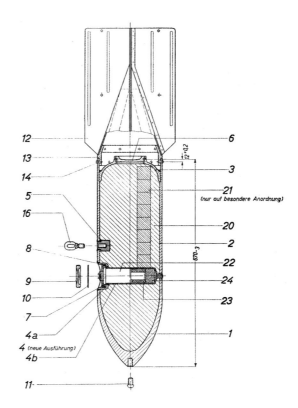

SC-50 JA (Güteklasse 1)

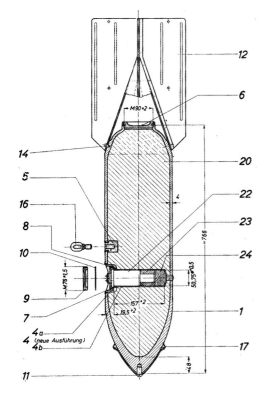

SC-50 JB (Güteklasse 1)

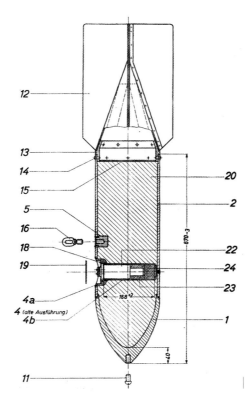

SC-50 B (Güteklasse III)

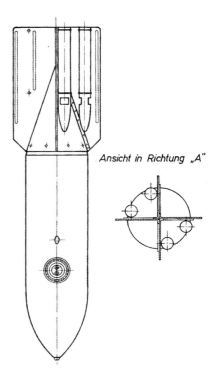

SC-50 mit Gerät Jericho

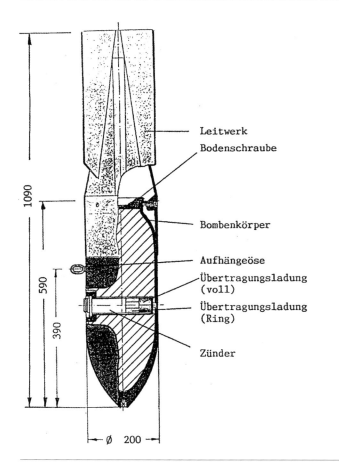

Leitwerk
Bodenschraube
Bombenkörper
Aufhängeöse
Übertragungsladung (voll)
Übertragungsladung (Ring)
Zünder

1090
590
390
Ø 200

Splitterbombe SD-50 (Mehrzweckbombe)

Bomb weight:	54kg (119 lb) maximum
Explosive weight:	16kg (35.2 lb)
Explosive filling:	Fp 02, Fp 60/40, or Amatol 39
Fuze type:	AZ (25)B and C electrical impact fuze, super-fast eAZ (55) impact fuze
Bomb dimensions:	1,090 x 280mm (42.9 x 11in)
Body diameter:	200mm (7.87in)
Use:	Against troops, aircraft, vehicles, normal buildings, aircraft hangars and industrial installations
Remarks:	Jettisoned from all internal and external weapon racks up to 50kg (110 lb). Made in three versions: Stahlguss (Stg) cast steel, Preßstahl (Pr) moulded steel, and Rohr (L) tubing.

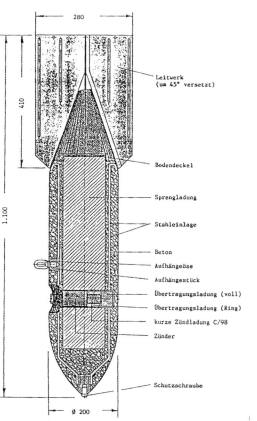

280
410
1.100

Leitwerk (um 45° versetzt)
Bodendeckel
Sprengladung
Stahleinlage
Beton
Aufhängeöse
Aufhängestück
Übertragungsladung (voll)
Übertragungsladung (Ring)
kurze Zündladung C/98
Zünder
Schutzschraube

Ø 200

Splitterbombe SBe-50 E

Bomb weight:	60kg (132 lb)
Explosive filling:	5.5kg (12.1 lb) Ammonal D or 3.0 to 5.4kg (6.6 to 11.9 lb) Ammonal DJ (various weights quoted)
Fuze type:	El.AZ (55) electrical impact fuze
Bomb dimensions:	1,100 x 280mm (43.3 x 11in)
Body diameter:	200mm (7.87in)
Use:	Against living and unarmoured targets
Remarks:	Jettisoned from all internal and external weapon racks up to 50kg (110 lb). Made in six versions (A I and II, C I and II, D and E).

Übungsbombe ZC-50 A

Bomb weight: 50kg (110lb)

Explosive weight: None. Filled with glass phials of red and white smoke producers

Fuze type: None

Bomb dimensions: 1,091 x 280mm (42.95 x 11in)

Body diameter: 200mm (7.87in)

Use: As with SC-50 and SD-50 for training purposes

Remarks: Four different models of this cement bomb. Also ZC-50 L with pyrotechnic flare in tail, burning up to 40 seconds, and ZC-50 C.

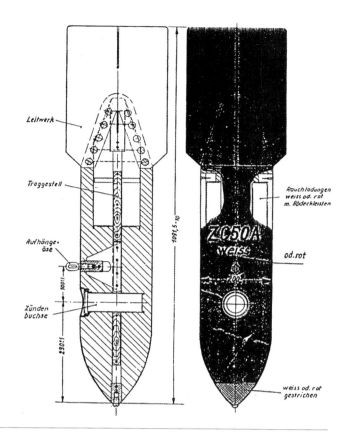

Splitterbombe SD-50 it

Bomb weight: 50kg (110lb)

Explosive weight: 29.2kg (64.4lb)

Explosive filling: Tritolo, S 20 or VP with central cylinder of moulded Tritolo

Fuze type: Mechanical tail fuze with windmill and impact mechanism

Bomb dimensions: 1,029 x 252mm (40.5 x 9.9in)

Body diameter: 252mm (9.9in)

Use: Against small merchant vessels, towns, industrial and road and rail installations

Remarks: Captured Italian bombs (Bomba 50 T)

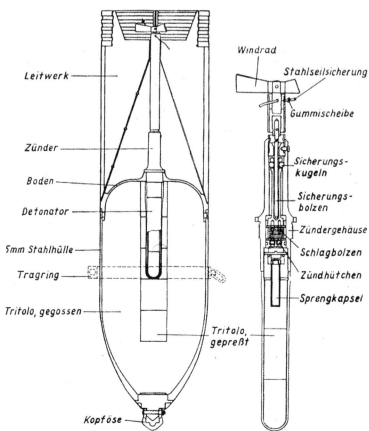

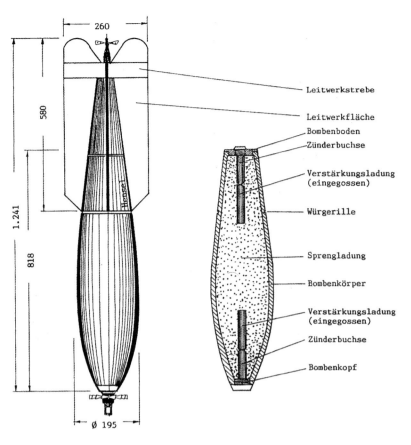

Splitterbombe SD-50 frz

Bomb weight:	57kg (126 lb)
Explosive weight:	19.4kg (42.8 lb)
Explosive filling:	Seven different explosive fillings
Fuze type:	mle. 24/31 H 21 or A nose fuze, or mle. 24 M 38 SR base fuze
Bomb dimensions:	1,241 x 260mm (48.9 x 10.24in)
Body diameter:	195mm (7.68in) maximum
Use:	Against troop concentrations, vehicles and parked aircraft
Remarks:	Captured French bombs. Jettisoned from AB-500-3A Abwurfbehälter.

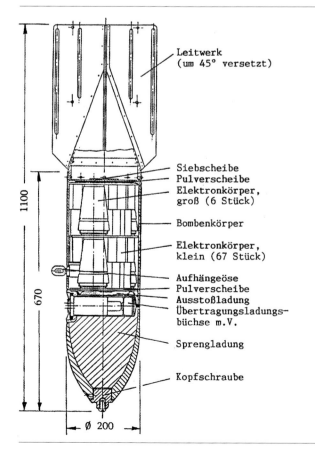

Combined Spreng- & Brandbombe C-50

Bomb weight:	c50kg (110 lb)
Explosive weight:	6kg (13.2 lb)
Explosive filling:	Fp 60/40; Schwarzpulver (blackpowder) expulsion charge
Incendiary filling:	73 Elektron incendiary pellets: 6 x 1,070gm + 67 x 55gm of total weight 10.105kg (22.28 lb)
Fuze type:	AZ (28) A electrical impact fuze turned through 180°.
Bomb dimensions:	1,100 x 280mm (43.3 x 11in)
Body diameter:	200mm (7.87in)
Use:	Against factories and silos (in low-level attack)
Remarks:	Only bombs of Güteklasse I used. Dry storage due to moisture sensitivity.

Liquid Brandbombe
Brand C-50 A

Bomb weight:	c41kg (90.4 lb)
Explosive weight:	0.03kg (0.066 lb)
Explosive filling:	Granatfüllung Grf. 88
Incendiary filling:	12kg (26.5 lb) liquid filling with phosphor igniters in glass phials
Fuze type:	El.AZ (25) B -D electrical impact fuze
Bomb dimensions:	1,100 x 280mm (43.3 x 11in)
Body diameter:	200mm (7.87in)
Use:	Against all targets where an incendiary effect is to be expected

Remarks:
Up until October 1942, Brand C-50 A bombs were filled with phosphorus/carbondisulphide solution poured into the incendiary mixture. (Bomb inscription reads: Attention! Protect against solar heat). Older version usable to -10°C, newer version to –30°C.

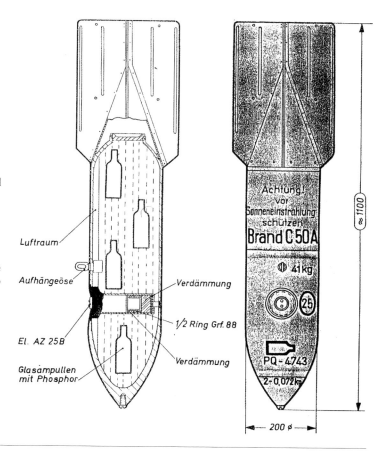

Liquid Brandbombe
Brand C-50 B

Bomb weight:	36kg (79.4 lb)
Explosive weight:	No information
Incendiary filling:	17kg (37.5 lb) filling with two glass bottles filled with phosphor
Fuze type:	El.AZ (25) B -D electrical impact fuze
Bomb dimensions:	1,100 x 280mm (43.3 x 11in)
Body diameter:	200mm (7.87in)
Use:	Against all targets where an incendiary effect is to be expected
Remarks:	Rounded-off bomb nose with large locking screw. Easier to manufacture, it replaced the Brand C-50 A. Burned for 10-15 mins, covering an area of c15m (60ft) diameter.

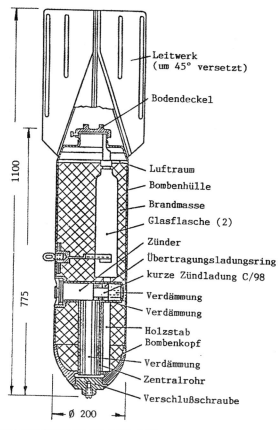

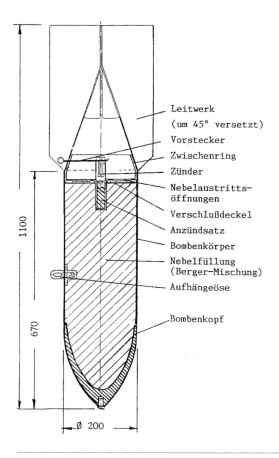

Leitwerk
(um 45° versetzt)
Vorstecker
Zwischenring
Zünder
Nebelaustritts-
öffnungen
Verschlußdeckel
Anzündsatz
Bombenkörper
Nebelfüllung
(Berger-Mischung)
Aufhängeöse

Bombenkopf

1100
670
Ø 200

Nebelbombe NC-50

Bomb weight:	51kg (112.4lb)
Explosive weight:	None
Smoke filling:	24kg (52.9lb) hexachlorethane-zinc mixture
Fuze type:	AZ (36) mechanical base impact fuze
Bomb dimensions:	1,100 x 280mm (43.3 x 11in)
Body diameter:	200mm (7.87in)
Use:	For blinding and confusing the enemy and for camouflaging own troops

Remarks:
Bomb bodies as SC-50 B but without lateral fuze pockets. Use in ground operations as long-burning smoke candle possible. Mean burning time 20 minutes with bomb in vertical position. Covers an area 500m (1,640ft) long, up to 40m (131ft) high and up to 20m (66ft) wide. Jettisoned similar to SC-50.

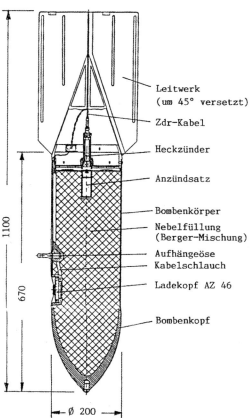

Leitwerk
(um 45° versetzt)
Zdr-Kabel
Heckzünder
Anzündsatz
Bombenkörper
Nebelfüllung
(Berger-Mischung)
Aufhängeöse
Kabelschlauch
Ladekopf AZ 46
Bombenkopf

1100
670
Ø 200

Nebelbombe NC-50 D

Bomb weight:	63kg (138.9lb)
Explosive filling:	None
Smoke filling:	33kg (72.75lb) hexachlorethane-zinc mixture
Fuze type:	AZ (46) mechanical impact fuze with electrical cocking mechanism
Bomb dimensions:	1,100 x 280mm (43.3 x 11in)
Body diameter:	200mm (7.87in)
Use:	For blinding and confusing the enemy and for camouflaging own troops
Remarks:	Tailfins with arrester plate. Camouflage area similar to NC-50 which it replaced.

Floating Nebelbombe NC-50 D See

Bomb weight:	22kg (48.5 lb)
Explosive filling:	None
Smoke filling:	8kg (17.6 lb) hexachlorethane-zinc mixture for grey-white fog screen
Fuze type:	AZ (46) mechanical impact fuze with electrical cocking mechanism
Dimensions:	1,120 x 280mm (44.1 x 11in)
Body diameter:	200mm (7.87in)
Use:	For hiding naval operations and blinding enemy coastal batteries.

Remarks:
Successor to NC-50 C. Tailfins with arrester plate. Mean smoke time 8-10 minutes. Essentially similar are the NC-50 C See and NC-50 W-C, used as floating signal for ditched aircrews. The recognition cloud is coloured yellow.

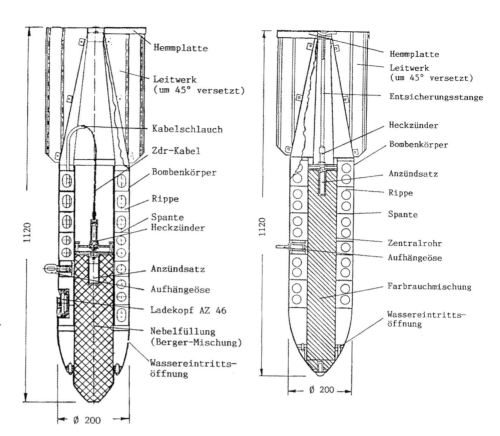

Blitzlichtbombe Bl C-50

Bomb weight:	c36kg (79.4 lb)
Explosive filling:	None
Flare powder:	4kg (8.8 lb) pyrotechnic aluminium; blackpowder bursting charge
Fuze type:	ZtZ (9) or ZtZ (89) mechanical time fuze
Bomb dimensions:	1,100 x 280mm (43.3 x 11in)
Body diameter:	200mm (7.87in)
Use:	For aircraft night photography
Remarks:	Light intensity 60 million HK = Hefner-Kerze (candela or candlepower) for 5 secs illumination. Jettison height 1,000-7,000m (3,280-22,965ft).

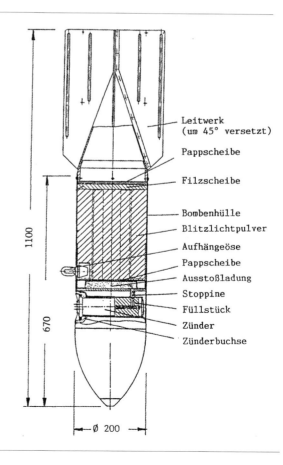

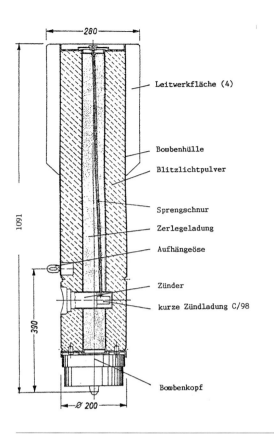

Blitzlichtbombe Bl C-50 A

Bomb weight:	47kg (103.6 lb)
Explosive filling:	None
Flare powder:	17kg (37.5 lb) pyrotechnic aluminium; blackpowder bursting charge
Fuze type:	ZtZ (9) or ZtZ (89) mechanical time fuze
Bomb dimensions:	1,091 x 280mm (42.95 x 11in)
Bomb diameter:	200mm (7.87in)
Use:	For aircraft night photography
Remarks:	Light intensity 500 million HK for 0.3 secs. Jettison altitude, up to 8,000m (26,250ft). Further variants were the Bl 50 B of 14.5kg (91.5 lb) weight, 14kg (30.9 lb) pyrotechnic aluminium, concrete nose; and the Bl 50 C of 62.6kg (138 lb) weight, c35kg (77 lb) aluminium granules and concrete nose. Fuzes were: for Bl 50 B: ZtZ (9), (89) B or C, for Bl 50 C: ZtZ (9), (9)A, (89) B or C.

Image labels: Leitwerkfläche (4), Bombenhülle, Blitzlichtpulver, Sprengschnur, Zerlegeladung, Aufhängeöse, Zünder, kurze Zündladung C/98, Bombenkopf

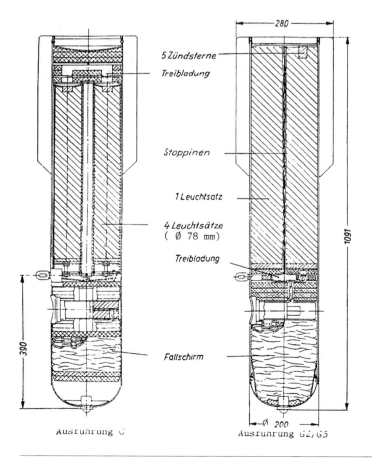

Parachute-Leuchtbombe LC-50 C & LC-50 F Versions A to C, and G2 to G5

Bomb weight:	19kg (41.9 lb) LC-50 F (version A) of 12/1940 33kg (72.8 lb) LC-50 F (version B) of 12/1940 29kg (63.9 lb) LC-50 F (version C) of 04/1942 40kg (88.2 lb) LC-50 F (version C & G) later 42kg (92.6 lb) LC-50 F (version F/G5) later
Explosive filling:	None [3gm blackpowder in fuze]
Flare filling:	29kg (63.9 lb) magnesium granulate, sodium nitrate, calcium oxalate and magnesium stearate [version G5 = 28kg (61.7 lb)]
Fuze type:	ZtZ (9) or ZtZ (59) B time fuze ZtZ (9), (9)A, (89) B or C in LC-50 F/G5
Bomb dimensions:	1,091 x 280mm (42.95 x 11in)
Body diameter:	200mm (7.87in)
Use:	For illuminating bombing targets and tactical battlefield reconnaissance at night
Remarks:	Flare body dropped with parachute. Light intensity: 800,000 HK (LC-50 F/C) Light intensity: 1.4 million HK (LC-50 F/G) Illumination duration: 2 to 5 mins.

Image labels: 5 Zündsterne, Treibladung, Stoppinen, 1 Leuchtsatz, 4 Leuchtsätze (Ø 78 mm), Treibladung, Fallschirm, Ausführung C, Ausführung G2/G5

Splitterbombe SD-70
(Mehrzweckbombe)

Bomb weight: c66kg (145.5 lb)

Explosive weight: 24kg (52.9 lb)

Explosive filling: Fp 60/40

Fuze type: El.AZ (25) B or C, El.AZ (55) electrical impact fuze, or eAZ (55) B super-fast impact fuze

Bomb dimensions: 1,090 x 240mm (42.9 x 9.45in)

Body diameter: 200mm (7.87in)

Use: Against living and lightly armoured targets, railway installations and smaller industrial targets

Remarks: Replaced the SC-50 and SD-50. Jettisoned from all internal and external 50kg (110 lb) bomb racks. Also with Stabo (spike-nose) and telescope fuze.

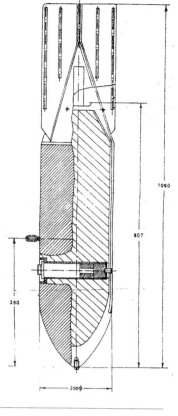

Bombenvorsatzkörper BVK-70

(superimposed nose penetration charge)

Bomb weight: No information

Explosive filling: No information

Fuze type: No information

Bomb dimensions: No information

Body diameter: 200mm (7.87in)

Use: Against living and strongly-armoured targets

Remarks: SD-70 bomb with projecting hollow-charge warhead. Penetration capability: 200mm (7.87in) armoured steel or 800mm (31.5in) of concrete.

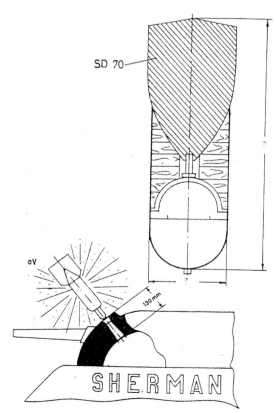

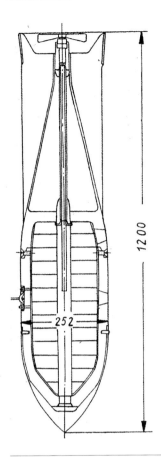

Panzerbrandbombe 70 JP

Bomb weight:	74.5kg (164.2 lb)
Explosive filling:	None
Incendiary filling:	13 Thermite discs, together weighing 36.6kg (80.7 lb). Bomb casing of Elektron.
Fuze type:	Mechanical tail fuze
Bomb dimensions:	1,200 x 252mm (47.2 x 9.9in)
Body diameter:	252mm (9.9in)
Use:	Against towns, industrial and warehouse installations.
Remarks:	Bomb nose with screw-on steel cap. Captured Italian bomb.

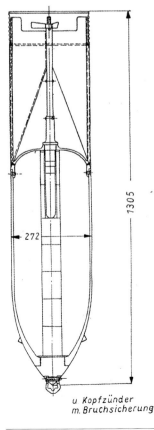

u Kopfzünder
m. Bruchsicherung

Minenbombe SC-100 it (Italian)

Bomb weight:	100kg (220.5 lb)
Explosive weight:	46.5-49.5kg (102.5-109.1 lb) Tritolo S.20, VP or Amatol 70/30 with moulded Tritolo central cylinder
Fuze type:	Mechanical nose fuze with windmill and o.V. (immediate) impact detonation, plus mechanical tail fuze with windmill and impact mechanism
Bomb dimensions:	1,305 x 272mm (51.4 x 10.7in)
Body diameter:	272mm (10.7in)
Use:	Against merchant ships, towns, industrial and railway installations
Remarks:	Captured Italian bomb. Intended for use from German air-dropped containers.

Splitterbombe SD-100 it (Italian)

Bomb weight:	109kg (240.3 lb)
Explosive weight:	27.3kg (60.19 lb)
Explosive filling:	Tritolo S.20 or VP with moulded Tritolo central cylinder
Fuze type:	Mechanical tail fuze with windmill cocking mechanism
Bomb dimensions:	1,260 x 254mm (49.6 x 10.0in)
Body diameter:	254mm (10.0in)
Use:	Against towns, bridges, industrial and railway installations
Remarks:	Captured Italian bomb. Intended for use from German air-dropped containers.

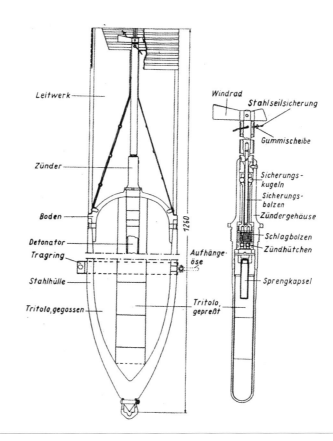

Splitterbombe SD-200 frz (French)

Bomb weight:	225kg (496 lb)
Explosive weight:	107kg (236 lb)
Explosive filling:	MMN or six other fillings
Fuze type:	Nose fuze A, base fuze 3B or mle. 24 M 38 SR
Bomb dimensions:	1,682 x 370mm (66.22 x 14.57in)
Body diameter:	370mm (14.57in) maximum
Use:	Against towns, bridges, industrial and railway installations
Remarks:	Captured French bomb with altered suspension lug.

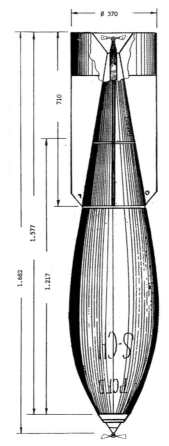

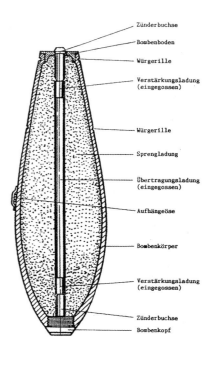

Panzersprengbombe PC-200 RS

Bomb weight:	No information
Explosive weight:	No information
Explosive filling:	No information
Fuze type:	No information
Bomb dimensions:	No information
Body diameter:	No information
Use:	Against bunkers and armour-plated warships
Remarks:	Experimental only. [Solid-propellant diglycol rocket unit at rear to increase impact velocity. Earlier experimental bombs were the PC-20 RS and SD 70 RS – Translator]

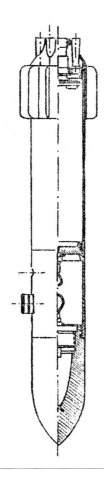

Minenbombe SC-250

Bomb weight:	245-256kg (540-564 lb) with Fp 02
Explosive weight:	125-130kg (276-287 lb) with
Explosive filling:	Trialen 105, Fp 02, Fp 60/40, Fp 50/50, Amatol 39, 40 or 41, Ammonal D, J, or DJ1
Fuze type:	Electrical impact fuze El.AZ (25) B, C or D, El.AZ (28) A, El.AZ (38) and (55) A; electro-mechanical LZtZ (17) A and B time fuze; electro-chemical LZtZ (57) time fuze; special fuze (50) B and Y and ZusZ (40) auxiliary fuze
Bomb dimensions:	1,640 x 512mm (64.57 x 20.16in)
Body diameter:	368mm (14.5in)
Use:	Against railway installations, embankments, flyovers, underpasses, large buildings, and below-ground installations up to 8m (26.3ft) depth. With annular nose ring, against sea targets. From December 1942, also used as a depth-charge filled with Trialen 106.
Remarks:	Produced in three quality grades (Güteklassen) and various types of manufacturing methods and inner linings, also with M 90 x 3 attachment for Stabo with telescopic fuze; with 'Jericho Trumpet' and dropped with Electron incendiary bombs. Used as depth-charge with shortened tail surfaces as also without them.

Labels on SC-250 diagram:

Leitwerk (um 45° versetzt)
Bodendeckel
Stützring
Sprengstoff
Zünder
Übertragungsladung (Ring)
Übertragungsladung
Bombenmantel
Kopfring
Bombenspitze

Schrauben
Aufhängestück
Aufhängeöse
Gewindering
Druckring
Mundlochhülse
Rohr mit Boden
Schutzschraube

SC-250 JA (Güteklasse I)

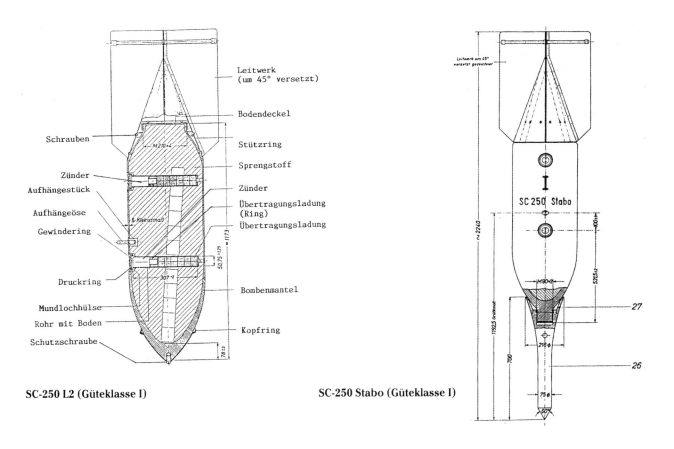

SC-250 L2 (Güteklasse I)

Leitwerk (um 45° versetzt)
Bodendeckel
Stützring
Sprengstoff
Zünder
Übertragungsladung (Ring)
Übertragungsladung
Bombenmantel
Kopfring

Schrauben
Zünder
Aufhängestück
Aufhängeöse
Gewindering
Druckring
Mundlochhülse
Rohr mit Boden
Schutzschraube

SC-250 Stabo (Güteklasse I)

SC 250 Stabo

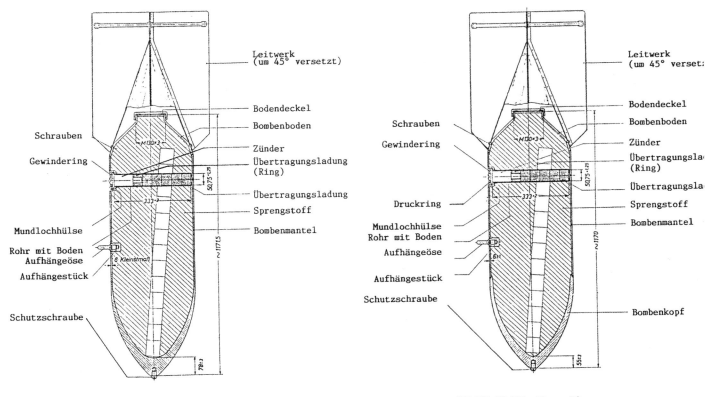

SC-250 JB (Güteklasse II)

Leitwerk (um 45° versetzt)
Bodendeckel
Bombenboden
Zünder
Übertragungsladung (Ring)
Übertragungsladung
Sprengstoff
Bombenmantel

Schrauben
Gewindering
Mundlochhülse
Rohr mit Boden
Aufhängeöse
Aufhängestück
Schutzschraube

SC-250 JC (Güteklasse II)

Leitwerk (um 45° verset…)
Bodendeckel
Bombenboden
Zünder
Übertragungsla… (Ring)
Übertragungsla…
Sprengstoff
Bombenmantel
Bombenkopf

Schrauben
Gewindering
Druckring
Mundlochhülse
Rohr mit Boden
Aufhängeöse
Aufhängestück
Schutzschraube

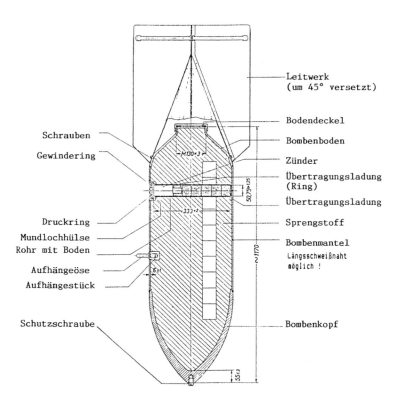

SC-250 J/2 (Güteklasse II)

SC-250 B (Güteklasse III; SC-250 K similar)   **SC-250 with 'Jericho Trumpets'**

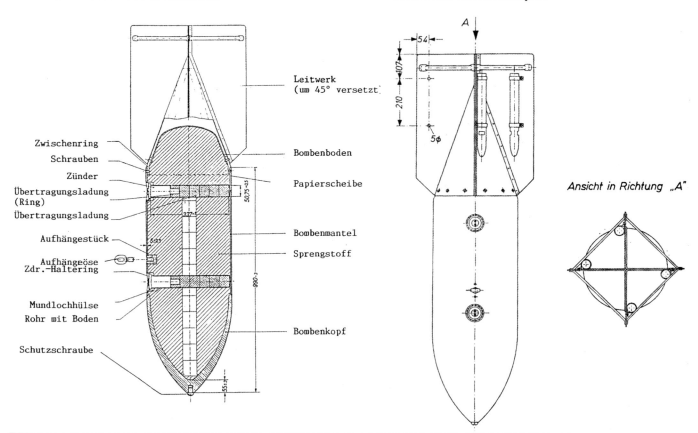

Splitterbombe SD-250
(Mehrzweckbombe)

Bomb weight:	250kg (551 lb) +/-12kg (26.5 lb)
Explosive weight:	80kg (176 lb)
Explosive filling:	Fp 60/40 or Amatol 39
Fuze type:	Electrical impact fuze El.AZ (25)B or C, El.AZ (55), or super-fast eAZ (55)A.
Bomb dimensions:	1,638 x 512mm (64.5 x 20.2in)
Body diameter:	368mm (14.5in)

Use:
In low-level attack against industrial complexes, railways and other traffic installations. Higher durability than the SC-250.

Remarks:
According to method of manufacture, these were: SD-250 (Pr) moulded steel, SD-250 (StG) one-piece cast steel, SD-250 JB 2-piece with nose of cast steel and tube casing, SD-250 Tel with 2.70m (8ft 10¼in) long telescopic rod. Jettisoned from ETC-500, 501, 502; Schloss 500 or ETC-2000, ESAC-250, L-Rost, PVC-1006.

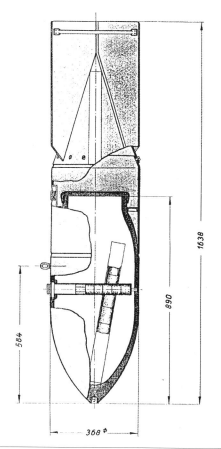

Splitterbombe SBe-250

Bomb weight:	229kg (505 lb)
Explosive weight:	48.54kg (107 lb)
Explosive filling:	Fp 02, Ammonal D or DJ
Fuze type:	electrical impact fuze (15) or El.AZ (28)
Bomb dimensions:	1,637 x 512.2mm (64.4 x 20.2in) SBe-250 C: 1,654 x 631mm (65.1 x 24.2in)
Body diameter:	370mm (14.6in)
Use:	Against living and unarmoured targets
Remarks:	Captured bombs were used by the Red Army also fitted with the all-ways AW-1 impact fuze.

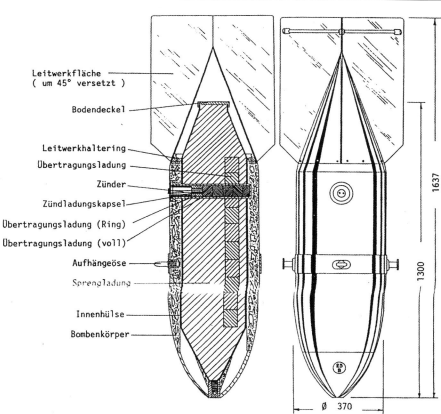

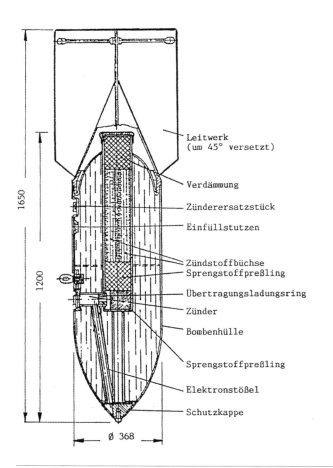

Leitwerk (um 45° versetzt)
Verdämmung
Zünderersatzstück
Einfüllstutzen
Zündstoffbüchse
Sprengstoffpreßling
Übertragungsladungsring
Zünder
Bombenhülle
Sprengstoffpreßling
Elektronstößel
Schutzkappe

Ø 368

Flammenbombe Flam C-250

Bomb weight:	125kg (276 lb)
Explosive weight:	1kg (2.2 lb) Fp 02
Flammable weight:	74kg (163 lb)
Filling:	mixture of 30% petrol + 70% crude-oil
Fuze type:	eAZ (26) super-fast electrical impact fuze
Bomb dimensions:	1,650 x 512.2mm (65 x 20.2in)
Body diameter:	368mm (14.5in)
Use:	For surprise attacks on living targets (marching columns, and the like); against troop barracks and industrial installations
Remarks:	Further developments were Flam C-250 B & C. Bomb wall thickness only 1.5-2.0mm. Had to be protected against solar heat and moisture.

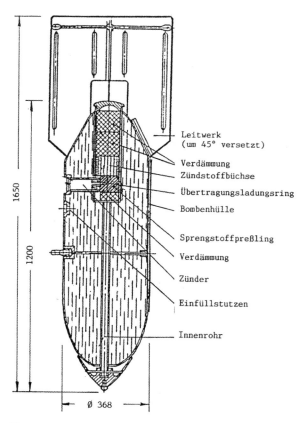

Leitwerk (um 45° versetzt)
Verdämmung
Zündstoffbüchse
Übertragungsladungsring
Bombenhülle
Sprengstoffpreßling
Verdämmung
Zünder
Einfüllstutzen
Innenrohr

Ø 368

Flammenbombe Flam C-250 B & C

Bomb weight:	110kg (242.5 lb)
Explosive weight:	0.6-0.65kg (1.32-1.43 lb) Fp 02
Flammable weight:	60kg (132 lb)
Filling:	mixture of petrol and crude-oil
Fuze type:	eAZ (26) super-fast electrical impact fuze
Bomb dimensions:	1,650 x 512.2mm (47.24 x 20.2in)
Body diameter:	368mm (14.5in)
Use:	For surprise attacks on living targets marching columns, and the like), against troop barracks and industrial installations.
Remarks:	Further developments of the Flam C-250.

Liquid Brandbombe
Brand C-250 A

Bomb weight:	185kg (408 lb)
Explosive weight:	0.19kg (0.42 lb) Fp 02
Incendiary weight:	65kg (143 lb)
Filling:	Incendiary, ignited by phosphorus glass phials
Fuze type:	El.AZ (25) B to D electrical impact fuze
Bomb dimensions:	1,640 x 512.2mm (64.57 x 20.2in)
Body diameter:	368mm (14.5in)
Use:	Deliberately-aimed drop on inflammable targets
Remarks:	Bomb stiffness and ballistics same as SC-250 K (Güteklasse III). Jettisoned from all fittings for 250kg (551 lb) bombs. Affected area of 30-40m (100-150ft) diameter burns for 10-20 minutes.

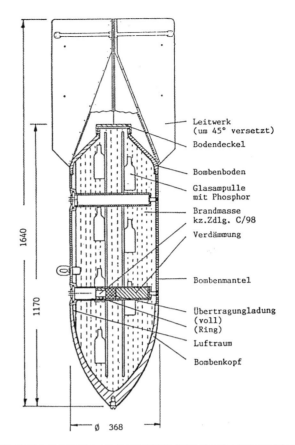

Leitwerk (um 45° versetzt)
Bodendeckel
Bombenboden
Glasampulle mit Phosphor
Brandmasse kz.Zdlg. C/98
Verdämmung
Bombenmantel
Übertragungladung (voll) (Ring)
Luftraum
Bombenkopf

1640
1170
Ø 368

Nebelbombe NC-250 S

Bomb weight:	185kg (408 lb)
Explosive weight:	3.2kg (7.05 lb) Fp 02
Smoke filling:	135kg (298 lb) chlor-sulphide acid and sulphur trioxide
Fuze type:	eAZ (26) super-fast impact fuze
Bomb dimensions:	1,650 x 512.2mm (65 x 20.2in)
Body diameter:	368mm (14.5in)
Use:	For instantaneous development of a fog/smokescreen of 500-1500m (1,640-4,920ft) length, 50-100m (165-330ft) width and 40-50m (130-165ft) height.
Remarks:	2mm thin-walled bomb body. Jettisoned from all bomb fittings for 250kg (551 lb) bombs.

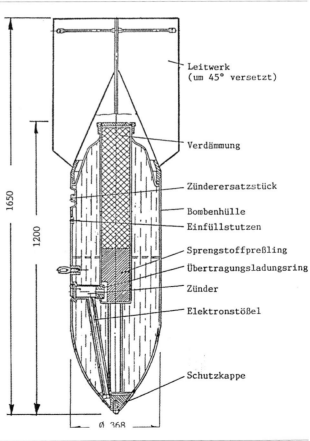

Leitwerk (um 45° versetzt)
Verdämmung
Zünderersatzstück
Bombenhülle
Einfüllstutzen
Sprengstoffpreßling
Übertragungsladungsring
Zünder
Elektronstößel
Schutzkappe

1650
1200
Ø 368

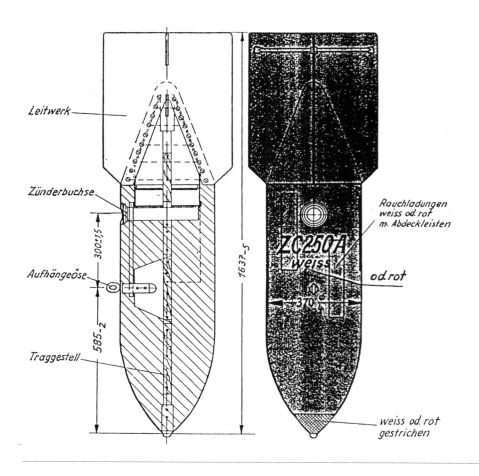

Übungsbombe ZC-250, ZC-250 A & ZC-250 M

Bomb weight:	250kg (551 lb)
Bursting charge:	0.075kg (0.165 lb) Grf 88 or 0.425kg (0.937 lb) Fp 02
Fuze type:	El.AZ C-50 (alias Zünder 5) electrical impact fuze. ZC-50 A and M without fuze
Bomb dimensions:	1,637 x 512.2mm (64.5 x 20.2in)
Body diameter:	368mm (14.5in)
Use:	As SC-250 and SS-250 for training purposes.
Remarks:	Jettisoned from all fittings for 250kg (551 lb) bombs.

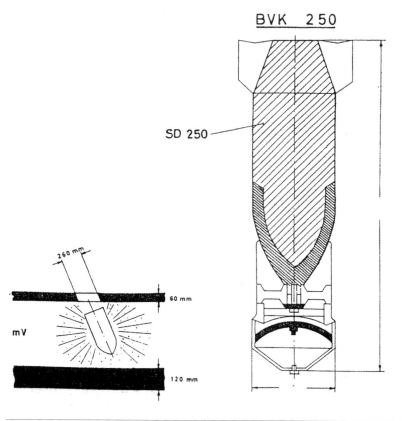

Bombenvorsatzkörper BVK-250

(Superimposed nose penetration attachment)

Bomb weight:	No information
Explosive weight:	No information
Fuze type:	No information
Bomb dimensions:	2,000 x 512.2mm (78.74 x 20.2in)
Body diameter:	368mm (14.5in)
Use:	Against living and strongly-armoured targets, ships
Remarks:	SD-250 bomb with projecting hollow-charge attachment ahead of nose. Penetration capability 60-120mm (2.36-4.72in) armoured steel. Experimental only.

Splitterbombe SD-250 HL

Bomb weight:	No information
Explosive weight:	No information
Fuze type:	No information
Bomb dimensions:	1,600 x 512.2mm (63 x 20.2in)
Body diameter:	368mm (14.5in)
Use:	Against strongly-armoured or concreted targets
Remarks:	Penetration ability between 60-120mm (2.36-4.72in) armoured steel. Experimental only.

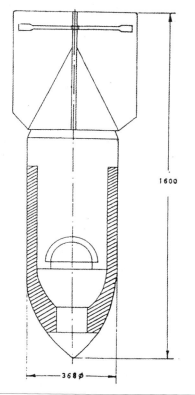

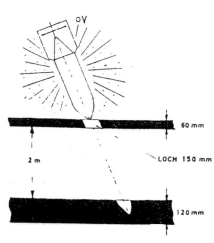

Hohlladungssprengbombe SH-250

Bomb weight:	No information
Explosive weight:	50kg (110lb)
Explosive filling:	Fp 50/50 + Fp 02 fuze charge
Fuze type:	Electrical base fuze
Bomb dimensions:	1,639 x 512mm (64.53 x 20.16in)
Use:	Against living targets, fixed installations and all sea targets
Remarks:	Proposed as a substitute for the SD-250 at the beginning of 1942. Had a calculated penetration capability of at least 300mm (11.8in) armoured-steel and 3,000mm (118.1in) concrete.

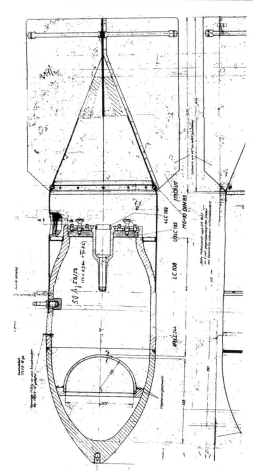

Minenbombe SC-500

Bomb weight:	480-520kg (1,058-1,146 lb)
Explosive weight:	250-260kg (551-573 lb)
Explosive filling:	Fp 02, Fp 60/40, Fp 50/50, Amatol 39, 40, 41, D, J or DJ1, or Trialen (exclusively against sea targets)
Fuze type:	El.AZ (25) B or C, El.AZ (38) or (55) electrical impact fuze
Bomb dimensions:	1,957 x 640mm (77 x 25.2in) SC-500 J = 2,010 x 470mm (79.1 x 18.5in)
Body diameter:	470mm (18.5in)
Use:	Against fixed airfield installations, hangars, assembly halls, flyovers, underpasses, high-rise buildings and underground installations. With screw-on nose ring, against sea targets
Remarks:	Produced until August 1942 with a fuze box. Several variants in Güteklasse I and III. Jettisoned from ETC-500, 501, 502, Schloss 500 in Schloss rack or ETC-2000, PVC-1006.

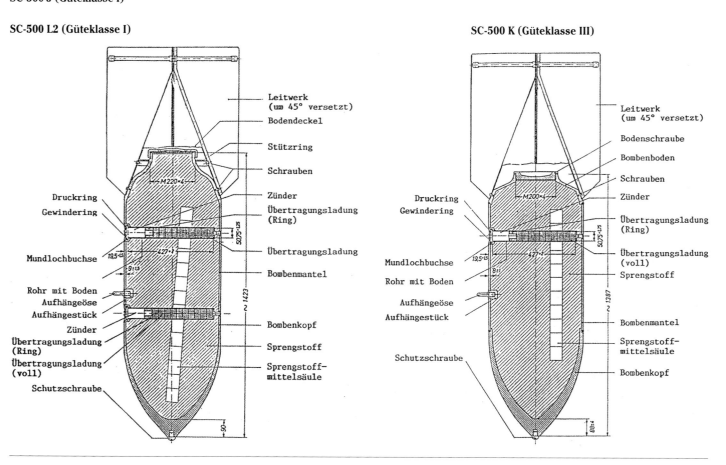

SC-500 J (Güteklasse I)

SC-500 L2 (Güteklasse I)

SC-500 K (Güteklasse III)

SC-500 B (Güteklasse III)

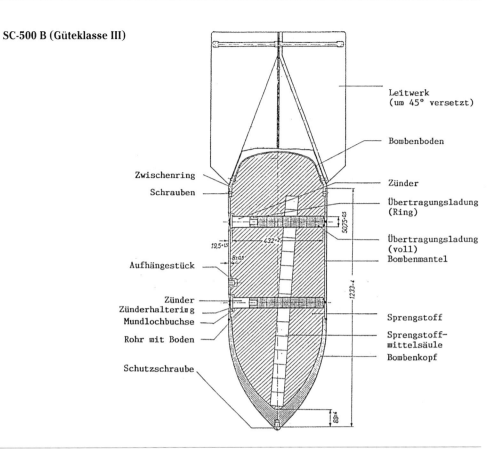

Leitwerk
(um 45° versetzt)

Bombenboden

Zünder

Übertragungsladung
(Ring)

Übertragungsladung
(voll)
Bombenmantel

Sprengstoff

Sprengstoff-
mittelsäule

Bombenkopf

Zwischenring

Schrauben

Aufhängestück

Zünder
Zünderhaltering
Mundlochbuchse
Rohr mit Boden

Schutzschraube

Minenbombe SC-500 HL

Bomb weight:	No information
Explosive weight:	No information
Fuze type:	No information, but with time-delay
Bomb dimensions:	2,000 x 640mm (78.7 x 25.2in)
Body diameter:	447mm (17.6in)
Use:	Against strongly-armoured and concreted targets
Remarks:	Capable to penetrating 30 and 60mm (1.18 and 3.36in) armoured steel. Experimental only.

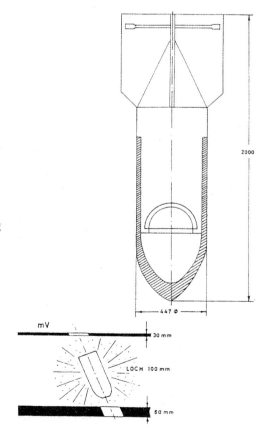

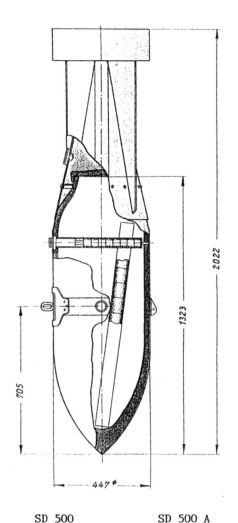

Left: **SD-500 A**

Below:
**The various
models of the
SD-500.**

Splitterbombe SD-500 (Mehrzweckbombe)

Bomb weight:	SD-500 = 457-503kg (1,008-1,109 lb)
	SD-500 A = 450kg (992 lb) in Stg, Pr & L.
	SD-500 B = 500kg (1,102 lb)
	SD-500 C = 485kg (1,069 lb)
	SD-500 E = 457-503kg (as above)

Explosive weight:	SD-500 = 75-180kg (165-397 lb), 90kg (198 lb)
	SD-500 A = 180kg (397 lb)
	SD-500 B = 180kg (397 lb)
	SD-500 C = 172kg (379 lb)
	SD-500 E = 75kg (165 lb)

Explosive filling: Fp 60/40

Fuze type:	SD-500 = El.AZ (25) B or (55);
	SD-500 A = El.AZ (25) A or C or (55);
	SD-500 B = El.AZ (25) D or (55) A, El.Z (50) +
	LZtZ (17) A or B;
	SD-500 C = El.AZ (25) D, (38) C or eAZ (55)A;
	SD-500 E = El.AZ (25) B or (55)

Bomb dimensions:	SD-500 = 2,007 x 396mm (79.0 x 15.6in)
	SD-500 A = 2,022 x 447mm (79.6 x 17.6in)
	SD-500 B = 2,007 x 396mm (79.0 x 15.6in)
	SD-500 C = 2,000 x 396mm (78.7 x 15.6in)
	SD-500 E = 1,744 x 396mm (68.7 x 15.6in)

Use: Against industrial installations, multi-storey factory buildings and ironwork constructions.

Remarks: Various models and methods of fabrication. Jettisoned from racks as SC-500. Penetrates 50mm (1.97in) armoured steel at minimum impact angle of 60° (SD-500 E). SD-500 C replaced SD-500, A, B and E, and partly the SC 500 J.

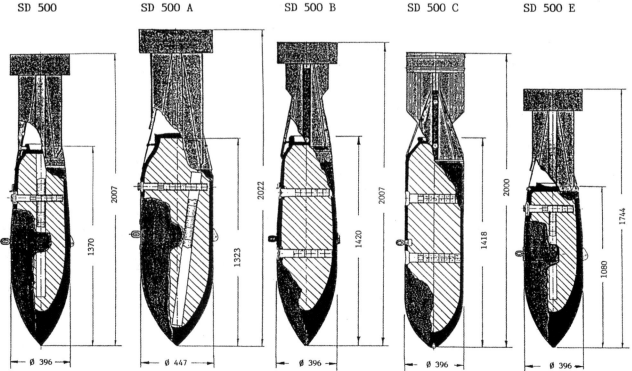

SD 500   SD 500 A   SD 500 B   SD 500 C   SD 500 E

Minenbombe SHL-500

Bomb weight:	No information
Explosive weight:	No information
Fuze type:	No information, but without time-delay
Bomb dimensions:	1,700 x 660mm (66.9 x 26.0in)
Body diameter:	660mm (26.0in)
Use:	Against fortified installations and sea targets
Remarks:	Capable of penetrating 700mm (27.6in) armoured steel and 3,500mm (137.8in) concrete. Experimental only.

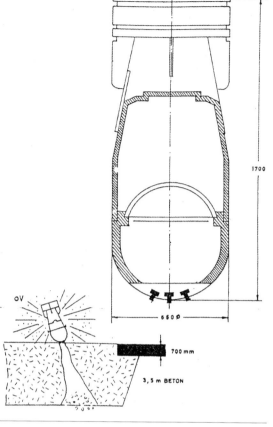

Panzersprengbombe PC-500 E & L

Bomb weight:	416-539kg (917-1,188 lb)
Explosive weight:	78-75kg (172-165 lb)
Explosive filling:	Fp 02, Fp 60/40 or Amatol
Fuze type:	El.AZ (25) B or (35) impact fuze
Bomb dimensions:	2,007 x 396mm (79.0 x 15.6in)
Body diameter:	396mm (15.6in) maximum
Use:	Against concrete bunkers, iron bridges, lightly-armoured warships, underground installations.
Remarks:	Used only in small numbers. Replaced by the PC-1000 and PC-1400.

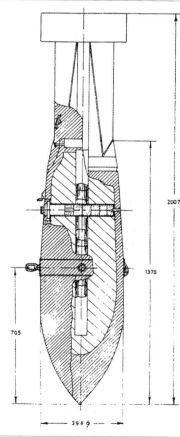

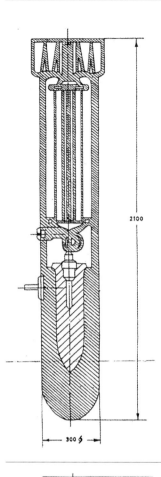

Panzerdurschlagsbombe
PC-500 RS

Bomb weight:	490-500kg (1,080-1,102 lb)
Explosive weight:	12-14kg (26.5-30.9 lb)
Explosive filling:	No information
Fuze type:	El.AZ (49) A1, B1 impact fuze
Bomb dimensions:	2,100 x 360mm (82.7 x 14.2in)
Body diameter:	300mm (11.8in)
Use:	Against concrete bunkers, armour-plated Warships and underground installations
Remarks:	Original design dates from 1939. Used only in small numbers. Replaced by the PC-1000 RS, likewise rocket-propelled.

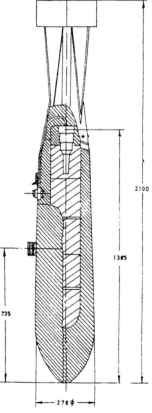

Panzerdurschlagsbombe
PD-500

Bomb weight:	500kg (1.102 lb)
Explosive weight:	32kg (70.6 lb), latterly 30kg (66 lb)
Explosive filling:	PMF 109
Fuze type:	El.AZ (49) P5 electrical impact fuze
Bomb dimensions:	2,100 x 330mm (82.7 x 13.0in)
Body diameter:	276mm (10.9in)
Use:	Jettisoned in level flight from altitudes above 3,400m (11,155ft) against armoured warships. Impact velocity 270m/sec (886ft/sec = 604mph).

Remarks:
Penetrates 140-160mm (5.5-6.3in) armoured steel at 60° impact angle, destruction through splinters and gas pressure. Jettisoned from ETC-500, 501, 502; Schloss 500 in rack, or ETC-2000, PVC-1006.

Flammenbombe Flam C-500 C

Bomb weight:	255kg (496 lb)
Explosive filling:	Fp 02
Incendiary filling:	157kg (346 lb) consisting of 30% petrol + 70% crude-oil
Fuze type:	El.AZ (25) A to D, or eAZ (26) electrical impact fuze
Bomb dimensions:	1,765 x 457mm (69.5 x 18.0in)
Body diameter:	457mm (18.0in)

Use:
For surprise attack on living targets (marching columns, troop barracks, artillery positions), also industrial installations with light roof construction, barrack blocks and other easily inflammable targets.

Remarks:
Production in spring 1943. Jettisoned from all racks for SC-500. The bomb develops a flame 30-40m (98-131ft) in diameter and 10-15 seconds duration. Had to be protected against solar heat and moisture. Ineffective at temperatures below –30°C.

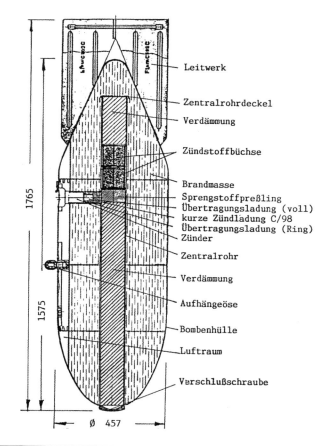

Streubrandbombe Streubrand C-500

Bomb weight:	c180kg (397 lb)
Explosive charge:	Explosive lead around bomb longitudinal axis

Explosive weight:
146kg (322 lb) consisting of 1,400 incendiary cans in 20% alcohol/methylated spirits solution of 29.2kg (64.4 lb) weight; phosphorus incendiary mass

Fuze type:	Mechanical ZtZ (89) B time fuze
Bomb dimensions:	1,750 x 640mm (68.9 x 25.2in)
Body diameter:	472mm (18.6in)

Use: Against widespread, lightly inflammable area targets (forests, dry grass, light wood constructions, fuel depots)

Remarks: Jettisoned from all racks for the SC-500. Streubrand C-500 II version has igniter with delayed-action in the incendiary cans. When dropped from 1,500m (4,920ft), fuze delay set for 4 secs; from above 5,000m (16,400ft), fuze delay is set for 25-33 secs. Storage in closed rooms away from sunlight at temperatures between +45°C and –5°C otherwise ineffective.

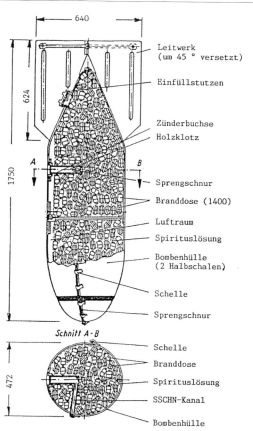

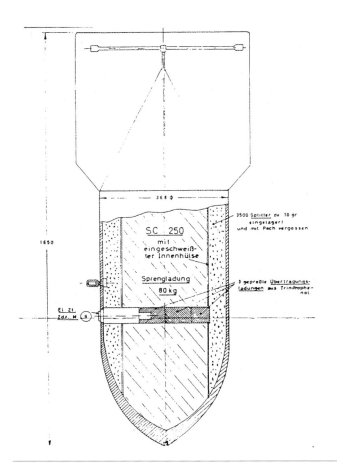

Shrapnellbombe Shr-500

Bomb weight:	c500kg (1,102 lb)
Explosive weight:	80kg (176 lb)
Explosive filling:	Surrounded by 3,500 splinters each of 10gm weight embedded in pitch + three compressed cylinders of Trinitrophenol
Fuze type:	El.ZtZ (9) electrical impact fuze
Bomb dimensions:	1,650 x 640mm (65.0 x 25.2in)
Body diameter:	368mm (14.5in)
Use:	Against air targets (bomber formations)
Remarks:	Consists of an SC-250 with additional outer casing described above.

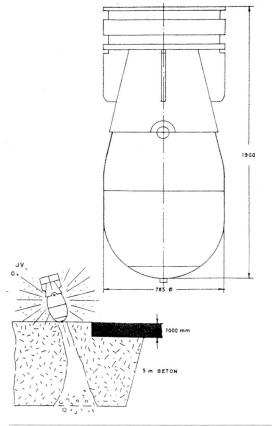

Hohlladungssprengbombe SHL-800

Bomb weight:	c800kg (1764 lb)
Explosive weight:	No information
Fuze type:	No information (but w/o delay in drawing)
Bomb dimensions:	1,900 x 785mm (74.8 x 30.9in)
Body diameter:	785mm (30.9in)
Use:	Against fortifications and sea targets
Remarks:	Capable of penetrating 1,000mm (39.4in) armoured steel and 5,000mm (197in) of concrete. Experimental only.

Großladungsbombe
SB-1000 & SB-1000 A

Bomb weight:	1,000kg (2.205 lb)
Explosive weight:	735kg (1.620 lb) Fp 60/40 or 800-850kg (1,764-1,874 lb) Trialen 106 or PMF 109
Fuze type:	eAZ (55)A with 165cm (65in) cable length
Bomb dimensions:	2,650 x 660mm (104.3 x 26.0in)
Body diameter:	660mm (26.0in)
Use:	Most destructive effect against built-up area targets

Remarks:
SB-1000 annular tail ring welded to bomb body. SB-1000 A has a bayonet-type tail surfaces lock. Jettisoned (without ignition current switch on Schloss) from Schloss 2000/XIII in ETC-2000/XIID and ETC 502 or other racks, strengthened PVC-1006 and ETC-500. From 1944, with fuze ignition current switch in Schloss 504, ETC-504 and Schloss 502 B. Not to be jettisoned below 700m (2,300ft). Self-detonation limit on water impact 1,000m (3,280ft).

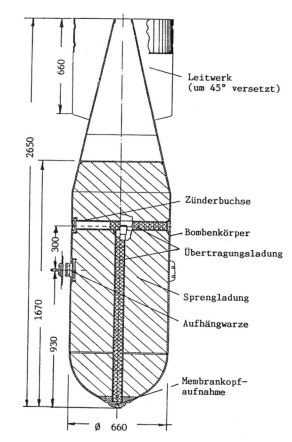

Leitwerk (um 45° versetzt)

Zünderbuchse

Bombenkörper

Übertragungsladung

Sprengladung

Aufhängwarze

Membrankopfaufnahme

Großladungsbombe
SC-1000 L & L2

Bomb weight:	993-1,027kg (2,189-2,264 lb)
Explosive weight:	530-590kg (1,168-1,300 lb) Fp 60/40 or Trialen 105; SC-1000 L2 = 620kg (1,367 lb)
Fuze type:	El.AZ (25) B, B2 or D, or El.AZ (55) electrical impact fuzes
Bomb dimensions:	2,580 x 654mm (101.6 x 25.75in) for SC-1000; 2,800 x 654mm (110.2 x 25.75in) for SC-1000 L2.
Body diameter:	654mm (25.75in)

Use: Against unarmoured sea targets, especially where a good underwater effect was expected. Also against unarmoured land targets.

Remarks: Against sea targets, with Trialen filling only. SC-1000 had one-piece drawn bomb body (Güteklasse I). Jettisoned from Schloss 2000 or ETC-2000, or strengthened PVC-1006 and ETC-500.

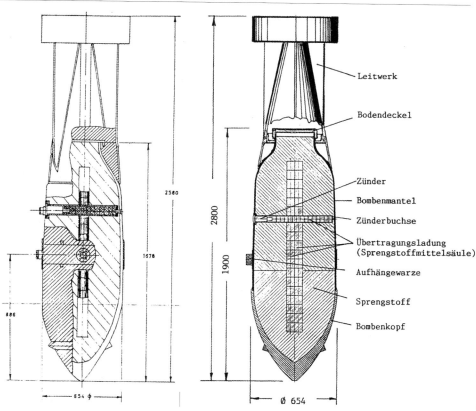

Leitwerk

Bodendeckel

Zünder

Bombenmantel

Zünderbuchse

Übertragungsladung (Sprengstoffmittelsäule)

Aufhängewarze

Sprengstoff

Bombenkopf

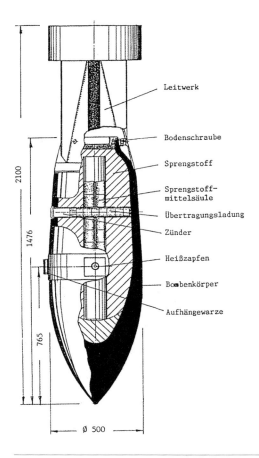

Leitwerk

Bodenschraube

Sprengstoff

Sprengstoff-
mittelsäule

Übertragungsladung

Zünder

Heißzapfen

Bombenkörper

Aufhängewarze

Ø 500

Panzersprengbombe PC-1000

Bomb weight:	938-1,042kg (2,068-2,297 lb)
Explosive weight:	152kg (335 lb)
Explosive filling:	Fp 60/40
Fuze type:	El.AZ (25) A to D, El.AZ (35) with interim fuze piece, or El.AZ (38).
Bomb dimensions:	2,100 x 500mm (82.7 x 19.7in)
Body diameter:	500mm (19.7in) maximum

Use:
Against concrete bunkers with up to 2m (6.56ft) wall thickness, iron bridges, lightly-armoured warships, underground installations up to 8m (26.25ft) below the surface.

Remarks:
Could penetrate 100mm (3.94in) armoured steel at minimum impact angle 60°. Jettisoned from Schloss 2000 or ETC-2000; strengthened PVC-1006 and ETC-500. Ring tail made of Elektron or sheet steel. One-piece casing with hardened nose.

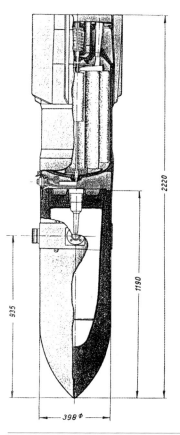

Panzerdurchschlagsbombe PC-1000 RS & PC-1000 RS-A

Bomb weight:	1,000kg (2,205 lb)
Explosive weight:	65kg (143 lb)
Explosive filling:	PMF 109
Fuze type:	El.AZ (49) or (49) B electrical special impact fuze

Bomb dimensions:
PC-1000 RS = 2,220 x 398mm (87.4 x 15.7in)
PC-1000 RS-A = 2,200 x 460mm (86.6 x 18.1in)

Body diameter: 398mm (15.7in)

Use: Against medium-strength bunkers, heavy cruisers, aircraft carriers and battleships (in level flight).

Remarks: Bomb body made of quality materials with a hardened nose; rocket propellant at rear. When jettisoned from 5,000m (16,400ft), is able to penetrate 180mm (7.1in) armoured steel at an impact angle of 60°. PC-1000 RS-A with capped rocket motor section and falls without propulsion. Jettisoned from Schloss 2000, ETC-2000 or PVC-1006. Drop altitudes between 1,000-8000m (3,280-26,250ft).

Panzerdurchschlagsbombe PD-1000

Bomb weight:	c1,000kg (2,205 lb)
Explosive weight:	65kg (143 lb)
Explosive filling:	PMF 109
Fuze type:	El.AZ (49) electrical impact fuze
Bomb dimensions:	2,645 x 440mm (104.1 x 17.3in)
Body diameter:	458mm (18.0in)
Use:	Jettisoned from high altitudes against armoured targets.
Remarks:	Manufactured in small numbers only.

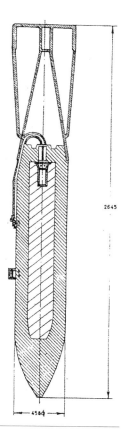

Henschel Hs 293 Powered Glide-bomb

Total weight:	1,045kg (2,304 lb) with underslung Walter HWK 109-507 rocket motor.
Weight at target:	967kg (2,132 lb)
Rocket motor:	78kg (172 lb) T-Stoff + Z-Stoff
Explosive weight:	500kg (1,102 lb)
Explosive filling:	Trialen 105
Fuze type:	El.AZ (38) B electrical impact fuze
Bomb dimensions:	3,100mm (122.0in) span; 3,819mm (150.4in) length; 1,100mm (43.3in) height
Wing area:	1.92m² (20.67ft²)
Body diameter:	470mm (18.5in)

Use: Against light-and medium-armoured sea targets. Remotely guided by missile controller after air-launch.

Remarks: Launched from He 177A-3, He 111 H-5, Fw 200 and Do 217. Impact circle 5 x 5m (16.4 x 16.4ft) when dropped from 12,000m (39,370ft) away. Several variants – from Hs 293A to Hs 293I.

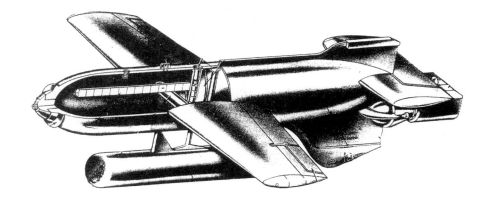

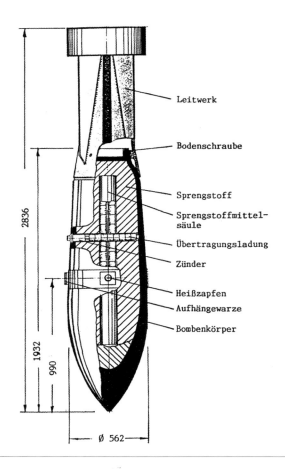

Panzersprengbombe PC-1400

Bomb weight:	1,353-1463 lb (2,983-3,225 lb)
Explosive weight:	320kg (705 lb)
Explosive filling:	Fp 60/40
Fuze type:	El.AZ (25) B, C or D; El.AZ (35) with Zwischenstück II interim fuze; El.AZ (38) C electrical impact fuze
Bomb dimensions:	2,836 x 562mm (111.7 x 22.1in)
Body diameter:	562mm (22.1in) maximum
Use:	Against armoured warships and fortified installations.

Remarks: Penetrates 110mm (4.3in) armoured steel at minimum impact angle 60°. Jettisoned from Schloss 2000, or ETC-2000, PVC 1006. For use against ships, made of alloyed steel Güteklasse I. When made of cast steel, no Quality Grade applied.

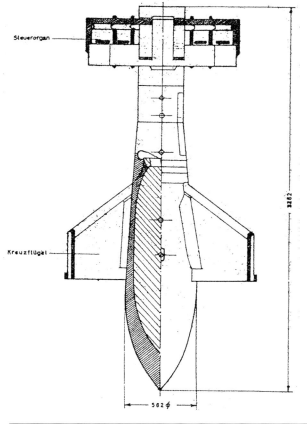

Gleitbombe PC-1400 X 'Fritz X'

Bomb weight:	1,650kg (3,638 lb)*
Explosive weight:	(1) 270kg (595 lb) with
Explosive filling:	(1) 50/50 Amatol/TNT
Explosive weight:	(2) 350kg (772 lb) with
Explosive filling:	Hexogen or Trialen (various data quoted)
Fuze type:	El.AZ (28)A, (35) or (38) electrical impact fuze.
Bomb dimensions:	1,352mm (53.2in) span 3262mm (128.4in) length 1,200 x 800mm (47.2 x 31.5in) for multi-sided tailspan and height
Body diameter:	562mm (22.1in) maximum
Use:	Against armoured warships. Remotely guided by controller in launch aircraft.

Remarks: Jettisoned from He 177, Do 217E, K and M. X-winged unpowered glide bomb. Impact circle 10m (32.8ft) diameter when dropped from 10,000m (10,930 yds) distance and 5,000m (16,400ft) altitude.

* In Fritz Hahn: Deutsche Geheimwaffen 1939-1945, p.297, weight = 1,570kg (3,461 lb) and explosive weight 320kg (705 lb). Designation SD-1400 X applied to early experimental models. Jettison heights up to 10,000m (32,800ft); maximum velocity 343m/sec (1,125ft/sec = 767mph). Sank Italian battleship *Roma*, damaged the battleship *Italia*, battleship *Warspite* and cruiser *Uganda* (UK), cruisers *Savannah* and *Philadelphia* (USA). Further developments were the PC-1500 X and 'Peter X' variants of 1,775-1,943kg (3,913-4,284 lb) weight – Translator.

Panzersprengbombe PC-1600 and PC-1600 A

Bomb weight:	1,600kg (3,527 lb)
Explosive charge:	230kg (507 lb)
Explosive filling:	PMF 109
Fuze type:	El.AZ (49) P16 electrical impact fuze
Bomb dimensions:	2,812 x 536mm (110.7 x 21.1in)
Body diameter:	536mm (21.1in)
Use:	Intended for use against large armoured targets such as warships up to battleship size.
Remarks:	Jettisoned from heights of 4,000-6,000m (13,120-19,700ft). Penetrated 180mm (7.1in) armour plating at 60° impact angle. Replaced PC-1400. Jettisoned from Schloss 2000 or ETC-2000, PVC-1006. The PC-1600 A was derived from PC-1800 RS without rocket.

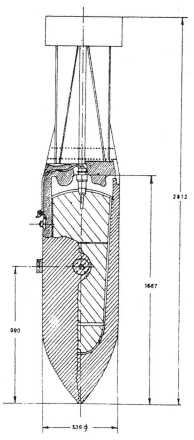

Splitterbombe SD-1700 (Mehrzweckbombe)

Bomb weight:	1,624-1,784kg (3,580-3,933 lb)
Explosive weight:	720kg (1,587 lb)
Explosive filling:	Fp 60/40
Fuze type:	El.AZ (28) B/6
Bomb dimensions:	3,300 x 660mm (129.9 x 26.0in)
Body diameter:	660mm (26.0in)
Use:	Against warships up to small cruiser size, heavy old-type cruisers and industrial installations.
Remarks:	Jettisoned in diving or level flight from Schloss 2000, or ETC-2000, PVC 1006. Penetrated 60mm (2.36in) armoured steel at 60° angle.

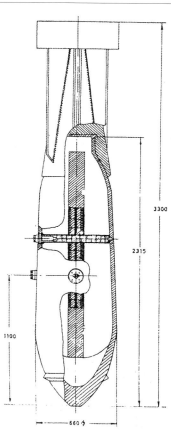

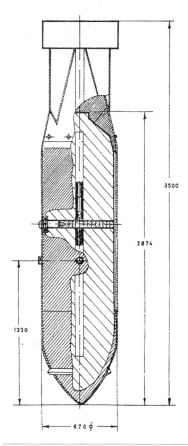

Minenbombe SC-1800

Bomb weight:	1,767-1,879kg (3,896-4,142 lb)
Explosive weight:	1,000kg (2,205 lb) Fp 60/40 or 1,100kg (2,425 lb) Trialen 105
Fuze type:	El.AZ (25) C or D, El.AZ (28) B/0.7; initially El.AZ (25) B electrical impact fuze
Use:	Against building complexes and large merchant vessels. (Strong high-explosive effects against sea targets; high pressure-wave destructive effect).
Remarks:	SC-1800 with Trialen filling used against land targets with no-delay fuze setting only. Nose ring. Jettisoned from Schloss 2000, ETC-2000, PVC 1006.

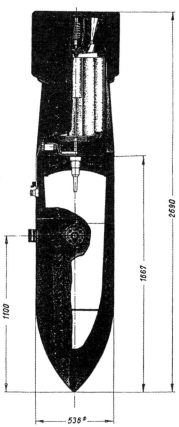

Panzersprengbombe PC 1800 RS

Bomb weight:	1,800kg (3,968 lb)*
Explosive weight:	220kg (485 lb)*
Explosive filling:	PMF 109
Fuze type:	El.AZ (49) C electrical impact fuze
Bomb length:	2,690mm (105.9in)
Body diameter:	536mm (21.1in)

Use: Against bunkers and battleships. Jettisoned only in diving flight at 50° angle (only after special training).

Remarks: one-piece thick-walled bomb body with rocket propellant burning for 3 secs duration. At 60° minimum impact angle, could penetrate 180mm (7.1in) armoured steel. Released from Schloss 2000 or ETC-2000, PVC-1006.

*Author also quoted bomb weight 2,057kg (4,535 lb) and explosive weight 360kg (794 lb) both in brackets behind the above data, but with no explanation. In Fritz Hahn: Deutsche Geheimwaffen 1939-1945, loaded weight = 2,115kg (4,663 lb), explosive weight = 230kg (507 lb), and impact speed 972km/h (604mph) for the PC 1800 RS 'Panther' – Translator.

Panzerdurchschlagsbombe PD-1800 RS

Bomb weight:	c1,800kg (3,968 lb)
Explosive weight:	No information
Explosive filling:	No information
Fuze type:	El.AZ (49) electrical impact fuze
Bomb length:	3,080mm (121.3in)
Body diameter:	450mm (17.7in)
Use:	Against bunkers and battleships
Remarks:	One-piece thick-walled bomb body with solid-propellant rocket motor. Manufactured in small numbers only.

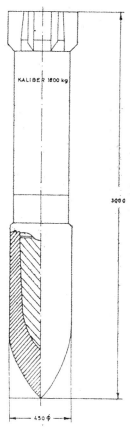

Minenbombe SC-2000

Bomb weight:	c2,000kg (4,409 lb)
Explosive weight:	No information
Explosive filling:	No information
Fuze type:	El.AZ (25) D or (28) electrical impact fuze
Bomb dimensions:	3,500 x 440mm (137.8 x 17.3in)
Body diameter:	440mm (17.3in)
Use:	Against building complexes and large merchant vessels.
Remarks:	With nose ring. Produced in small numbers only.

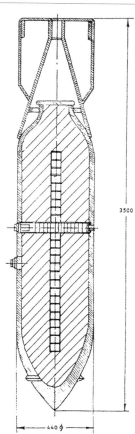

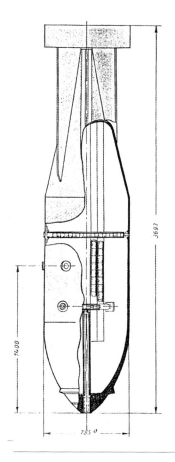

Großladungsbombe SB-2500 & SB-2500 (A1)

Bomb weight:	SB-2500 = 2,430-2,570kg (5,357-5,666lb)*
Explosive weight:	SB-2500 = 1,570-1,710kg (3,461-3,770lb)* SB-2500 (A1) = 1,950-2,000kg (3,990-4,409lb)*
Explosive filling:	Fp 60/40 (both variants). From December 1942, with Trialen 105 exclusively for merchant ships.
Fuze type:	El.AZ (25)B, C, or D in conjunction with AZ (24)C. El.AZ (28)A still partially used in 1943.
Bomb dimensions:	SB-2500 = 3,693 x 785mm (145.4 x 30.9in) SB-2500 (A1) = 3,895 x 825mm (153.3 x 32.5in)
Use:	Against towns and industrial installations (severest pressure-wave destructive effect)
Remarks:	SB-2500 A1 bomb body of one-piece cast aluminium (1943 manufacture). SB-2500 had steel body and reduced dimensions.(Used in He 177 and Do 217). Jettisoned from Schloss 2000 or 3000.

* In Karl W Pawlas: Munitions Lexikon Band 3, p.56, bomb weight: SB-2500 =
2,370kg (5,225lb); SB-2500 (A1) = 2,500kg (5,512lb). Explosive weight SB-2500
= 1,570kg (3,461lb); SB-2500 (A1) = 2,000kg (4,409lb). SB-2500 made of
welded sheet steel with welded cast steel nose and nose ring. The SB-2500 (A1)
was of one-piece cast aluminium or welded aluminium sheet casing with
welded nose of Bondur – Translator.

Minenbombe SC-2500

Bomb weight:	No information*
Explosive weight:	1,700kg (3,748lb)
Explosive filling:	Trialen 105
Fuze type:	El.AZ (25) D or El.AZ (28) electrical impact fuze
Bomb dimensions:	3,895 x 829mm (153.3 x 32.6in)
Body diameter:	829mm (32.6in)
Use:	Against building complexes and merchant vessels
Remarks:	Experimental models only.

* Bomb weights have been quoted as 1,950kg (4,300lb), and 2,500kg (5,512lb)
for Großladungsbombe SC-2500 – Translator.

Gleitbombe PD-2500 X

Bomb weight:	c2,500-2,600kg (5,512-5,732 lb)
Explosive weight:	No information
Explosive filling:	No information
Fuze type:	No information
Bomb dimensions:	3,500mm (137.8in) length
Body diameter:	510mm (20.1in)
Use:	Against armoured warships. Remotely guided.
Remarks:	Similar to PC-1400 X. X-winged glide-bomb.

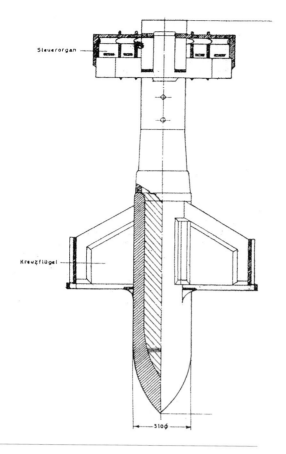

Großladungsbombe SA-4000

Bomb weight:	3,360kg (7,407 lb)
Explosive weight:	c2,700kg (5,952 lb)
Explosive filling:	Amatol 50/50*
Fuze type:	eAZ (55)A super-fast electrical impact fuze
Bomb dimensions:	4,445 x 952mm (175 x 37.5in)
Body diameter:	952mm (37.5in)
Use:	Intended for use against towns and industrial installations.
Remarks:	Development was abandoned in favour of smaller Minenbomben. Manufactured only experimentally. Also designated as 'geballte Ladung' (concentrated warhead).

*Intended for use by the He 177, one SA-4000 variant consisted of five cylinders each of 1,000mm (39.4in) diameter and overall length 4,000mm (157.5in) made of Nipolit explosive. Was to have been dropped by 1,600mm (63in) diameter parachute. – Translator

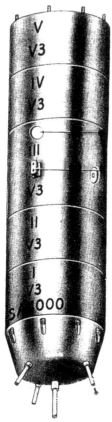

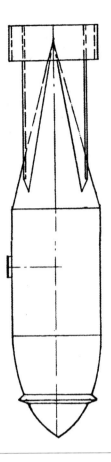

Minenbombe SC-5000

Bomb weight:	5,000kg (11,023 lb)
Explosive weight.	No information
Explosive filling:	No information
Bomb dimensions:	5,250 x 920mm (206.7 x 36.2in)
Body diameter:	920mm (36.2in)
Use:	Against towns and industrial installations and large sea targets.
Remarks:	None*

* Described as a Großladungsbombe, the accompanying drawing dated from December 1940 – Translator.

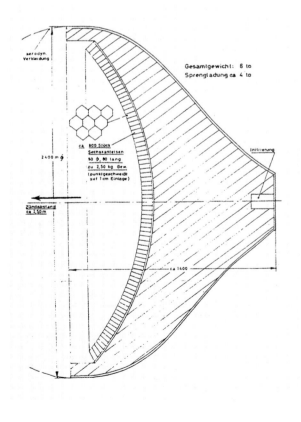

Hohlladungsbombe SHL-6000

Bomb weight:	6,000kg (13,230 lb)
Explosive weight:	4,000kg (8,818 lb)
Explosive filling:	No information
Fuze type:	No information
Bomb dimensions:	3,900 x 2,400mm (153.5 x 94.5in)
Explosive dimensions:	1,400 x 2,400mm (55.1 x 94.5in)
Use:	Against industrial installations, bridges and large ship targets.
Remarks:	Hollow-charge warhead with aimed splinter effect. Intended for use with the Heinkel He 177.

Weapon Detail Part Two

Abwurfbehälter
(Air-Dropped Containers)

Bündel Bd C-10
(Bundle for 5 x SC-10 Bombs)

Container weight:	c52kg (115 lb)
Bomb load:	5 x SC-10 Splitterbomben
Fuze type:	Electro-pyrotechnic ZtZ (69)C (Bündel)
Explosive charge:	1kg (2.2 lb) Fp 60/40 per bomb
Container dimensions:	584.4 x 360mm (23 x 14.2in)
Use:	Dropped as a cluster from all aircraft equipped with ETC-50. Used against living and unarmoured targets.
Remarks:	Consists of base plate, upper frame and enclosing central belt and suspension loop. A similar bundle is the Bd frz 10 for holding 4 x SD-10 frz French Splitter- or Brandbomben.

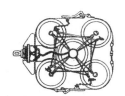

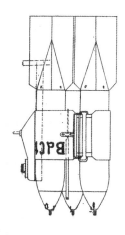

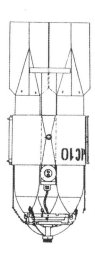

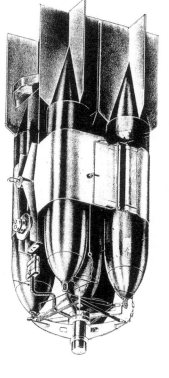

Abwurfbehälter AB-23

Container weight:	full c60kg (132 lb) empty 14kg (30.9 lb)
Bomb load:	23 x SD-2 Splitterbomben
Fuze type:	Electro-pyrotechnic ZtZ (79) A or B
Container dimensions:	1,105 x 203mm (43.5 x 8.0in)
Use:	Dropped from all aircraft equipped with Schloss 50/X, ETC-50 and ESAC-250/IX. Used against living and non-armoured targets.

Remarks: Introduced at beginning of 1942. Container is in two folding halves.

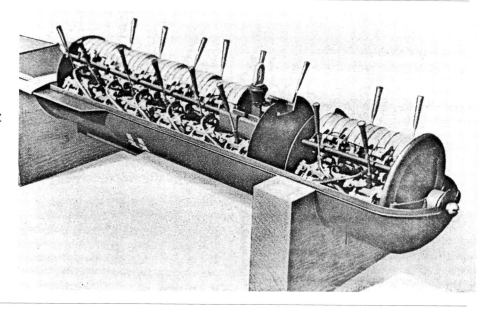

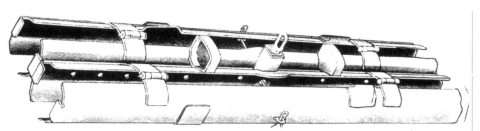

Abwurfbehälter AB-24

Container weight:	full c56kg (123.5 lb) empty 8kg (17.6 lb)
Bomb load:	24 x SD-2 Splitterbomben
Fuze type:	None
Overall dimensions:	1,100 x 180mm (43.3 x 7.1in)
Use:	Dropped from all aircraft equipped with ETC-50 against living and non-armoured targets.
Remarks:	Spring-operated container doors

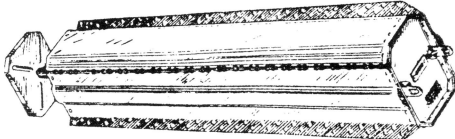

Brandbomben-Schüttkasten BSK-36
(Multi-bomb container for incendiaries)

Container weight:	Between 42 and 46kg (92.6 and 101.4 lb)
Bomb load:	36 x B-1 E Elektron Brandbomben or 16 x B-2 E Elektron Brandbomben
Fuze type:	Mechanical or electro-pyrotechnical time fuze
Container dimensions:	1,143 x 203mm (45 x 8in)

Use: Dropped from all aircraft equipped with Schloss 50 and ESAC-250/IX against easily inflammable targets.

Remarks: Container made of sheet aluminium.

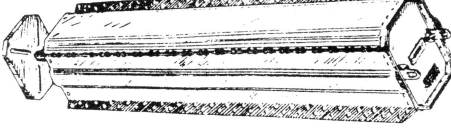

Three-sided Abwurfbehälter

Container weight:	c46 to 48kg (101.4 to 105.8 lb)
Bomb load:	36 x B-1 E Elektron Brandbomben
Fuze type:	Mechanical time fuze
Container dimensions:	1,067 x 216mm (42 x 8.5in)
Use:	Dropped from all aircraft equipped with ETC-50 or ESAC-250/IX against easily inflammable targets
Remarks:	Container made of sheet aluminium.

Abwurfbehälter AB-36

Container weight:	full 42.5kg (93.7 lb) empty 6.5kg (14.3 lb)
Bomb load:	36 x B-l E Elektron Brandbomben
Fuze type:	Mechanical time fuze
Container dimensions:	1,067 x 203mm (42 x 8in)
Use:	Dropped from all aircraft equipped with ETC-50 against easily inflammable targets
Remarks:	Container made of sheet steel.

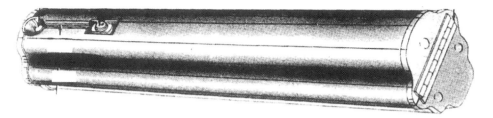

Abwurfbehälter AB-42

Container weight:	Full, between 43.5 and 59kg (95.9 and 130.1 lb) Empty 4.4kg (9.7 lb)
Bomb load:	42 x B-1 E Elektron Brandbomben or 42 x B-1.3 E Elektron Brandbomben
Fuze type:	Electro-pyrotechnic ZtZ (69) B time fuze
Container dimensions:	1,105 x 197 x 229mm (43.5 x 7.76 x 9.0in)

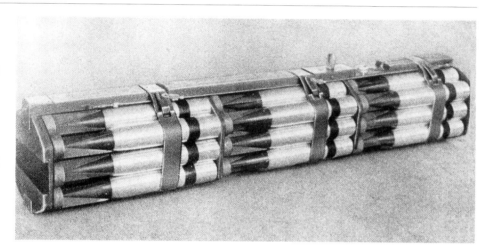

Use: Dropped from all aircraft equipped with ETC-50. Most favourable release altitude 2,000m (6,560ft), against easily inflammable targets

Remarks: Supporting parts made of wood.

Abwurfbehälter AB-70-3

Container weight:	Full 52kg (114.6 lb) Empty 8kg (17.6 lb)
Bomb load:	22 x SD-2B Stör Splitterbomben
Fuze type:	Electro-pyrotechnic ZtZ (69) D time fuze
Container dimensions:	1,010 x 190.5mm (39.8 x 7.5in)
Use:	Dropped from all aircraft equipped with ETC-50 or mining thoroughfares, troop encampments and airfields
Remarks:	Container of tension- frame construction.

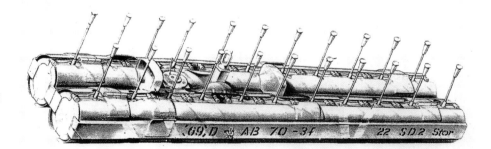

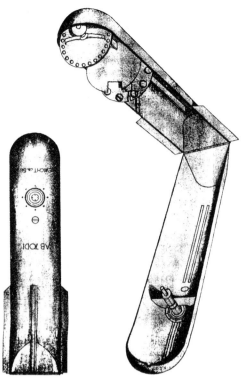

Abwurfbehälter AB-70

Container weight:
Full 56kg (123.5 lb) with 50 x SD-1
Empty 16 to 18kg (35.2 to 39.7 lb)

Bomb load:
50 x SD-1 Splitterbomben or 23 x SD-2 Stör Splitterbomben or 3 x Mark 3S Seemarkierungskörper (sea marker buoys)

Fuze type:
Electro-pyrotechnic ZtZ (79) A or B time fuze

Container dimensions:
1,105 x 203mm (43.5 x 8.0in)

Use:
Dropped from all aircraft equipped with ETC-50 against living and unarmoured targets and for position-marking at sea

Remarks:
Container in shell-form of two folding halves.

Variants:
AB-70-1 – with 3 x Mark 3S; AB-70-5 – with
50 x SD-1*; AB-70-D1 – with 23 x SD-2B Stör

* Could also house 23 x SD 2B Stör Splitterbomben equipped with ZtZ (89) B harassment fuzes. Weight of bombs 46kg (101.4 lb); container weight full 60kg (132 lb). High-level launch: up to 6,000m (19,685ft), low-level launch: not below 150m (492ft) – Translator.

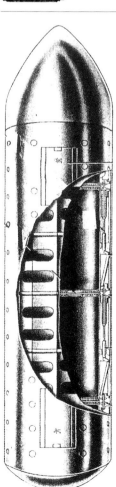

AB-250-1

Abwurfbehälter AB-250

Container weight:
Full 210-274kg (463-604 lb) Empty c50kg (110 lb)

Bomb load:
AB-250-1: 242kg (534 lb) with 96 x SD-2 Splitterbomben;
AB-250-2: 215kg (474 lb) with 224 x SD-1 Splitterbomben;
AB-250-2: 280kg (617 lb) with 144 x SD-2 Splitterbomben;
AB-250-2: 210kg (463 lb) with 40 x D-4 HL Splitterbomben;
AB-250-2: 220kg (485 lb) with 17 x SD-10 A Splitterbomben;
AB-250-2: 270kg (595 lb) with 28 x SD-10 C Splitterbomben;
AB-250-2: 154kg (340 lb) with 34 x Mark 3 B Bodenmarkierungskörper;
AB-250-3: 114kg (251 lb) with 28 x Mark 2 S Seemarkierungskörper;
AB-250-3: 256kg (564 lb) with 108 SD-2 Zt Splitterbomben;
AB-250-kz: 90kg (298 lb) with 41 x Mark 2 L Luftmarkierungskörper;
AB-250 kz: 85kg (187 lb) with 18 x Mark 3 B Bodenmarkierungskörper

Fuze type:
Electro-pyrotechnic ZtZ (69) E, D or D1, ZtZ (79) A,
or Mechanical ZtZ (89) time fuze

Container dimensions:
1,618 x 373mm (63.7 x 14.7in) AB-250-1: 1,632 x 381mm (64.25 x 15in)

Use:
Dropped from all aircraft intended to release 250kg (551 lb) bombs (except the He 111 equipped with ESAC-250/IX) in diving or level flight against living and unarmoured ground and air targets, as well as for target-marking and anti-tank use.

Remarks:
Air-dropped containers are in form of folding Half-shells, except for AB-250-1.

Note: Boden = ground; Luft = air; See = sea;
Markierungskörper = marker body

**AB-250-2 with
40 x SD-4 HL**

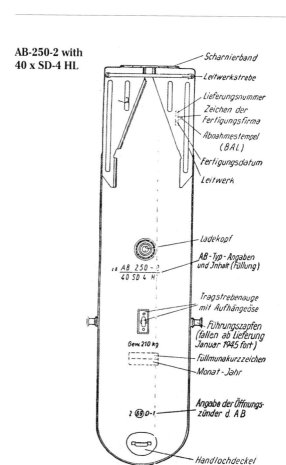

Scharnierband
Leitwerkstrebe
Lieferungsnummer
Zeichen der
Fertigungsfirma
Abnahmestempel
(BAL)
Fertigungsdatum
Leitwerk

Ladekopf

AB-Typ-Angaben
und Jnhalt (Füllung)

AB 250-2
40 SD 4 H

Tragstrebenauge
mit Aufhängeöse

Führungszapfen
(fallen ab Lieferung
Januar 1945 fort)

Gew 210 kg

Füllmunakurzzeichen
Monat-Jahr

Angabe der Öffnungs-
zünder d. AB

2 (69)D-1

Handlochdeckel

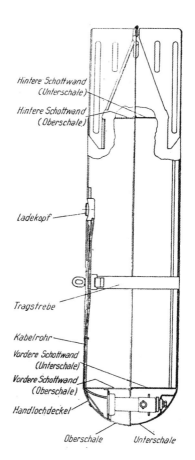

Hintere Schottwand
(Unterschale)

Hintere Schottwand
(Oberschale)

Ladekopf

Tragstrebe

Kabelrohr

Vordere Schottwand
(Unterschale)

Vordere Schottwand
(Oberschale)

Handlochdeckel

Oberschale   Unterschale

**AB-250-2 with
224 x SD-1**

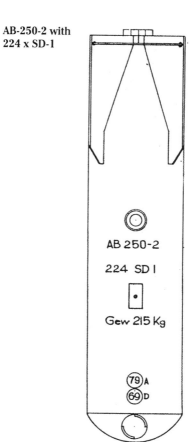

AB 250-2

224 SD I

Gew 215 Kg

(79)A
(69)D

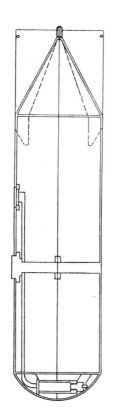

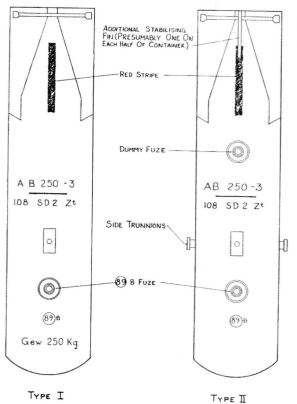

ADDITIONAL STABILISING
FIN (PRESUMABLY ONE ON
EACH HALF OF CONTAINER.)

RED STRIPE

DUMMY FUZE

A B 250 -3
108 SD2 Zt

AB 250 -3
108 SD2 Zt

SIDE TRUNNIONS

(89) B FUZE

(89)B   (89)B

Gew 250 Kg.

TYPE I   TYPE II

**AB-250-3 with
108 x SD-2
Type I & II**

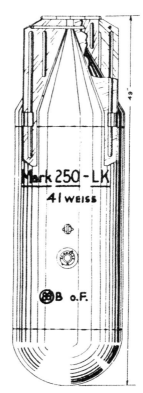

Mark 250-LK

41 WEISS

(89)B o.F.

**AB-250 kz with 41
Mark 2 L
(old designation:
Mark 250 LK)**

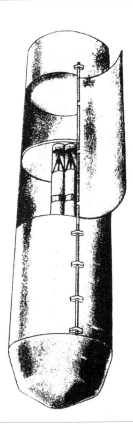

Brandbomben-Schüttbehälter BSB-360
(Multi-bomb container for incendiary bombs)

Container weight:	Full 435kg (959 lb) Empty 75kg (165 lb)
Bomb load:	360 x B-1 E Elektron Brandbomben
Fuze type:	No information
Container dimensions:	2,362 x 500mm (93 x 19.7in)
Use:	Dropped in level flight against easily inflammable targets
Remarks:	Thin-walled container made of sheet steel.
Similar containers:	BSB-700 and BSB-1000.

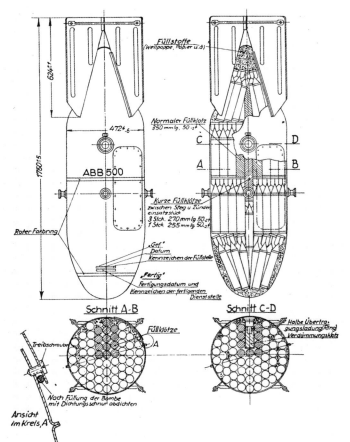

Abwurfbehälter ABB-500

Container weight:	Full c200kg (441 lb) Empty: 39kg (86 lb)
Bomb load:	140 x B-1 E Elektron Brandbomben
Fuze type:	Electro-pyrotechnic ZtZ (79) or (79) A or Mechanical ZtZ (89) time fuze
Container dimensions:	1,760 x 472mm (69.3 x 18.6in)
Use:	Dropped from all aircraft equipped to release 500kg (1,102 lb) bombs
Remarks:	Container is opened along the welded seam by a small explosive charge (with o.V setting) maximum 4.5 secs, and (with m.V. setting) maximum 33 secs after jettison, whereby the incendiary bombs are catapulted out. Dropped in level flight around 5,000m (16,400ft); in a dive, around 1,000m (3,280ft).

Note: o.V. setting = without time-delay, m.V. setting = with time-delay

Abwurfbehälter AB-500

Container weight: Full 220-470kg (485-1,036 lb)
Empty: 20kg (44 lb)

Bomb load: AB-500-1: 400kg (882 lb) with SD-4 HL Splitterbomben;
AB-500-1: 470kg (1,036 lb) with 37 x SD-10 A Splitterbomben;
AB-500-1: 340kg (750 lb) with 170 B-1.3 E + 14 x B-1.3 EZ Brandbomben;
AB-500-1: 415kg (915 lb) with 392 x SD-1 Splitterbomben;
AB-500-1: 350kg (772 lb) with 116 x B-2 EZ Elektron Brandbomben;
AB-500-1: 190kg (419 lb) with 44 x Mark 2S Seemarkierungskörper;
AB-500-1: 280kg (617 lb) with 58 x Mark 3B Bodenmarkierungskörper;
AB-500-1B: 370kg (816 lb) with 28 x SD-10 frz Splitterbomben;
AB-500-1D: 430kg (948 lb) with 24 x SD-15 Splitterbomben;
AB-500-3A: 250kg (551 lb) with 4 x SD-50 frz Splitterbomben;
AB-500-3B: 220kg (485 lb) with 4 x SD-50 Splitterbomben;
AB-500-3B: 300kg (661 lb) with 4 x SD-70 Splitterbomben

Fuze type: Electro-pyrotechnic ZtZ (69) D, D-1 and E or Mechanical ZtZ (89) B time fuze

Container dimensions: 2,362 x 500mm (93 x 19.7in)

Use: Dropped from all aircraft equipped to release 500kg (1,102 lb) bombs against living and unarmoured targets, as well as for anti-tank use and as target-markers.

Remarks: Container made in folding half-shell form.

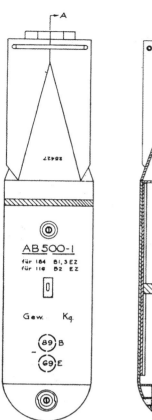
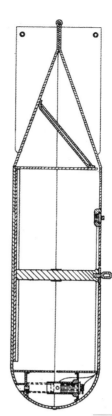

Above, right: AB-500-1 for 184 x B-1.3 EZ or 116 x B2 EZ Brandbomben

Right: AB-500-1 for 37 x SD-10 A Splitterbomben

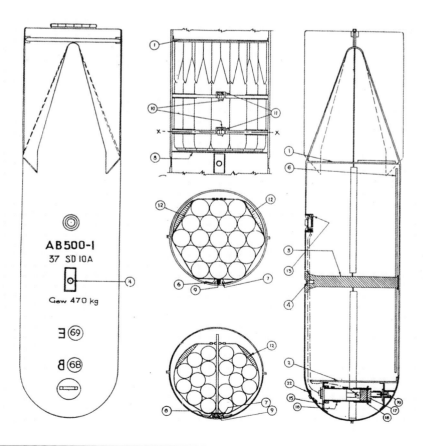

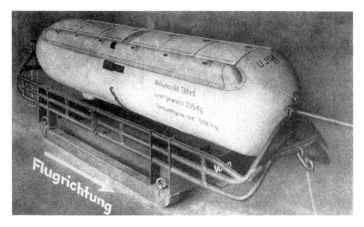

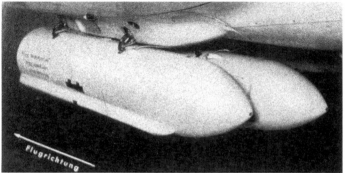

Brandbomben-Schüttbehälter BSB-700
(Multi-container for incendiary bombs)

Container weight:	Full 905kg (1,995 lb); Empty: 200kg (441 lb)
Bomb load:	700 x B-1 E Elektron Brandbomben (Model XII)
Fuze type:	Electro-mechanical release
Container dimensions:	3,150 x 660mm (124 x 26in)
Use:	Dropped from all aircraft equipped with ETC-2000/XIIA and PVC-1006 L and B against easily inflammable targets.
Remarks:	Sheet steel and dural light metal construction in three segments each of six chambers for enclosing the incendiary bombs. A similar container is the BSB-1000.

Abwurfbehälter AB-1000

Container weight:	Full 922-960kg (2,033-2,094 lb) Empty: 162kg (357 lb)
Bomb load:	AB-1000-2: 955kg (2,105 lb) with 550 x B-1.3 E + 60 B-1.3 EZ incendiaries; AB-1000-2: 960kg (2,116 lb) with 238 x B-1.3 E + 248 B-2 EZ incendiaries; AB-1000-2: 922kg (2,033 lb) with 1,000 x SD-1 Splitterbomben; AB-1000-3: 615kg (1,356 lb) with 192 x Mark 3B Bodenmarkierungskörper
Fuze type:	Two electro-pyrotechnic ZtZ (69) D; 1 mechanical ZtZ (89) A time fuze
Container dimensions:	3,277 x 660mm (129 x 26in)
Use:	Dropped from all aircraft fitted with Schloss 2000/XII in ETC-2000/XII and ETC-502 and similar bomb racks. Added later were Schloss 504 and ETC-504 with delivery of attachment loop for the AB-1000-2. Used against living, unarmoured, and easily inflammable targets and as ground target-markers.
Remarks:	Container is of stiffened frame construction with spaces left and right for contents divided by transverse walls. Jettisoned at high altitude. A mixture of SC-1000 and AB-1000 was also possible.

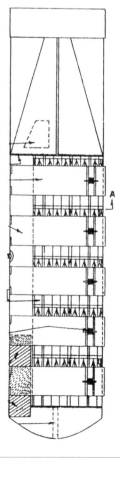

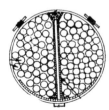

Mischlastabwurfbehälter 1,000kg

(Temporary substitute also with LMB air-dropped mine casing)

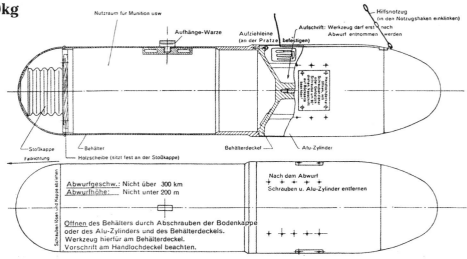

Container weight:	Full 1,000kg (2,205 lb) Empty 200kg (441 lb) including 50kg (110 lb) parachute
Contents load:	c800kg (1,764 lb) of munitions and supplies
Fuze type:	No information
Container dimensions:	5,040 x 660mm (198.4 x 26in) for LM B
Use:	For dropping ammunition and supplies to ground troops. Shock-absorber nosecap; when not installed, nose filled with wood. Jettisoned at not less than 200m (656ft) and not over 300km/h (186mph). Was replaced by container of wood construction.

Mischlastbehälter 1000

(Mixed-load container)

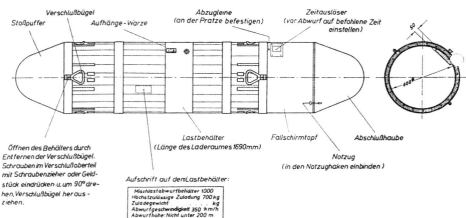

Container weight:	Full 1,000kg (2,205 lb) Empty 280kg (617 lb) including 75kg (165 lb) parachute
Contents load:	720kg (1,587 lb) ammunition and supplies of all kinds Useful internal space 460 litres contained in space 1,690 x 600mm (66.5 x 23.6in)
Fuze type:	No information
Container dimensions:	3,174 x 660mm (125 x 26in)

Use: For dropping ammunition and supplies to ground troops. Wooden construction with metal frame.

Remarks: Container inscription: Not to be released below 300m (984ft) and above 350km/h (217mph). Jettison was also possible later from heights over 1,000m (3,280ft) and at low level above 100m (328ft).

Weapon Detail Part Three

Zünder (Fuzes)

Glossary

Zünder (Z)	fuze (or fuse), igniter, exploder	Sonderzünder	special fuze
Aufschlagzünder (AZ)	impact or contact or percussion fuze	Störzünder	anti-removal deterrent or harassment fuze
Doppelzünder (Dopp.Z)	double or twin fuze	Zeitzünder (ZtZ)	time-delay fuze
Elektrischer Aufschlagzünder (El.AZ)	electrical impact fuze	Zusatzzünder (ZusZ)	auxiliary fuze.
Empfindlicher Aufschlagzünder (eAZ)	sensitive or super-fast impact fuze	m.V.	mit Verzögerung (time-delay setting)
		o. V.	ohne Verzögerung (without time-delay)
Langzeitzünder (LZtZ)	long-delay time fuze	V.Z	Vorzugszünder (safety time-delay setting)

Aufschlagzünder AZ C-10 (h.u.t) alias Zünder (3)

Mechanical impact fuze without explosive content, safe for transportation, handling and loading.

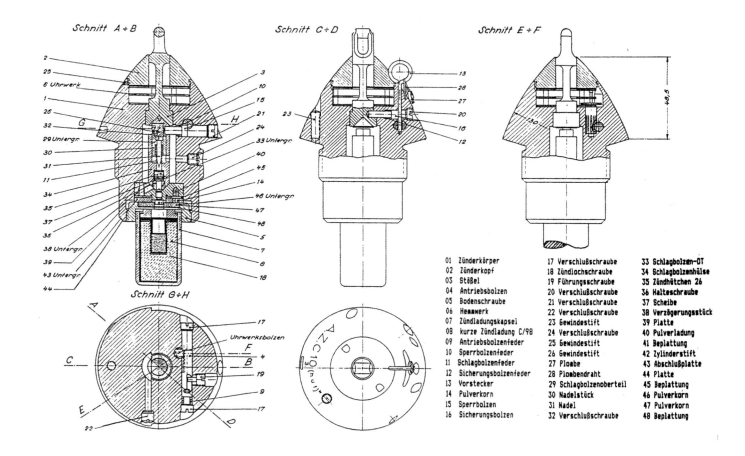

01	Zünderkörper	17	Verschlußschraube	33	Schlagbolzen-ÖT
02	Zünderkopf	18	Zündlochschraube	34	Schlagbolzenhülse
03	Stößel	19	Führungsschraube	35	Zündhütchen 26
04	Antriebsbolzen	20	Verschlußschraube	36	Halteschraube
05	Bodenschraube	21	Verschlußschraube	37	Scheibe
06	Hemmwerk	22	Verschlußschraube	38	Verzögerungsstück
07	Zündladungskapsel	23	Gewindestift	39	Platte
08	kurze Zündladung C/98	24	Verschlußschraube	40	Pulverladung
09	Antriebsbolzenfeder	25	Gewindestift	41	Beplattung
10	Sperrbolzenfeder	26	Gewindestift	42	Zylinderstift
11	Schlagbolzenfeder	27	Ploabe	43	Abschlußplatte
12	Sicherungsbolzenfeder	28	Ploabendraht	44	Platte
13	Vorstecker	29	Schlagbolzenoberteil	45	Beplattung
14	Pulverkorn	30	Nadelstück	46	Pulverkorn
15	Sperrbolzen	31	Nadel	47	Pulverkorn
16	Sicherungsbolzen	32	Verschlußschraube	48	Beplattung

Elektrischer Aufschlagzünder El.AZ C (50) alias Zünder (5)

Electrical impact fuze without explosive content, safe for transportation, handling and loading.
Variable o.V or m.V setting.

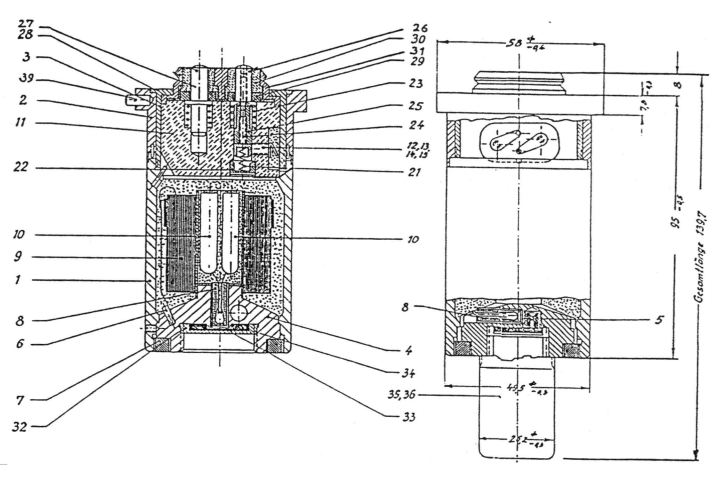

Elektrischer Zeitzünder El.ZtZ (9) and (9)A

Electrical time fuze without explosive content, safe for transportation, handling and loading.
Fuze delay time can be set in flight from 8 to 40 seconds. The El.ZtZ (9)A has a delay time from
4 to 20 seconds.

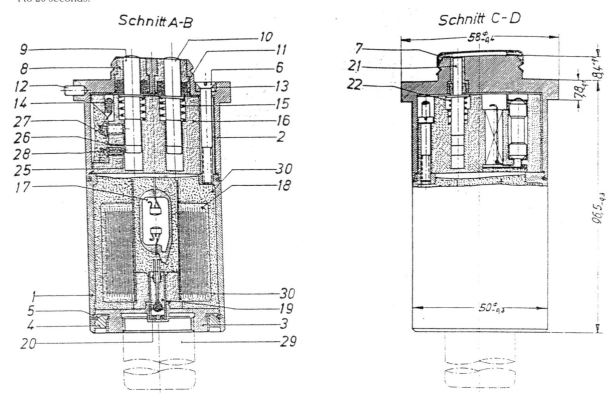

Aufschlagzünder AZ 8312 alias Zünder (13)A

Mechanical impact fuze without explosive content, safe for transportation, handling and loading.
Used in B-1 E, B-1 EZ, B-1.3 E and B-1.3 EZ Elektron Brandbomben.

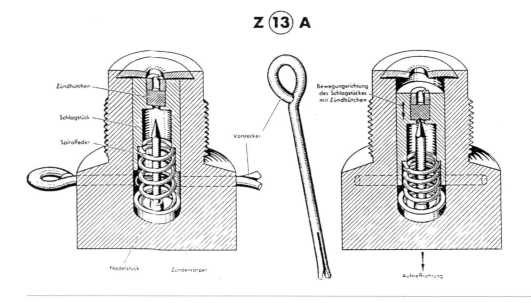

Elektrischer Aufschlagzünder El.AZ C(50) alias Zünder (15)

Electrical impact fuze without explosive content, safe for transportation, handling and loading.
Choice of m.V or o.V fuze setting can be set in flight, also with V.Z. safety delay time.

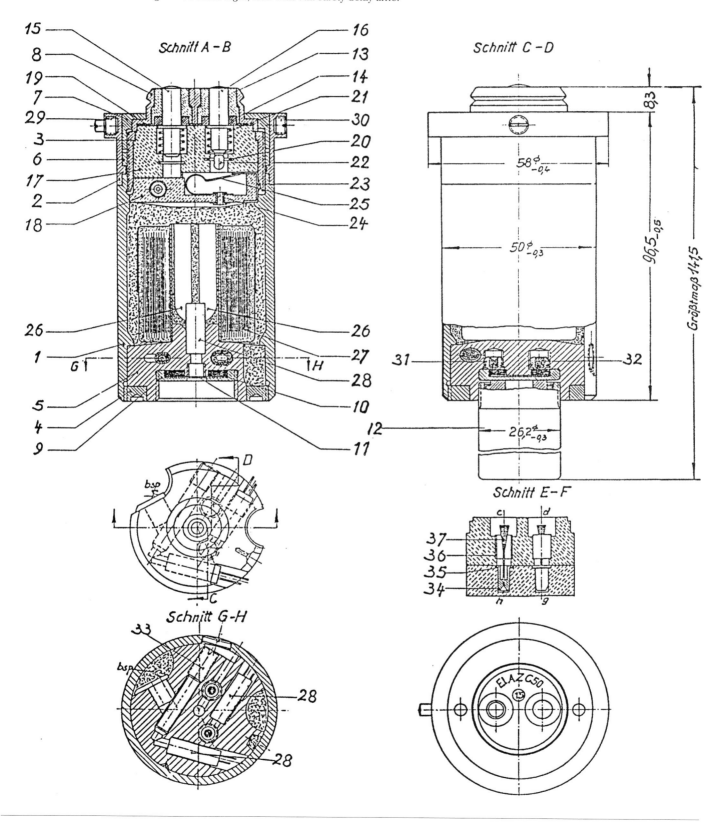

Langzeitzünder L.ZtZ (17) A and (17) B

Electro-mechanical long-delay time fuzes without explosive content, both fuzes safe for transportation, handling and loading. The two fuzes differ in their delay times as follows: LZtZ (17) A = 2 to 72 seconds and LZtZ (17) B = 5 to 120 minutes. Installation in conjunction with Zusatzzünder ZusZ (40) auxiliary fuze.

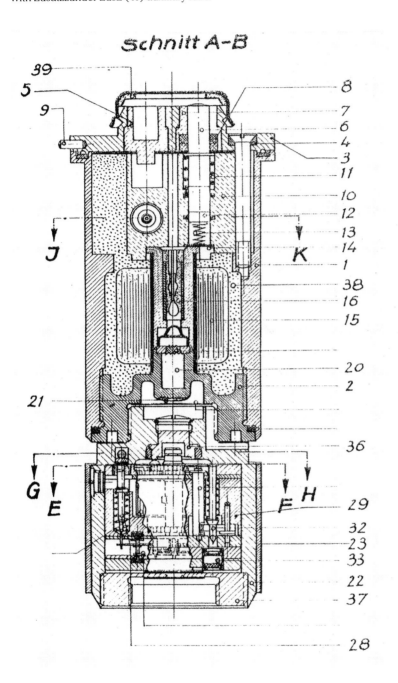

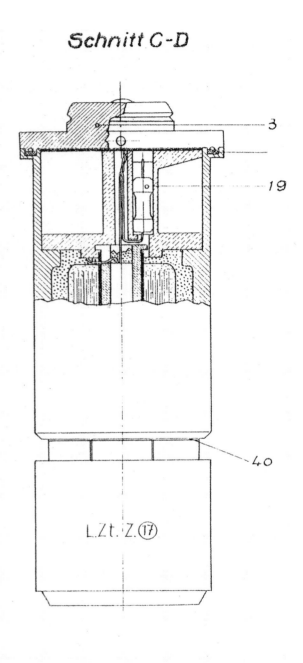

Langzeitzünder L.ZtZ (17) Bm

Mechanical long-delay time fuze without
explosive content, safe for transportation,
handling and loading. Time setting can be
varied between 5 to 20 minutes. Used as
Zerstörerzünder (destruction fuze) with
Sondermunition (special weapons).
[One example was the Fieseler Fi 103 (V-1)
flying-bomb – Translator]

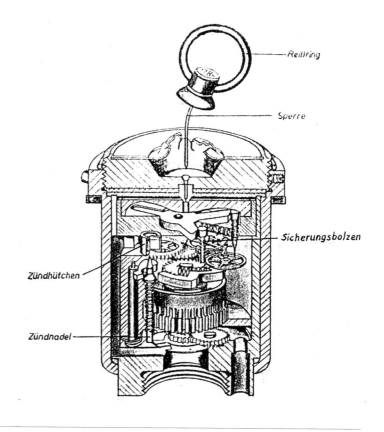

Aufschlagzünder
AZ (23) A and AZ (23) B

Mechanical all-ways super-fast impact fuze
without explosive content, safe for transportation, handling and loading. The AZ (23) B has
a long safety cable 170mm (6.7in) in length.
Used in chemical-filled Brand CH-4 bombs.

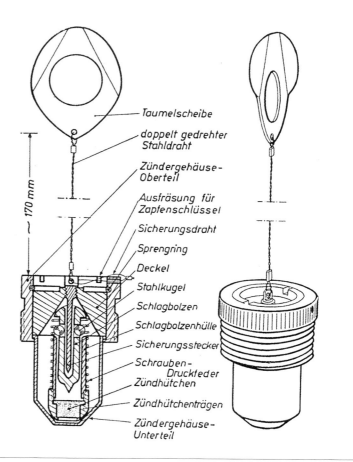

Aufschlagzünder AZ (24) A and AZ (24) A*

Mechanical impact fuze without explosive content, both fuzes safe for transportation, handling and loading.
Equipped with explosive capsule of 10 seconds safety delay time. Other than impact, a rupture ignition is also available.

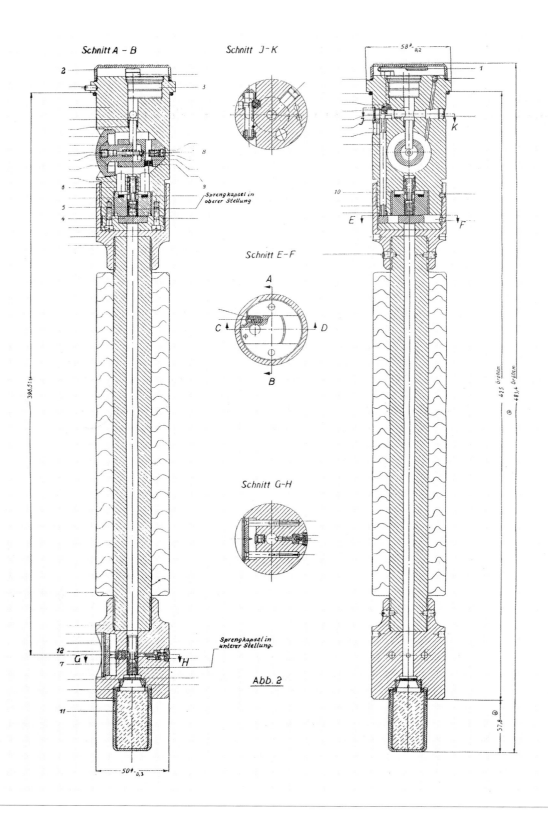

Schnitt A – B

Schnitt J – K

Sprengkapsel in
oberer Stellung

Schnitt E – F

Schnitt G – H

Sprengkapsel in
unterer Stellung.

Abb. 2

Elektrischer Aufschlagzünder El.AZ (25) A, B and C

Electrical impact fuze without explosive content, safe for transportation, handling and loading. Can be set in flight for m.V., o.V. or VZ condition. Multi-purpose fuze for high-, low-altitude and diving flight release against land or sea targets. Versions A and B with increased low-temperature stability and constant safety arming time.

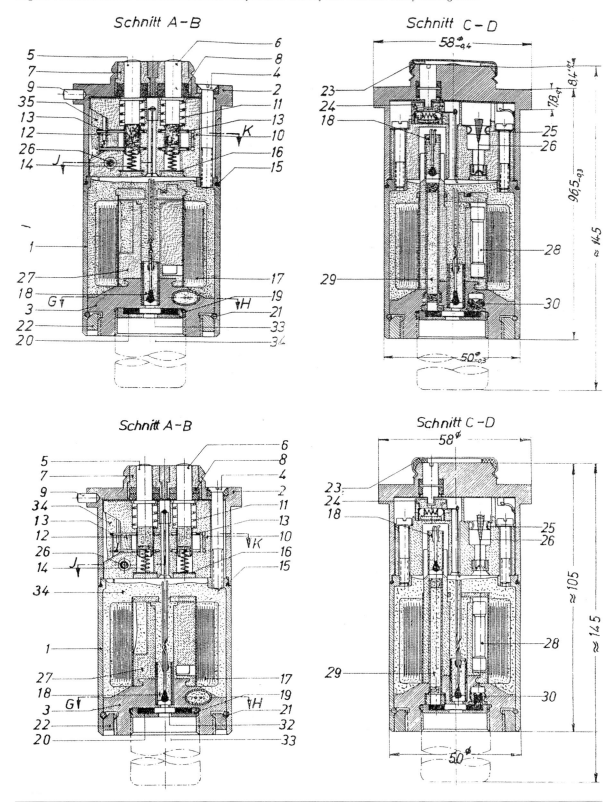

Empfindlicher Aufschlagzünder eAZ (26)

Electrical impact fuze without explosive content, safe for transportation, handling and loading.
Has additional highly-sensitive impact installation for one-sided impact. Instantaneous o.V. setting
only. Used in Flam C-250, Flam C-500 and NC-250 bombs.

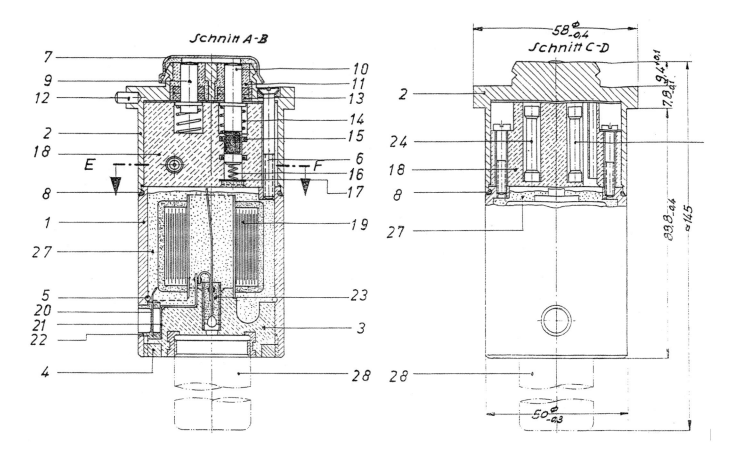

Elektrischer Aufschlagzünder El.AZ (28) A and B/6, B/2 and B/0.7

Electrical impact fuze without explosive content, safe for transportation, handling and loading for high-level and diving attacks with time delay setting of 0.12 seconds. The B/6, B/2 and B/0.7 with rupture feature are intended for thin-walled Minenbomben (high-explosive demolition bombs). [Also El.AZ (28) C/0.35 used in Bombentorpedo BT 200 (with 0.12 secs), in BT 400 (with 0.18 secs) and BT 700 (with 0.18 secs) time delay – Translator]

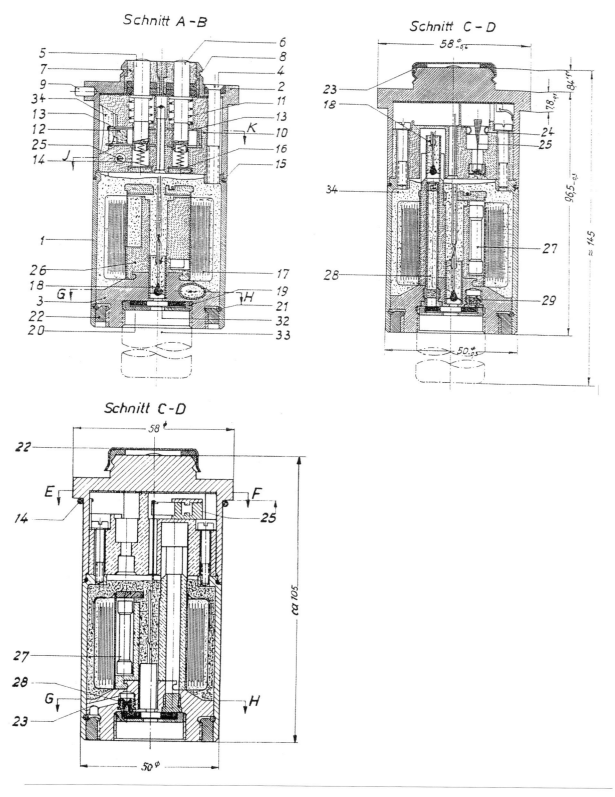

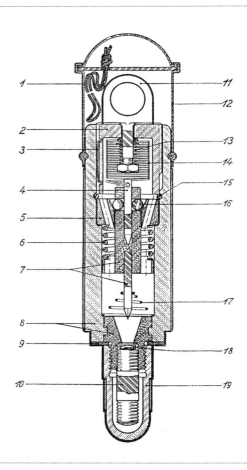

Zeitzünder ZtZ (29)

Pyrotechnic time fuze without explosive content, safe for transportation, handling and loading with self-arming and delayed-action capsules.

Zünder (31)

Ripcord fuze without explosive content, safe for transportation, handling and loading. Fuze armed when parachute opens. [Used in Mark L2 Luftmarkierungskörper (air-marker body) – Translator]

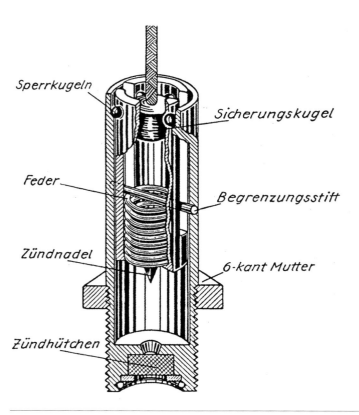

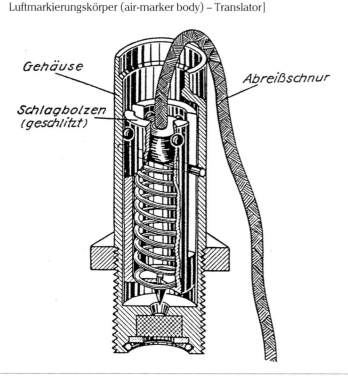

Elektrischer Aufschlagzünder El.AZ (35)

Electrical impact fuze without explosive content, safe for transportation, handling and loading. For high-level and diving attack. Used only with m.V. setting. Special fuze for Panzersprengbomben (armour-piercing high-explosive bombs). Substitute fuze for El.AZ (25) B and C.

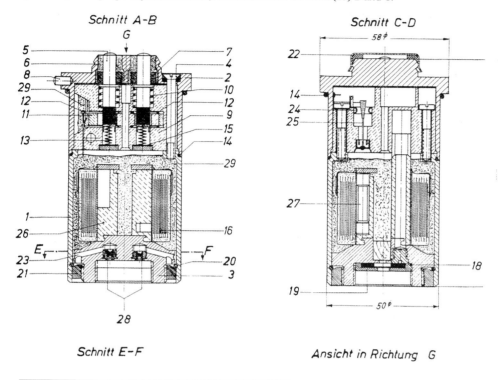

Elektrischer Aufschlagzünder El.AZ (38)

Electrical impact fuze without explosive content, safe for transportation, handling and loading. For high- and low-level and diving attack and can be set in flight for o.V or m.V fuze setting; three variations. Minimum horizontal release height 20m (66ft).

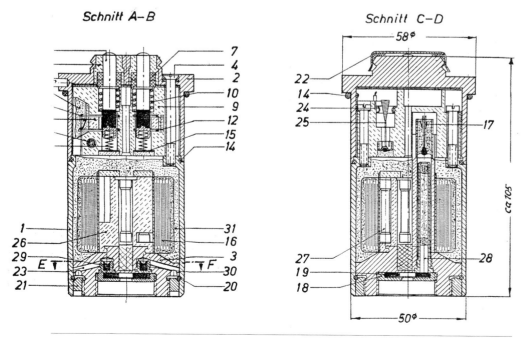

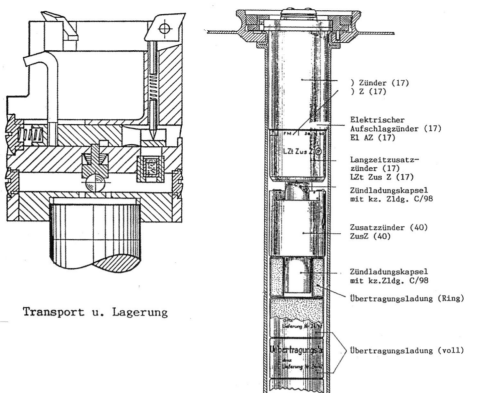

Transport u. Lagerung

) Zünder (17)
) Z (17)

Elektrischer
Aufschlagzünder (17)
El AZ (17)

Langzeitzusatz-
zünder (17)
LZt Zus Z (17)

Zündladungskapsel
mit kz. Zldg. C/98

Zusatzzünder (40)
ZusZ (40)

Zündladungskapsel
mit kz.Zldg. C/98

Übertragungsladung (Ring)

Übertragungsladung (voll)

Zusatzzünder ZusZ (40)

Mechanical fuze without explosive content, safe for transportation, handling and loading. Is primed upon impact, and by removal of the Langzeitzünder (17) time fuze, causes immediate bomb detonation. Used in conjunction with LZtZ (17) A or B.

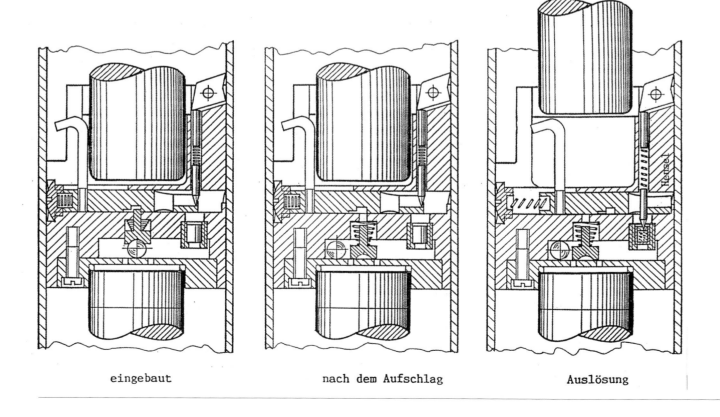

eingebaut   nach dem Aufschlag   Auslösung

Doppelzünder Dopp.Z (41) and (41) A

Mechanical clockwork double fuze without explosive content, safe for transportation, handling and loading, with selectable setting possibility prior to loading with the pre-extended impact bolts. Minimum release altitude with o.V. setting 25m (82ft); below that, with V.Z. safety delay setting.

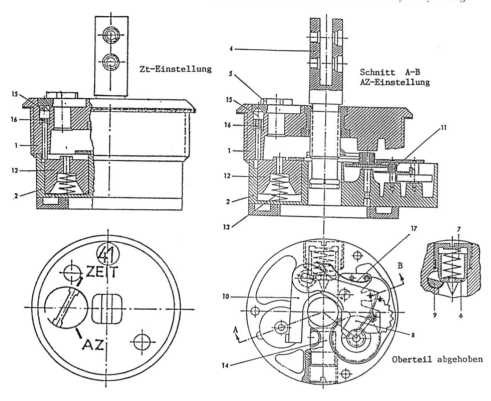

Zusatzzünder ZusZ (42)

Auxiliary mechanical fuze without explosive content, safe for transportation, handling and loading. Primed on impact of the bomb and upon removal of the Langzeitzünder causes bomb to detonate. A further development of the ZusZ (40), used in conjunction with the LZtZ (17) A or B time fuze.

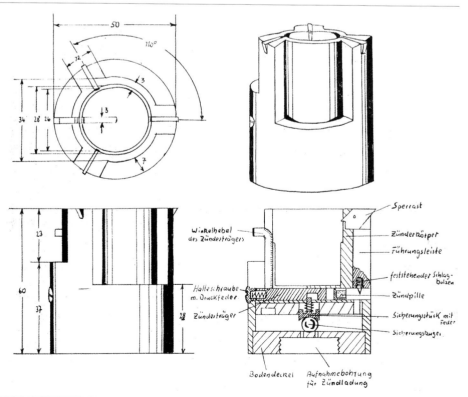

Elektrischer Aufschlagzünder El.AZ (45) A

Electrical impact fuze without explosive content, safe for transportation, handling and loading. For high-level and diving attack with selection in flight of either o.V. or m.V. fuze setting. A reserve fuze of simple construction, designed to bridge the gap in the event of production shortfall of the El.AZ (25) fuze.

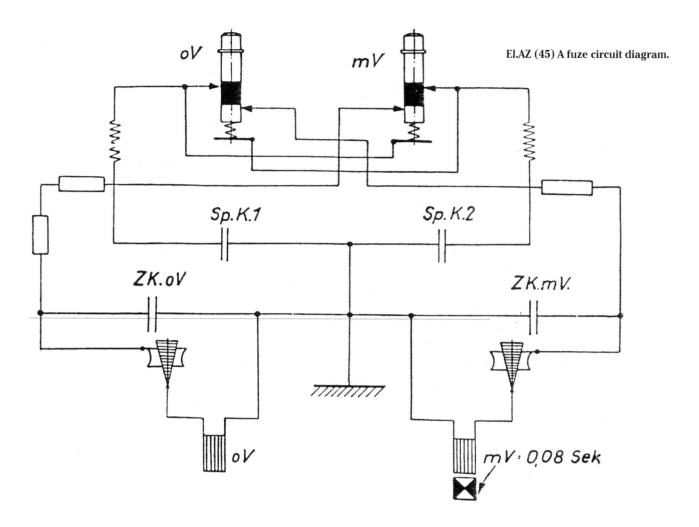

El.AZ (45) A fuze circuit diagram.

Aufschlagzünder AZ (46)

Mechanical impact fuze without explosive content, safe for transportation and loading.
Safety mechanism disengaged by a pyrotechnic charge.

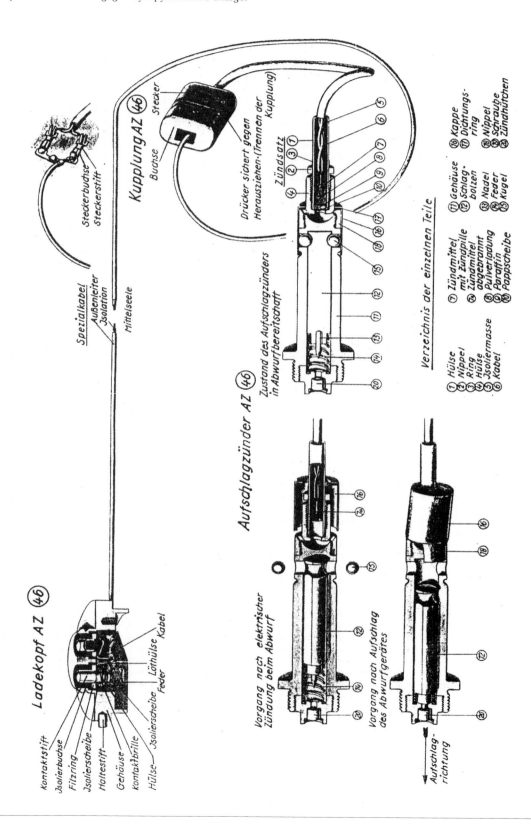

Kupplung AZ (46)

Stecker
Buchse
Steckerbuchse
Steckerstift

Drücker sichert gegen
Herausziehen (Trennen der
Kupplung)

Zündsatz

Spezialkabel
Außenleiter
Jsolation
Mittelseele

Aufschlagzünder AZ (46)

Zustand des Aufschlagzünders
in Abwurfbereitschaft

Vorgang nach elektrischer
Zündung beim Abwurf

Vorgang nach Aufschlag
des Abwurfgerätes

Aufschlag-
richtung

Ladekopf AZ (46)

kontaktstift
Jsolierbuchse
Filzring
Jsolierscheibe
Haltestift
Gehäuse
kontaktbrille
Hülse
Jsolierscheibe
Feder
Löthülse
Kabel

Verzeichnis der einzelnen Teile

① Hülse
② Nippel
③ Ring
④ Hülse
⑤ Jsoliermasse
⑥ Kabel

⑦ Zündmittel mit Zündpille
⑦a Zündmittel abgebrannt
⑧ Pulverladung
⑨ Paraffin
⑩ Pappscheibe

⑪ Gehäuse
⑫ Schlagbolzen
⑬ Nadel
⑭ Feder
⑮ Kugel

⑯ Kappe
⑰ Dichtungsring
⑱ Nippel
⑲ Schraube
⑳ Zündhütchen

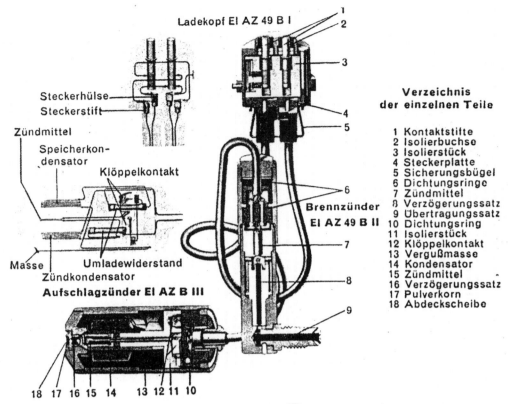

Ladekopf El AZ 49 B I

Steckerhülse
Steckerstift
Zündmittel
Speicherkon-
densator
Klöppelkontakt

Masse
Umladewiderstand
Zündkondensator

Aufschlagzünder El AZ B III

Brennzünder
El AZ 49 B II

**Verzeichnis
der einzelnen Teile**

1 Kontaktstifte
2 Isolierbuchse
3 Isolierstück
4 Steckerplatte
5 Sicherungsbügel
6 Dichtungsringe
7 Zündmittel
8 Verzögerungssatz
9 Übertragungssatz
10 Dichtungsring
11 Isolierstück
12 Klöppelkontakt
13 Vergußmasse
14 Kondensator
15 Zündmittel
16 Verzögerungssatz
17 Pulverkorn
18 Abdeckscheibe

18 17 16 15 14   13 12 11 10

Elektrischer Aufschlagzünder El.AZ (49) and (49) C

Electrical fuze without explosive content, safe for transportation, handling and loading. Special fuze used in PC-RS bombs. The El-AZ (49) C for the PC-1800 RS. Similar types are: El.AZ (49) P5 and P16 fuzes.

Einbau und Lage des :El AZ ⑨ in der PC 1000 RS

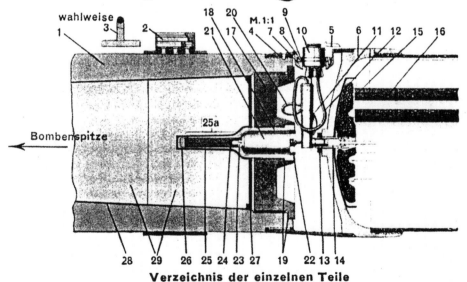

wahlweise

M.1:1

25a

Bombenspitze

28   29   26 25 24 23 27   19   22 13 14

Verzeichnis der einzelnen Teile

1 Hülle	12 Kabel mit Stecker	22 Gewindering
2 Aufhängewarze	13 Ringmutter	23 Lederabdichtscheibe
3 Aufhängeöse	14 Buchse	24 Zündpille
4 Zwischenring	15 Anfeuerungssatz	25a Zündladung B (kompl.)
5 Halteblech	16 Treibladungs-Pulverstange	25 Zündmittel
6 Deckel	(Röhrenpulver)	26 Holzklötzchen
7 Mundlochhülse	17 Bodenschraube	27 Pappscheibe z. Abdichten
8 Gewindering	18 Bodenlochbuchse	d. Sprengladung
9 Druckring	19 Dichtungsgrenze	28 Papphülle für Sprengladun
10 Ladekopf El AZ 49 B I	20 Kabel mit Stecker	29 Sprengladung
11 Brennzünder El AZ 49 B II	21 Aufschlagzünder	

Elektrischer Sonderzünder El.Z (50) and (50) B

Vibration-sensitive and storage-dependent electrical special fuze without explosive content, safe for transportation, handling and loading. Made detonable by the screw-on Zündladung C/98 ignition charge. Fuze is ready 9 seconds after impact. Fuze reacts to vibration and becomes effective with the impact of successive bombs. Renewed bombing of the area only in high-level attack. Version (50) B from 1943 had exchangeable battery.

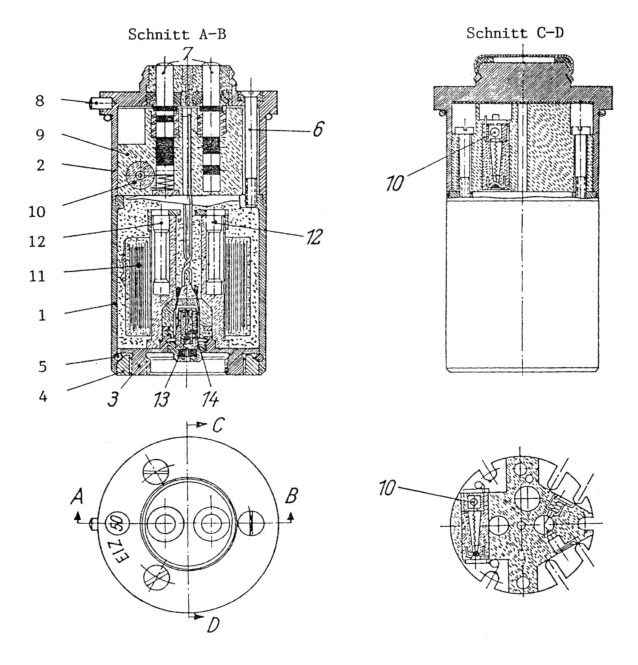

Elektrischer Sonderzünder El.Z (50) Y

Electrical special anti-removal fuze that externally resembled the Sonderzünder (50), but at any attempt to disarm, was immediately activated and exploded the bomb.

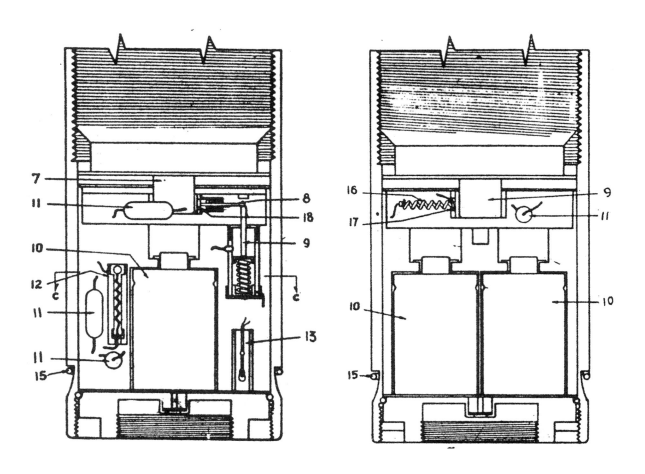

Elektrischer Aufschlagzünder El.AZ (55)

Electrical impact fuze without explosive content, safe for transportation, handling and loading. For high- and low-level and diving attack, with o.V. or m.V. fuze setting selectable in flight. With m.V. setting, safety time delay V.Z. = 14 seconds.

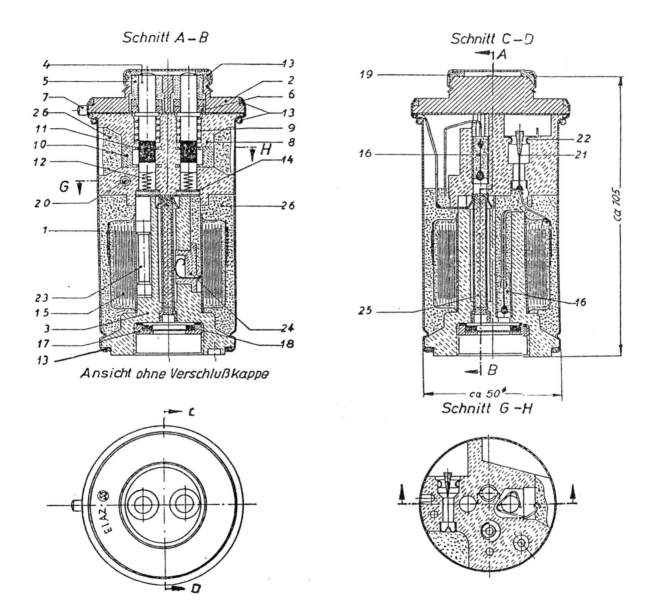

Empfindlicher Aufschlagzünder eAZ (55) A

Highly-sensitive (super-fast) impact fuze without explosive content, safe for transportation, handling and loading. For high- and low-level and diving attack. Could be selectively set in flight for o.V. or m.V. fuze setting prior to jettison, the latter with 14 seconds safety delay time. Similar to the El.AZ (55), it consists of a side-impact fuze with, at the nose of the bomb, a diaphragm connected with the fuze by a cable.

eAZ (55) A circuit diagram

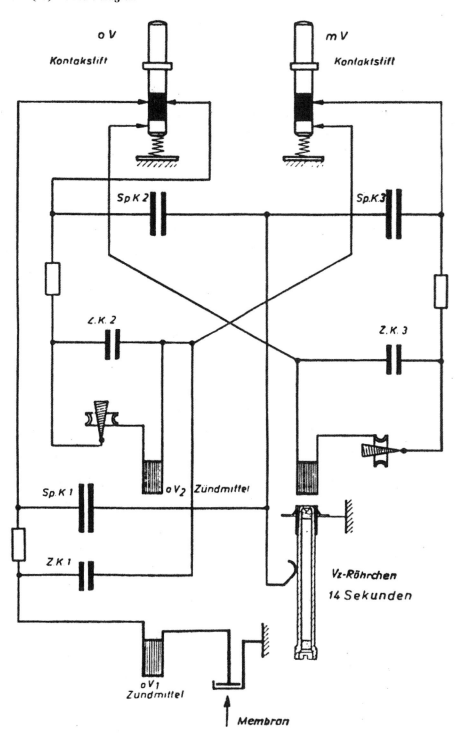

Langzeitzünder LZtZ (57)

Chemical time fuze without explosive content, safe for transportation, handling and loading. Electrical priming, with effective time delay between 1 and 100 hours, divided into three time groupings. Detonative effectiveness strengthened by attachment of the short C/98 fuze charge.

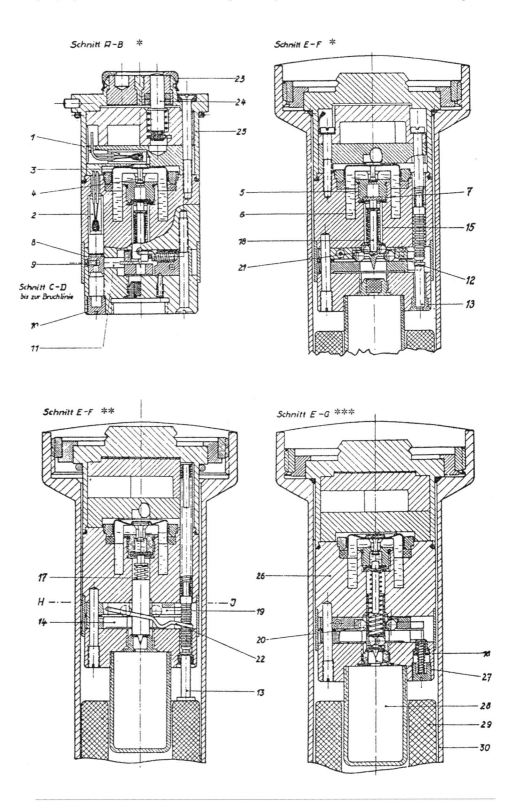

Zeitzünder El.ZtZ (59)A and B

Electro-pyrotechnic time fuze without explosive content, safe for transportation, handling and loading. Fuze time setting can be varied in flight between 13 and 57 seconds. Ignition of both powder charges takes place electrically after jettison. The ZtZ (59) B fuze has three time settings:12, 41, and 58 seconds).

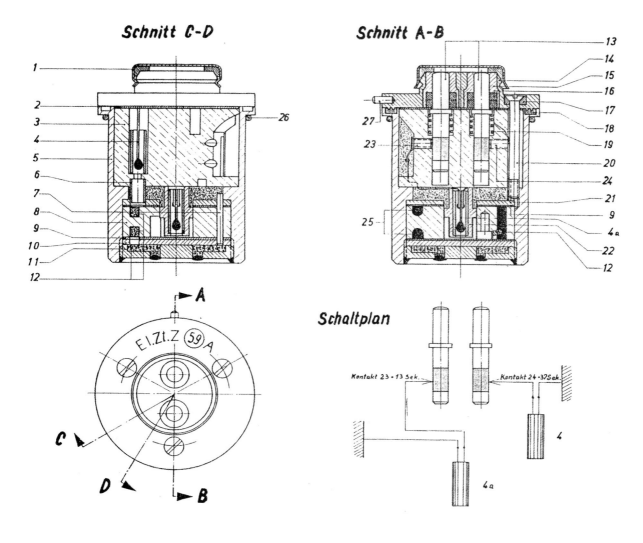

Aufschlagzünder AZ (63)

Mechanical-pyrotechnic impact fuze without explosive content, safe for transportation, handling and loading with a cable-connected time mechanism.

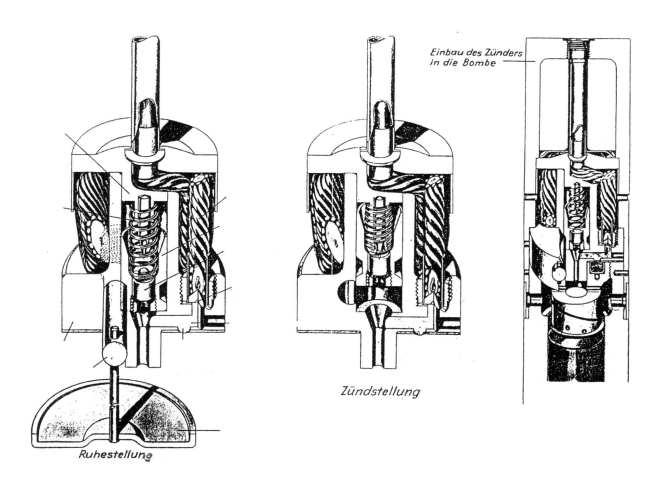

Einbau des Zünders in die Bombe

Zündstellung

Ruhestellung

Empfindlicher AufschlagzündereAZ (66) and (66) A

Sensitive (super-fast) impact fuze without explosive content, safe for transportation, handling and loading.
Its effectiveness is based on the principle of magnetic ignition/contact. Replaced the AZ C-10 (h.u.t.) impact fuze.

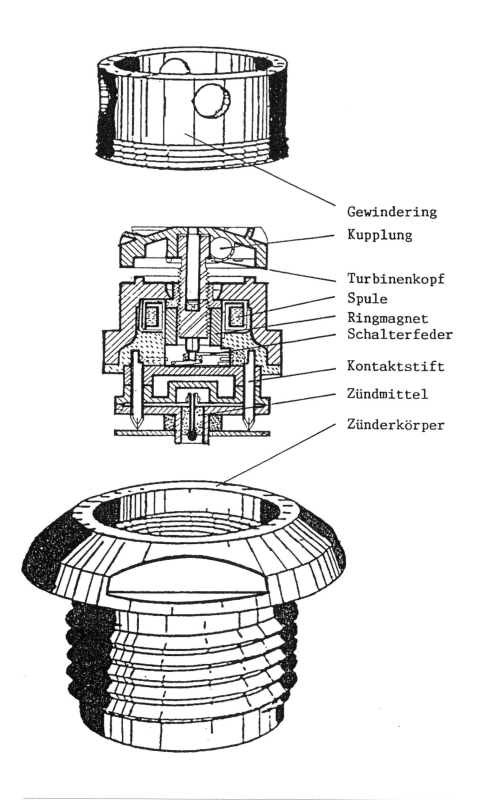

Gewindering

Kupplung

Turbinenkopf
Spule
Ringmagnet
Schalterfeder

Kontaktstift

Zündmittel

Zünderkörper

Langzeitzünder LZtZ (67)

Mechanical long-delay time clockwork fuze differing externally from the (41)A fuze only by the (67) inscription. The positioning bolts are included as dummies as a deception measure. By unwinding the screw thread, the safety mechanism is disengaged according to the setting, and bomb explodes 5,10,15, 20, 25, or 30 minutes after jettison.

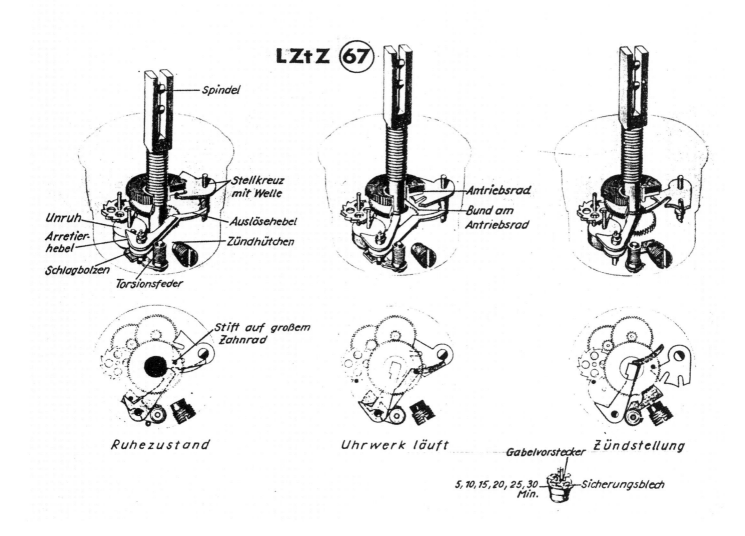

LZtZ (67)

Spindel
Stellkreuz mit Welle
Auslösehebel
Zündhütchen
Unruh
Arretierhebel
Schlagbolzen
Torsionsfeder

Antriebsrad
Bund am Antriebsrad

Stift auf großem Zahnrad

Ruhezustand

Uhrwerk läuft

Zündstellung

Gabelvorstecker
5, 10, 15, 20, 25, 30 Min.
Sicherungsblech

Zeitzünder ZtZ (69) B, C, D, D1 and E

Electro-pyrotechnic time fuze without explosive content, safe for transportation, handling and loading in all its variants. Priming takes place electrically. The variants differ in their time-delay setting (from 0.7 to 5.5 seconds).

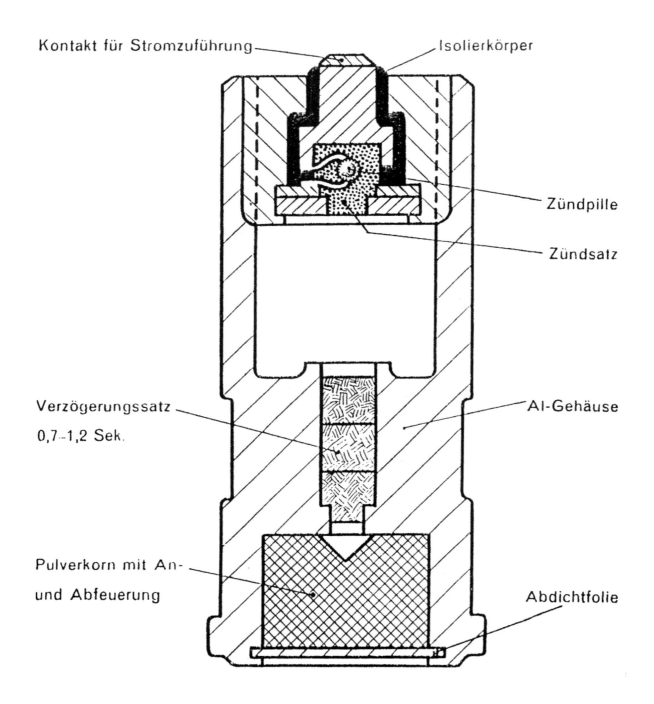

Störzunder Z (70) A

Chemical harassment (anti-removal or interference-shielded) storage-dependent fuze without explosive content, safe for transportation, handling and loading. Time delay from 4 to 30 hours.

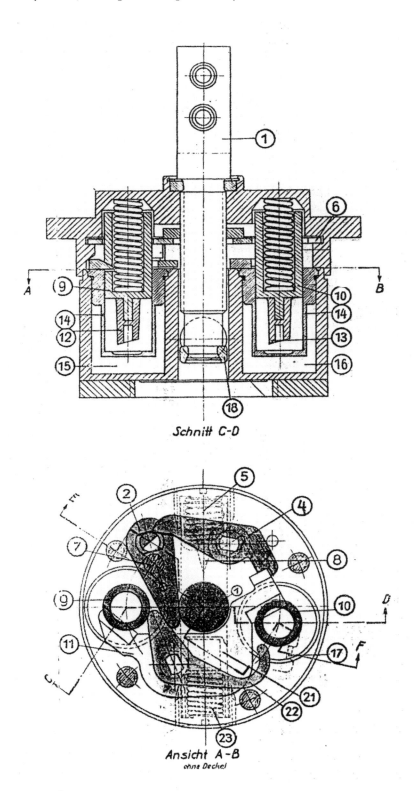

Schnitt C-D

Ansicht A-B
ohne Deckel

Störzünder Z (70) B

Mechanical harassment fuze without explosive content, safe for transportation, handling and loading. Made effective by screw-on attachment of the small Zündladung 34 ignition charge. Has a pre-stressed impact bolt which, when clock runs out and subsequent impact, reacts even to the slightest vibration or movement and explodes the (SD-2) bomb with a l second delay. Similar fuzes are the Zünder Z (70) B1 and B2.

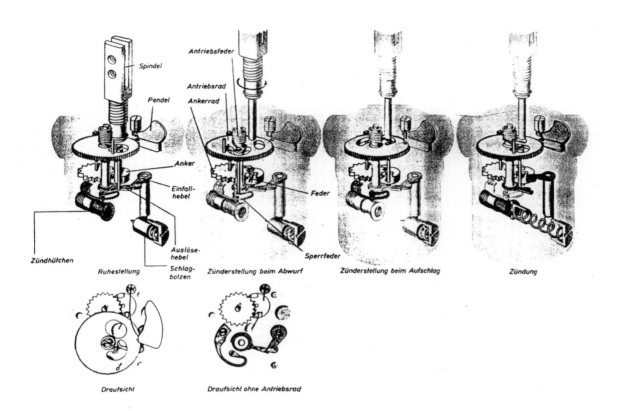

Spindel
Pendel
Anker
Einfall-hebel
Zündhütchen
Auslöse-hebel
Schlag-bolzen
Ruhestellung

Antriebsfeder
Antriebsrad
Ankerrad
Feder
Sperrfeder
Zünderstellung beim Abwurf

Zünderstellung beim Aufschlag

Zündung

Draufsicht

Draufsicht ohne Antriebsrad

Aufschlagzünder AZ (73),(73) A, A2, A3, & B

Mechanical diaphragm impact fuze without explosive content, safe for transportation, handling and loading. For one-sided impact. Individual variants differ minimally in design. With the AZ (73) B impact fuze, the membrane is modified as a semi-circular cap and primed with a shear-pin, the fuze cap being moveable in position.

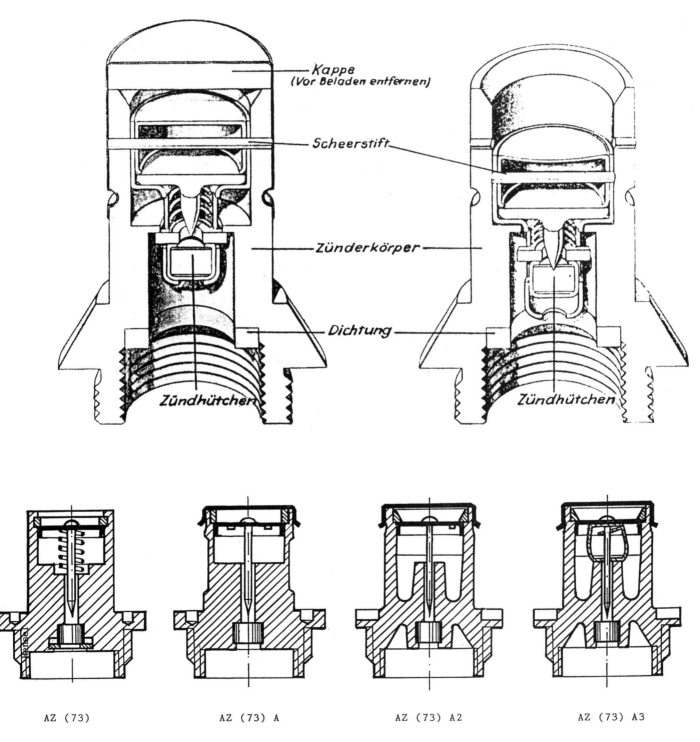

Sectional views of the AZ (73) to AZ (73) A3 fuzes

Zeitzünder (79) and (79) A

Electro-pyrotechnic time fuze without explosive content, safe for transportation, handling and loading. Two ignition settings can be selected in flight, and is immediate from battery power.

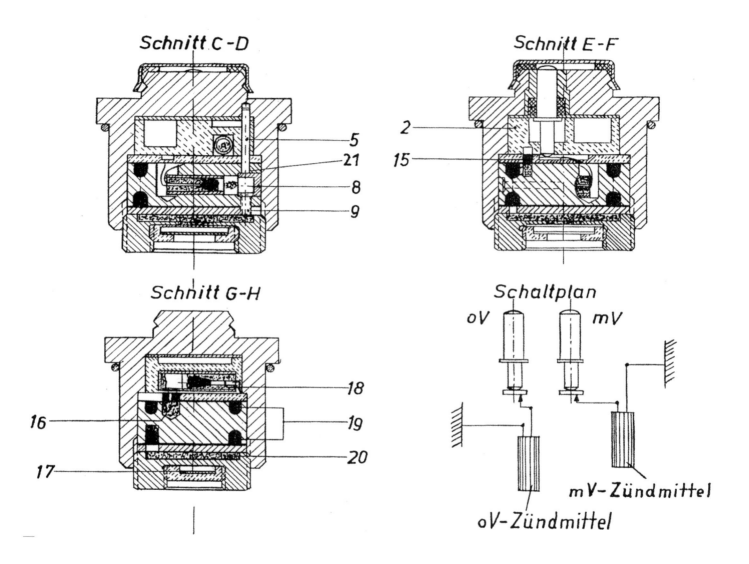

Aufschlagzünder AZ (80)

Mechanical impact fuze without explosive content, safe for transportation, handling and loading, made effective in conjunction with the small fuze charge. Used in guided bombs as a safety fuze in the event of failure of the electrical impact fuze.

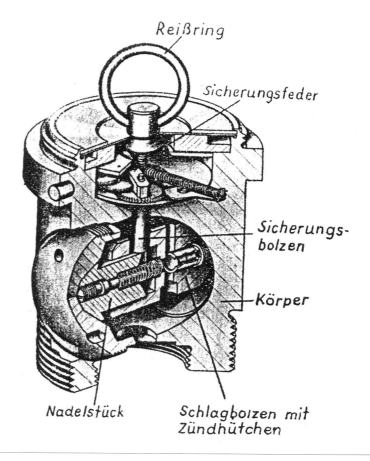

Empfindlicher Aufschlagzünder eAZ (86)

Sensitive (super-fast) electrical impact fuze without explosive content, safe for transportation, handling and loading. Used in the SD-50 Tel, SD-70 Tel, and newer models of the SD-250 Tel fitted with the nose telescopic extension.

eAZ (86) fuze

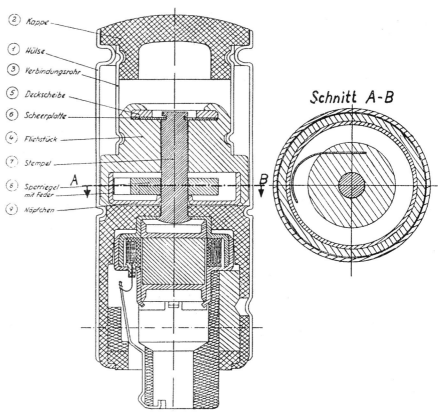

Fuze used in Tel bombs

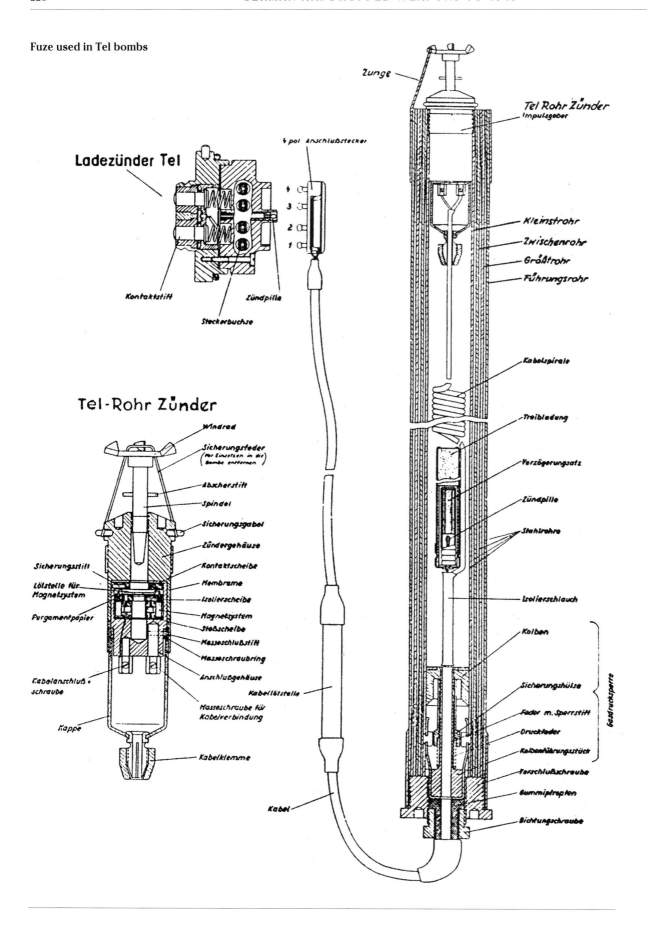

Zeitzünder ZtZ (89) A, B, C and D

Mechanical time fuze without explosive content, safe for transportation, handling and loading. Delay times between 4 and 60 seconds. Time-delay mechanism is set prior to loading in the aircraft (except for Heinkel He 111 with ESAC-250/IX).

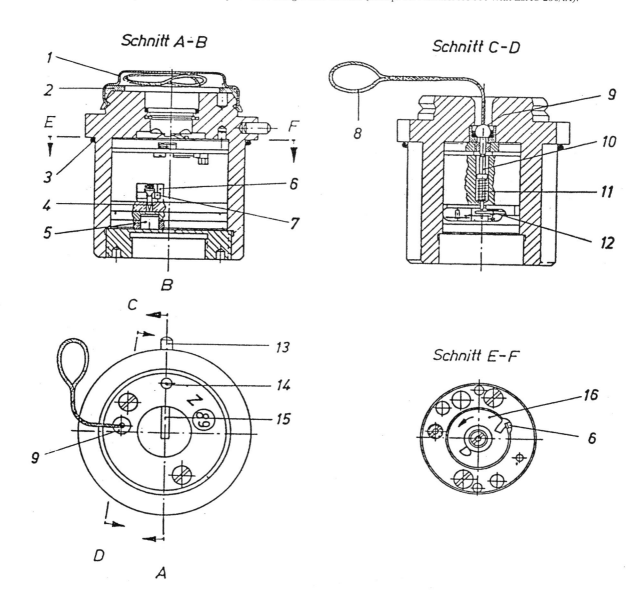

Schnitt A-B

Schnitt C-D

Schnitt E-F

Weapon Detail Part Four

Examples of Bomb Explosive Effects

Top: **September 1939. The wreckage of Polish aircraft that were severely damaged in a German air raid, removed from the airfield runway.**

Above: **June 1940. This French Maginot-Line bunker was severely damaged by artillery fire (see observation tower) and by a bomb hit (roofing). Although the bomb impacted at an angle and slithered on, the detonative effect caused subsequent damage.**

Left: **September 1939. The impact of a 500kg *Minenbombe* threw the Polish 'General Sosnovski' armoured train off the tracks.**

Above: **June 1940. A water-filled bomb crater near to a Maginot-Line complex.**

Right: **A German bomb toppled this Unic P107 BU tracked vehicle of the French artillery and severely damaged it (crater visible at right).**

Below: **Likewise toppled over from the detonation of a German air-dropped bomb is this 12.1 tonne heavy Charléger FCM 36 of a French tank battalion. May 1940 photo.**

This heavy French B-1 bis tank suffered damage as a result of German air raid on the Belgian small town of Beaumont. Photo taken May 1940.

A French forward airfield after a German air raid. Seen is a damaged Loiré- et-Olivier LeO-451.

July 1941. This photo emphasizes the heavy detonation pressure effect of German high-explosive demolition bombs. The light GAS truck, complete with a coupled 4.5cm Pak 37 was toppled over and heavily damaged. In the background is a Ba-10 armoured scout-car.

July 1941. A Junkers Ju 87 'Stuka' dive-bomber at lower right after attacking a Russian supply-column thoroughfare.

A view from the ground. The force of the explosion overturned this Russian fuel tanker. Subsequent fires turned it into a burnt-out wreck.

A direct hit from a bomb destroyed this Stalin-Line bunker. This photo of July 1941 clearly shows the effect of air-dropped concrete-smashing bombs.

Above left: **The destructive effects and crater from a large-calibre German high-explosive bomb that fell on a village street in southern Russia.**

Above right and below: **In the town of Smolensk after a German air raid. From the largely wooden-built houses, only the walled chimney stacks remain.**

The scene on Soviet airfields following the surprise opening attacks in Luftwaffe air raids on 22nd June 1941 when the Red Air Force suffered heavy losses.

Appendix One

Toxic Chemical Bomb Fillings

The *Kampfstoffe* fillings in bombs and artillery shells consisted of injurious or toxic gases, liquids or powders of a chemical or biological nature, most but not all of which produced lethal effects for human beings. First used during World War One by Germany and France in ground operations (but not air-dropped in both World Wars), the earliest bore designations in Germany signified by a coloured Kreuz (cross) code. Many further and much more lethal substances were developed in the years that followed until 1945, but for space reasons, only some of the more pertinent are included here.

Weißkreuz (White Cross)
An eye irritant consisting of Bromines such as Bromessigester, (Bromethylacetate), Bromazeton (Bromacetone) and Chlorazetophenon (Chloroacetophenol). The least dangerous, it is used in the form of CS teargas in several police forces throughout the world. One of the eye irritants was also known as 'Omega' or O-Salz (Chlorazetophenon) which required seven chemicals in its preparation. Weißkreuz was used in the KC-250, KC-500 and KC-1800 bombs. Bromine itself, dissolved in water or solvents, develops a reddish-brown poisonous vapour causing choking and attacks the skin and breathing organs. Leading to hallucinations, sleeplessness, and lack of concentration, it is lethal in high concentrations such as in Brombenzylcyanide.

Blaukreuz (Blue Cross)
These were nose and throat irritants that held Arsenic compounds known as Arsines. Arsine or Arsenic trihydride, was a strongly poisonous gas smelling of garlic. Upon breathing in, it causes nausea, asphyxia and often, death. The irritant was known as a 'mask-breaker' since, upon breathing in even the slightest quantity, caused the gas-mask wearer to rip it off and thus inhale even more of the substance. Arsenic in the form of Arsenic trioxide (white arsenic) is a highly poisonous white, tasteless, odourless powder. Was produced as a dust which affected the breathing system and used in KC-50 bombs. Blaukreuz chemicals included Clark I (alias C-1), consisting of Diphenylaminechloride

which affected the eyes, throat and lungs. Further developments were Clark II, a Diphenylarsenic cyanide, and the similar Clark III. Arsenic poisoning itself leads to disorientation, cramps, circulatory disturbances, liver and kidney ailments, and eventually, death. Blau*salz* on the other hand, is Potassium ferrocyanide, whilst Blau*säure* is Cyanide acid, a poisonous eye and skin irritant. Other Blaukreuz substances manufactured were known as A-Öl, made from eight chemicals, and Adamsit (named after the US chemist Adams), a Phenolarsenic chloride.

Grünkreuz (Green Cross)
Suffocating for the lungs, these gases consisted of Phosgene, Öl-F, Perstoff (alias K-Stoff), Klop or Chlorpikrin. Used in KC-50, KC-250 II, KC-250 III, KC-500, KC-1000 and KC-1800 bombs. Phosgene (Carbonyl chloride) is a colourless gas smelling of rotten hay, that derives from the decomposition of Chloroform, Trichloroethylene and Carbontetrachloride. Used in World War One, after several hours of lung damage, led to death. A Diphosgene, Öl-F was made from Chlorine and Carbon monoxide. Klop or Chlorpikrin (Chloropikrin), a Trichloromethane or Nitrochloroform, is a poisonous liquid that produces skin blisters. The gases irritate the eyes and breathing tract. Other Grünkreuz substances included Stickstoff-*Lost* (Nitrogen-*Lost* or T-9), the latter described in the next heading. Perstoff, in the form of the Perchlormethylmercaptane oily liquid, forms toxic vapours similar to tear-gas.

Gelbkreuz (Yellow Cross)
These were of the well-known corrosive Senfgas (mustard-gas), which not only attacked the skin but also clothing. Other substances developed later on included *Lost* (Dichloroethylsulphide) – a mustardgas named after the chemists **Lo**mmel and **St**einkopf. *Lost* was initially followed by *Oxol-Lost* (alias Senf-OL), made from Chlorine and Calcium carbonate, but far more lethal in its effectiveness. Since its usefulness as a gas deteriorated with falling temperatures (for example at -15°C), various mixtures with Arsenic and Clark were tried. Initially, other toxic chemicals such as Arsenic and Diphenylarsenic chloride were

mixed with it. Thinning with Nitrobenzol (Nitrobenzene) produced a mixture effective at -20°C, and became known as *Winterlost* (alias OKM). Effectiveness at still lower temperatures up to -35°C was achieved by mixing the normal Dichloroethylenesulphide with Diisopropylfluorphosphate. Other mixtures were *Zäh-Lost* that contained wax and synthetic products, but which was limited in its storage capability and was succeeded by *Propyl-Lost*. A simpler method of manufacture on a chlorine-sulphur basis resulted in *D-Lost* or Direct-*Lost* that needed seven chemicals in its manufacture but used far fewer raw materials than was required to produce *Oxol-Lost*. A Stickstoff-*Lost* (Nitrogen-*Lost*) was Nitrosenf (T-9), a Trichloroethylamine odourless gas that required eleven chemicals to produce. When breathed in, resulted in death within 5 minutes. Because of its effect on the lungs, it belonged to the rün (green) category. A mixture of Grün with arsenic came under the Gelb (yellow) category, as also substances from Blau (blue) mixed with *Oxol-Lost*. Gelbkreuz mixtures were used in KC-250, KC-250 II, KC-500 and KC-500 II bombs. In France, the mustardgas was called Yperit.

Buntkreuz (Multi-coloured Cross)
Consisted of a Blaukreuz and Grünkreuz mixture. Used in KC-250 II and KC-250 III bombs filled with Tabun.

Tabun (T-83)
One of the newer nerve gases that were designated as 'Trilonen', this liquid Phosphoric acid ester was a compound of Phosphoricacid-cyanide-dimethylamide-ethyl ster that was first laboratory-tested in 1936 and needed eight chemicals to make it. A brownish liquid that slowly dissipates into the atmosphere, it thus remained long in the vicinity. Extremely poisonous, it attacks the skin, brain and nervous system causing paralysis and death. A variant known as Tabun-A contained 5% Chlorbenzol (Chlorobenzene), whilst Tabun-B contained 20% Chlorbenzol. Together with Sarin and Soman, it belonged to the Grün 3 class of toxic chemicals. Tabun-filled artillery shells were discovered by the British in 1945.

Sarin (T-144)
Named after the chemists **S**chrader, **A**mbros, **R**itter and **Lin**de, it was even more poisonous than Tabun. A colourless, almost odourless gas, it also penetrated the skin. Chemically, it was a Methylphosphoricacid-fluoro-isopropylester and required 7 chemicals in its manufacture. A variant that required only five raw materials – Chlorine, Isopropylalcohol, Hydrogen fluoride solution, Methanol and Phosphor-trichloride, was known as Sarin-2.

Soman (T-300)
Discovered in 1944 and the most poisonous of all substances developed until 1945, it required 8 chemicals in its preparation – Chlorine, Isopropylalcohol, Methanol, Phosphor trichloride, Sodium, Sodium hydroxide solution and Sodium fluoride. As a skin irritant, was twice as powerful as Sarin, but when breathed in, was ten times more deadly. Chemically, it was known as Methylfluorphosphansäure-pinakolyl-ester (Pinacolyl-methyl-phosphoro-fluoridate). Produced only in limited quantities.

As indicated above, many of the toxic substances bore a T designation, and included T-46, T-113, T-150, T-155 and T-500, too numerous to be gone into here. Although Tabun and other 'nerve gases' were produced for bomb fillings, none were actually used by Germany in World War Two for fear of similar retaliation by the Allies.

At the end of World War Two, a total of 43,714 tons of chemical warfare weapons, most of which were bombs, were found in the British Zone of Germany. Since most poison gases are inflammable, these were normally disposed of in Great Britain by burning. This method, however, proved unsuitable for German bombs as many contained explosive igniters weighing up to 15.5kg (34 lb), as in the KG-250 III Gr. bombs. A large majority of such bombs were thus prepared for dumping at sea, where they were scuttled at depths not less than 1,800ft, well away from seaside beaches and with due consideration for fish life. Due to the need for extreme precautionary measures, this work continued until June 1947 when all had been dealt with.

The figure for normal high-explosive and incendiary bombs disposed of by the British alone was 163,660 tons, including almost 56,000 tons of bombs found in Belgium, Denmark, Holland and Norway. Figures for bombs disposed of by the other powers were not available at the time of writing. More details of the high-explosive and/or chemical substances and their production quantities are to be found in the books listed at the end of Appendix 2.

Appendix Two

Composition of Explosives in Bombs

Up to the end of World War Two, well over one hundred explosive compounds used by the HWA and Luftwaffe had been compiled in a numbered table, a separate list of numbers having been applied by the Kriegsmarine for their explosives. The most commonly used in bomb fillings was No 14 Füllpulver (filling powder) Fp 02 = Trinitrotoluol (TNT), the table having started with No 1. Others in the table were Trialen 105, 106, 107, and PMF 109, the digits signifying their respective code number. Most of the German bomb explosive fillings mentioned in this book (plus a few others) are included in the table at the top of the following page:

Trotyl (powder)
60% TNT + 40% Ammonalsalpeter. Was replacement for Nitroglycerine. Contained metallic salts to reduce smoke, much less than Schwarzpulver (blackpowder) in artillery shells. Stable, it protected gun barrels and was used in early bombs.

Hexogen
An extremely powerful and poisonous explosive, it was made from Hexamethylene-tetramine and Nitric acid with additives of Formaldehyde and Ammonium nitrate. As it is highly sensitive to shock, it had to be phlegmatised (tamed) for storage purposes with 5% wax. Normally a white powder, when phlegmatised with wax, had a blue colour. The addition of Aluminium powder or granules increased its gas explosive energy effects. Used mainly in bombs, LTs and sea mines. [A similar explosive used in bombs in the U.K was RDX = Cyclotrimethylene-trinitramine.]

Hexamin
Highly explosive like TNT, was used to fill torpedoes and sea mines. Was more difficult to fabricate and was shock-sensitive. Mixed with 36-40% TNT content + 10% Aluminium powder, became the basis for the Ammonal group of explosives.

Ammonal
High-explosive powder with Aluminium powder mixture content. The Al powder burns at a very high temperature and greatly increases the high-explosive energy. Although detonation velocity is reduced, pressure effect duration is increased. Used in torpedoes, low-level bombs, air-dropped LTs, and missiles.

Ammonpulver
Consisting 50% Ammonsäure (acid) + 22% Diglycol + 22% Nitrocellulose + 5% Hydrocellulose + 1% Centralite (called Carbamite = Diethyl-diphenyl urea in U.K.) After manufacture, it was covered with Diglycol as the powder was moisture-sensitive.

Nipolit
An extremely powerful explosive, developed by Dr von Holt of the WASAG (Westfälisch-Anhaltische Sprengstoff AG) had no need for a metal casing. Was used in spe-

cial bombs, the X-4 air-to-air rocket and unmanned Lippisch 3/L winged missile.

Nitropenta

Consists of Penta-erythritol-tetranitrate. A very powerful explosive producing similar effects to Hexogen. Preferably used in small-calibre bullets and projectiles, but also in Granaten and Bomben. Its effects in mines was increased with Aluminium powder.

Salz (literally: salt)

Camouflage name given to several explosive compounds, among them MAN-Salz, a monomethylammonium that was very moisture-sensitive; TETRA-Salz, a Tetramethylammoniumnitrate, and PH-Salz, composed of Ethylenediaminnitrate.

Diamin

Comprised 53.5% Ammonalnitrate+ 45% Ethylenediamindinitrate + 15% Aluminium.

The explosive fillings used in mines and torpedoes by the Kriegsmarine (Navy) were variations of SW = Schießwolle (gun-cotton). These had designations such as S 16 to S 20 and SW 36, the latter used from about 1940. For example, S 17 = 62% TNT + 23% Hexamin (Hexanitrodiphenylamine) + 15% Aluminium, and S 18 = 60% TNT + 24% Hexamin + 16% Aluminium. S 18 was an explosive filling in the *Flußmine* (river-mine) FM 1000 alias *'Sommerballon'* (Summer Balloon) intended to destroy hydro-electric power stations. SW 36 was detonated by an Aufschlagzünder (contact fuze) or by an MZ-Pi = Magnetzünder-Pistole (magnetic ignition pistol) in torpedoes.

The table at the bottom of this page provides principal characteristics of some explosives mentioned above.

Code	Explosive composition
Fp 02	100% Trinitrotuluol (TNT) or Tritolo (Italy). Also Fp 02 in phlegmatised form.
Fp 60/40	60% Trinitrotuluol + 40% Ammonsalpeter (ammonium saltpetre or nitrate)
Fp 60/40	(phlegmatised): with wax for storage stability.
Fp 50/50	50% Trinitrotuluol + 50% Ammonsalpeter
Fp 50/40/10	50% Trinitrotuluol + 40% Ammonsalpeter + 10% Aluminium powder
Fp 20/80	20% Trinitrotuluol + 80% Ammonsalpeter
Grf. 88	(Granatfüllung 88): 100% Pikrinsäure (picric acid or trinitrophenol)
HA 41	80% Hexogen + 20% Aluminiumpulver (powder)
HTA 15	45% Hexogen + 40% Trinitrotuluol + 15% Aluminiumpulver
PMF 109	80% Hexogen + 20% Aluminiumpyroschliff (shavings)
Amatol 39	50% Dinitrobenzol + 35% Ammonsalpeter + 15% Hexogen. Several variants.
Amatol 40	53% Dinitrobenzol + 30% Ammonsalpeter + 17% Hexogen
Amatol 41	52% Ammonsalpeter + 30% PH-Salz + 10% Hexogen + 6% Kalksalpeter (potassium nitrate) + 2% Montanwachs (mining-industry wax)
Amatol 44	45% Dinitrobenzol (Dinitrobenzene) + 35% Ammonsalpeter + 20% Hexanit
Ammonal D	90% Ammonsalpeter + 4% Aluminiumpyroschliff + 4% Napthaline + 2% Holzmehl (sawdust)
Ammonal DJ	70% Ammonsalpeter + 20% TNT +10% Aluminiumpyroschliff (shavings)
Ammonal DJ1	76% Ammonsalpeter + 20% TNT + 4% Aluminiumgries (grit)
Ammonal J	80% Ammonsalpeter + 20% TNT
Diglycol	Diethyleneglycoldinitrate. Replaced Nitroglycerine from about 1936.
Hexogen	Hexanitrodiphenylamine + TNT + Aluminium. Had other compositions.
Hexogen	(phlegmatised): was Hexogen with 5% wax for storage stability
Nipolit	45% PETN + 44% Diglycol + 5% Nitrocellulose + 2% Centralite.
Nitroglycerin	Glyceryl-trinitrate.
Nitropenta	Penta-erythritol-tetranitrate (alias PETN in U.K and PENT in Germany).
Pentol	70% Nitropenta + 30% Hexogen
Trialen 105	70% Trinitrotuluol + 15% Hexogen + 15% Aluminiumpulver
Trialen 106	50% Trinitrotuluol + 25% Hexogen + 25% Aluminiumsalpeter
Trialen 107	60% Trinitrotuluol + 20% Hexogen + 20% Aluminiumpulver
Trialen 105/109	50% Trialen 105 + 50% PMF 109.

For additional information on explosives and/or toxic chemicals, see:

Solid Propellent & Exothermic Compositions: James Taylor; George Newnes Ltd, London, 1959.

German Secret Weapons of the Second World War: Ian V Hogg; Greenhill Books, London, 1999, pp.183-191.

Deutsche Geheimwaffen 1939-1945: Fritz Hahn; Erich Hoffmann Verlag, Heidenheim, 1963, pp.238-252.

Waffen und Geheimwaffen des deutschen Heeres 1939-1945, Vol 1: Fritz Hahn; Bernard & Graefe Verlag, Koblenz, 1986, pp.213-235.

Die deutschen Waffen und Geheimwaffen des 2. Weltkrieges und ihre Weiterentwicklung: Rudolf Lusar: J F Lehmanns Verlag; 4th Edition, Munich, 1962, pp.280-288.

For highly interesting accounts on unexploded bombs disposal conducted by Royal Air Force personnel both during and after World War Two in the United Kingdom as well as in other European countries, illustrated with numerous photographs of German high-explosive and phosphorous bombs, air-dropped containers, several types of fuzes and even two poison-gas containers, the following are recommended reading – Translator:

RAF UXB: The Untold Story of RAF Bomb Disposal during World War 2, Vol 1: Jim Jenkinson; Woodfield Publishing, Bognor Regis, West Sussex, 1999.

UXB: Collected Stories of Bomb Disposal Experts, Vol 2: Jim Jenkinson; Woodfield Publishing, Bognor Regis, West Sussex, 2001.

Explosive	Weight (kg/litre)	Explosion heat (kcal/kg)	Explosion temperature	Detonation velocity (m/sec)
Trinitrotuluol	1.59	950	2,820°C	4,800
Nitroglycerine	1.60	1,485	3,950°C	8,000
Hexamin	1.67	1,035	3,450°C	7,100
Trotyl	1.67	980	2,800°C	6,900
Nitropenta	1.70	1,450	3,900°C*	8,400*
Picric acid	1.76	1,050	3,350°C*	7,300
Hexogen	1.82	1,365	3,800°C	8,400*

* various figures quoted.

Appendix Three

Sources and Literature

For readers wanting to know more about the exclusively German document sources, the following list of principal words is included to indicate the meaning of the titles.

Principal Terms

Abwurf	air-dropped, jettisoned, released
Abwurf (as prefix)	
-**behälter**	container
-**geräte**	devices, equipment
-**munition**	munitions, bombs, projectiles
-**waffe**	weapon
Allgemeine	general
Angaben	details, statements
Anlage	plant, works, installation
Anweisung	directive, instruction, order
Ausgabe	edition, issue
Bedienung(s)	servicing
Begriffe	definitions, concepts
Beladen	load, loading
Beschreibung	description
Bewaffnung	armament
Blindgänger	unexploded bomb
Blitzlichtbomben	flash-bombs
Brandbomben	incendiary bombs
Nebelbomben	smoke bombs
Sprengbomben	high-explosive bombs
Schüttbehälter	multi-bomb container
Bombenwurf	bomb jettison, release
Deckblatt	cover sheet
Einsatz	employment, use
Entwurf	draft, proposal
Erkennen	recognise, recognition of
Fertigmachen	preparation, make ready
Flugzeug	aircraft, airplane (USA)
gegen	against
Gerät(e)	equipment, device(s)
Grundbegriffe	basic concepts, ideas
Grundlagen	fundamentals, basics
Handbuch	handbook
Heft	book, volume
Inhalt	content(s)
Instandsetzung	preparation, repair
Konstruktion	design
Lösung	solution. As suffix:
Behelfs-	temporary, makeshift
Not-	emergency solution
Luft	air, airborne
Lufttorpedo	air-launched torpedo
Mischlast	mixed load
Mitteilungen	communication, notification
Munition	munitions, bombs, weapons
Nebelgerät	smoke or fog device
Seeziele	sea targets
Sonder	special
sowie	as well as, also
Stand	status as of (date)
Teil	part, portion
Vorwort	preface
Vernichten	destroy, destruction of
Waffen	weapons, ordnance
Wartung	maintenance
Wirkungsweise	effectiveness
Werkschrift	works document
Vorschrift	regulation, directive, order
Vorschrift (As suffix):	
Abbau-	dismantling
Bedienungs-	servicing, operating
Belade-	loading
Einbau-	installation
Wartungs-	maintenance
Zünder-	fuze, igniter
Zünder	fuze. As suffix:
Langzeit-	long time-delay
Sonder-	special
Stör-	harassment, anti-removal

Sources

L.DV. 8/1 (Entwurf)	Der Bombenwurf Teil 1 Grundbegriffe des Bombenwurfes, vom April 1941
L.DV. 8/8	Der Bombenwurf Teil 8 Der Bombenwurf gegen Seeziele, vom 7. Januar 1944
L.DV. 143/1	Vorschrift für das Fertigmachen der Abwurfmunition Teil 1 Fertigmachen der SC-10, vom 6. Mai 1940
L.DV. 143/2	Vorschrift für das Fertigmachen der Abwurfmunition Teil 2 Fertigmachen der SC-50, SC-250 und SC-10, vom 6. Mai 1940
L.DV. 143/3	Vorschrift für das Fertigmachen der Abwurfmunition Teil 3 Fertigmachen der SD-50, vom 1. Juli 1940
L.DV. 152 M.DV. 552	Entwurf einer Zündervorschrift (Nur für Abwurfmunition) Teil 1 Inhalt, Vorwort und allgemeine Begriffe, vom 16. Februar 1936
L.DV. 152 M.DV. 552	Entwurf einer Zündervorschrift (Nur für Abwurfmunition) Teil 2 Technische Grundlagen der mechanischen Zünder für Abwurfmunition, Dezember 1938
L.DV. 152	Entwurf einer Zündervorschrift (Nur für Abwurfmunition) Teil 3 Technische Grundlagen der elektrischen Zünder für Abwurfmunition, April 1938
L.DV. 152	Entwurf einer Zündervorschrift (Nur für Abwurfmunition) Teil 4
M.DV. 552	Zünder (3), AZ C 10 (h.u.t.)*, vom 16. Februar 1936
L.DV. 152	Entwurf einer Zündervorschrift (Nur für Abwurfmunition) Teil 5
M.DV. 552	Zünder (5), ELAZ C (5), vom 16. Februar 1936
L.DV. 152 M.DV. 552	Entwurf einer Zündervorschrift (Nur für Abwurfmunition) Anlage 1 zu Teil 5, Zünder (5), 1936
L.DV. 152 M.DV. 552	Entwurf einer Zündervorschrift (Nur für Abwurfmunition) Anlage 2 zu Teil 5, Zünder (5), 1936
L.DV. 152	Entwurf einer Zündervorschrift (Nur für Abwurfmunition) Teil 6
M.DV. 552	Zünder (9), ELAZ C (9), vom 9. September 1939
L.DV. 152	Entwurf einer Zündervorschrift (Nur für Abwurfmunition) Teil 7
M.DV. 552	Zünder (15), ELAZ C (50), vom 9. Juli 1937
L.DV. 152	Entwurf einer Zündervorschrift (Nur für Abwurfmunition) Teil 8
M.DV. 552	Zünder (25), ELAZ (25), vom 28. August 1939
L.DV. 152	Entwurf einer Zündervorschrift (Nur für Abwurfmunition) Teil 9
M.DV. 552	Zünder (26) B, ELAZ (26), vom 4. September 1939
L.DV. 152	Entwurf einer Zündervorschrift (Nur für Abwurfmunition) Teil 10

M.DV. 552	Zünder (29), ZtZ LC (10), vom 2. März 1939	L.DV.T.2088 A-4/Fl.	Ju 88 A-4 Bedienungsvorschrift - FL, vom 19. Juli 1941
L.DV. 152	Entwurf einer Zündervorschrift (Nur für Abwurfmunition) Teil 11	D (Luft)152/17	Entwurf einer Zündervorschrift (Nur für Abwurfmunition Teil 17
M.DV. 552	Zünder (28) A, ELAZ (28) A, vom 5. März 1940		Zusatzzünder (40), Zus.Z. (49) (Stand Juli 1941), vom 22. Juli 1944
L.DV. 152/12	Entwurf einer Zündervorschrift (Nur für Abwurfmunition) Teil 12	D (Luft) T 286	Abwurfbehälter AB-36 Beschreibung und Wirkungsweise, vom 1. Februar 1941
M.DV. 552	Zünder (17), Z (17), vom 9. November 1940	D (Luft) T 229/4	Bf 109 E Bedienungs- und Beladevorschrift für die Abwurfwaffe, vom 27. Juni 1940
L.DV. 152	Entwurf einer Zündervorschrift (Nur für Abwurfmunition) Teil 13	D (Luft) T 579/2	Bf 110 Bedienungs- und Beladevorschrift für die Abwurfwaffe, vom 8. Juli 1940
M.DV. 552	Zünder (28) B, ELAZ (28) B, vom 9. September 1940	D (Luft) T 579/6	Bf 110 Beschreibung, Ein- und Abbauvorschrift für die Abwurfwaffe, vom 17. Oktober 1944
L.DV. 152	Entwurf einer Zündervorschrift (Nur für Abwurfmunition) Teil 15	D (Luft) T 583/4b	He 111, H-4, P-4, H-5 und H-6 Bedienungs- und Beladevorschrift für die Abwurfwaffe
M.DV. 552	Zünder (35), ELAZ (35), vom 9. September 1940		Heft 5b: Einsatz des Brandbomben-Schüttbehälters BSB 700 B 1 EL/XII, vom 5. Februar 1941
L.DV. 152	Entwurf einer Zündervorschrift (Nur für Abwurfmunition) Teil 16	D (Luft) T 583/4c	He 111, H-5 Belade- und Bedienungsvorschrift für die Abwurfwaffe Heft c: Einsatz der Lufttorpedos LFT-5 und F-5 W, vom Dezember 1941
M.DV. 552	Zünder (38), ELAZ (38), vom 9. September 1940		
L.DV. 152/19	Entwurf einer Zündervorschrift (Nur für Abwurfmunition) Teil 19 Zünder (17) A, ELAZ (17) A und (17) B, ELAZ (17) B, vom 21. August 1941	D (Luft) T 583/4d	He 111, H-4, P-4, H-5 und H-6 Bedienungs- und Beladevorschrift für die Abwurfwaffen (Stand Mai 1942), vom 1. Dezember 1942
L.DV. 152	Entwurf einer Zündervorschrift (Nur für Abwurfmunition) Teil 21	D (Luft) T 2087 Teil 12 B	D-5 Ju 87 D-5 Flugzeug-Handbuch Teil 12 B, Abwurfwaffenanlage, vom 6. Dezember 1941
M.DV. 552	Zünder (55), ELAZ (55), vom 9. September 1940	D (Luft) T 2087	D-1 trop. Ju 87 D-1 trop. Flugzeug-Handbuch Teil 12 B, Abwurfwaffenanlage, vom 7. Dezember 1943
L.DV. 152	Entwurf einer Zündervorschrift (Nur für Abwurfmunition) Teil 22	D (Luft) T 2096	B-6 Ar 96 B-6 Flugzeug-Handbuch Teil 8 B, Abwurfwaffenanlage, vom 3. Juni 1944
M.DV. 552	Zünder (25) A, ELAZ (25) A, vom 8. Oktober 1940	D (Luft) T 2109 G-1 Teil 8	Bf 109 G-1 Flugzeughandbuch Teil 8 B Abwurfwaffenanlage, Ausgabe September 1943, Berlin 1943
L.DV. 152	Entwurf einer Zündervorschrift (Nur für Abwurfmunition) Teil 24		
M.DV. 552	Zünder (24) A, ELAZ (24) A, vom 26. Juli 1941	D (Luft) T G.Kdos 2177 A-3 Teil 12 c	He 177 A-3 Flugzeug-Handbuch Teil 12 c, Sonderwaffenanlage mit FuG 203 D (Stand August 1943), vom 25. Januar 1944
L.DV. 152/19	Deckblatt Nr. 5 zur L.DV. 152/19, vom August 1942		
L.DV. 152/20	Entwurf einer Zündervorschrift (Nur für Abwurfmunition) Teil 20 Elektrischer Sonderzünder (50), ELZ (50), vom 22. Oktober 1941	D (Luft) T 2190 A-5/ A-6 Teil 0	Fw 190 A-5/A-6 Flugzeug-Handbuch Teil 0, Allgemeine Angaben (Stand August 1943), Ausgabe Dezember 1943, vom 8. Dezember 1943
L.DV. 152/25	Entwurf einer Zündervorschrift (Nur für Abwurfmunition) Teil 25 Elektrischer Langzeitzünder (57) E, LZtZ (57), vom 8. Juli 1941	D (Luft) 4001	Schlachtfliegerbombe SD-2 mit Zünder (41) Beschreibung und Wirkungsweise, mit Anlage Störzünder (67) und (70) B, vom 11. Februar 1941
L.DV. 152/28	Entwurf einer Zündervorschrift (Nur für Abwurfmunition) Teil 28 Zünder (89), ZtZ (89), vom 10. März 1942	D (Luft) 4002	Erkennen und Vernichten von Bombenblindgängern SD-2, vom 16. Mai 1941
L.DV. 152/29	Entwurf einer Zündervorschrift (Nur für Abwurfmunition) Teil 29 Zünder (59) B, ELZtZ (59) B, vom 26. Oktober 1941	D (Luft) 4230	Bl C 50 Beschreibung, Wirkungsweise und Instandsetzung sowie Bedienung und Wartung der Blitzlichtbombe C-50, vom 25. Juli 1941
L.DV. 152/30	Entwurf einer Zündervorschrift (Nur für Abwurfmunition) Teil 30 Zünder (79), ELZtZ (79), vom 15. Januar 1942	D (Luft) 4300 Teil 1 Heft 2	Abwurfmunition für Bomben Munitions-Handbuch Teil 1 Minenbomben, Heft 2: SC-250, Ausgabe Dezember 1942
L.DV. 152/31	Entwurf einer Zündervorschrift (Nur für Abwurfmunition) Teil 31 Zünderanordnung (55), ELAZ (55) A, vom 12. Oktober 1942	D (Luft) 4300 Teil 1 Heft 3	Abwurfmunition für Bomben Munitionshandbuch Teil 1 Minenbomben, Heft 3: SC-500, Ausgabe 18. Dezember 1942
L.DV. 153	Entwurf einer Beschreibung und Bedienungsanweisung für das große Flugzeug-Nebelgerät S 200/V, Berlin 1937	D (Luft) 4310 Heft 1	Abwurfmunition - Nebelbomben Munitions-Handbuch Heft 1 NC-250 S, vom 13. Mai 1942
L.DV. 196 (Entwurf)	Beschreibung, Bedienungs- und Wartungsvorschrift des Munitionstransportwagen 11 (MT 11), August 1940	D (Luft) 4316 Teil 1 Heft 1	Abwurfmunition Bomben-Abwurfgeräte Munitions-Handbuch Abwurfgeräte für Sprengbomben, Heft 1: AB-23 SD-2, vom 5. Mai 1942
L.DV. 816	Entwurf einer Beschreibung und Bedienungsvorschrift für Abwurfgeräte Träg 5 Schloß 50/X, Träg 3 Schloß 50/X und Träg 4 Schloß 50/X		
L.DV. 4200	Die deutsche Abwurfmunition, vom 5. Juni 1943	D (Luft) T 5209	Kurzanweisung zum Beladen der Mischlastabwurfbehälter 1,000 kg (Behelfslösung mit LMB-Gefäß), vom Juni 1942
L.DV.T. 536	Beschreibung und Bedienungsvorschrift für das Abwurfgerät ESAC-250/IX und das Einheitsschloß C-50, vom 25. Juli 1941		

D (Luft) T 5215/2   Mischlast-Abwurfbehälter 1000 kg (Notlösung) Geräte-Handbuch (Stand Februar 1944), vom 31. März 1944

D (Luft) T 7225   BSB-700 B 1 EL/XII Beschreibung und Wirkungsweise des Brandbomben-Schüttbehälters BSB 700, vom 6. Januar 1941

D (Luft) T 7250   AB-42 Waffen-Handbuch Beschreibung und Wirkungsweise sowie Bedienung und Wartung des Abwurfbehälters, vom 29. September 1941

D (Luft) T 7251   ABB-500 Waffen-Handbuch Beschreibung und Wirkungsweise sowie Bedienung und Wartung des Abwurfbehälters 42, vom 9. September 1941

OP 1666   Volume 1, German Explosive Ordnance, Washington 1946

Ersatzteil-Liste   Fw 190 A und B Konstruktionsgruppe 8 Bewaffnung, Bremen o.J.

Ersatzteil-Liste   He 177 A-3 Bewaffnung, Rostock 1943

Firmenschrift   Ju 188 E-1 Flugzeug-Handbuch (Stand April 1943)

Technische Mitteilungen des Generals der Truppentechnik: Kurzbeschreibung italienischer Abwurfmunition, vom 15. Mai 1944

Technische Mitteilungen des Generals der Truppentechnik: Französische Abwurfmunition aus deutschen Abwurfwaffen, vom 10. Mai 1944

Werkschrift 2217 E-2, E-4, Teil 8 B Do 217 E-2, E-4 Flugzeug-Handbuch Teil 8 B, Abwurfwaffenanlage (Stand März 1942), vom 30. März 1942

Literature

Adler   Die Laufbahnen in der Luftwaffe; Berlin 1942

Åkesson, P, Bock, F and others   Burgwald - von der Luftmunitionsanstalt zum Ortsteil; Burgwald 1998

Béjeuhr, P P   Der Luft-Krieg; Dachau 1915

Boelcke, W A   Deutschlands Rüstung im Zweiten Weltkrieg; Frankfurt am Main 1969

Boog, H   Luftwaffe und unterschiedloser Bombenkrieg, in: Der Zweite Weltkrieg; München 1989

Buchbender, O, and Schuh, H   Die Waffe, die auf die deutsche Seele zielt - Psychologische Kriegführung 1939-1945; Stuttgart 1988

Churchill, W S   Der Zweite Weltkrieg; Bern, München, Wien 1996

Cooper, B and Batchelor, J   Bomber 1914-1939; München undated

Cooper, B and Batchelor, J   Bomber 1939-1945; München undated Die großen Luftschlachten des Zweiten Weltkrieges; Genf undated

Eichbaum   Das Buch von der Luftwaffe; Berlin undated
Eichholtz, D   Geschichte der deutschen Kriegswirtschaft 1939-1945, Band 1; Berlin (East) 1969

Eichholtz, D   Geschichte der deutschen Kriegswirtschaft 1939-1945, Band 2; Berlin (East) 1969

Feuchter, G W   Probleme des Luftkrieges; Potsdam 1939

Goebbels, J   Tagebücher 1945 Die letzten Aufzeichnungen; Hamburg 1977

Green, W and Swanborough, G   Wings of the Luftwaffe; London 1977

Griehl, M   Junkers Ju 87 'Stuka'; Stuttgart 1998

Groehler, O   Geschichte des Luftkrieges 1910 bis 1970; Berlin (East) 1977

Halder, F   Kriegstagebuch, Band III, Der Russlandfeldzug bis zum Marsch auf Stalingrad (22.6.41-24.9.42); Stuttgart 1964

Hackenberger, W   Deutschlands Eroberung der Luft; Siegen, Leipzig, Berlin 1915

Hillmann, B, Kluge, V et al   Lw.2/XI - Muna Lübberstedt Zwangsarbeit für den Krieg; Bremen 1996

Jendrek, G and Behme, J   Schriftenreihe Luftschutz Bd. 17: Mittel und Methoden des Schutzes gegen Massenvernichtungsmittel; Teil III: Die biologische Waffe und die Mittel und Methoden zur Bekämpfung biologischer Wirkungsmittel; Berlin (East) 1965

Joachimczyk, A M   Der Krieg in der Luft; Berlin 1914

Just, G   Stuka-Oberst Hans-Ulrich Rudel; Stuttgart 1983

Justrow, K   Der technische Krieg II. Band: Wirkung und Kampfesweise im Zukunftskrieg; Berlin 1939

Kesselring, A   Die deutsche Luftwaffe, in: Bilanz des Zweiten Weltkrieges; Oldenburg and Hamburg 1953

King, J B   Deutsche Geheimwaffen; München undated

Klein, Heinrich   Vom Geschoss zum Feuerpfeil; Neckargmünd 1977

Knobloch, Hans   Die Ballistik in der Luftwaffe vom Bomben werfen, Schießen und vom Treffen; Berlin 1942

Knobloch, Hans   Grundzüge der Ballistik des Bombenwurfs, in: Beiträge zur Ballistik und Technischen Physik, published by von Prof. Dr.-Ing. Hubert Schardin; Leipzig 1938 Luftschutz-Fibel; Berlin undated

Maie, K A   Die Luftschlacht über England, in: Der Zweite Weltkrieg; München 1989

Marquardt, Ernst   Bombenentwicklung 1925-1945, ungedrucktes Manuskript, no location, undated

Meinhardt, F   Schriftenreihe Luftschutz Bd. 11: Konventionelle Abwurfmittel; Berlin (East) 1962

Miranda, J and Mercado, P   Die geheimen Wunderwaffen des III. Reiches; Illertissen 1995

Müller, Wolfgang   Zielgeräte für den Bombenwurf aus dem Horizontalflug, in: Beiträge zur Ballistik und Technischen Physik, published by von Prof. Dr.-Ing. Hubert Schardin; Leipzig 1938

Nowarra, H   Die deutsche Luftrüstung 1933-1945, Band I-IV; Koblenz 1993

Anonymous   Der Luftkrieg 1914-1915, Leipzig 1915

Price, A   Das letzte Jahr der deutschen Luftwaffe Mai 1944 - Mai 1945; Wölfersheim 1998

Rudel, H-U   Mein Kriegstagebuch; Wiesbaden and München 1987

Schliephake, H   Flugzeugbewaffnung; Stuttgart 1977

Schneider, H   Flugzeug-Typenbuch; Leipzig 1944

Speer, A   Erinnerungen; Frankfurt a.M., Berlin 1998

Stüwe, B   Erprobungsstelle West; Augsburg 1998

Unger, H   Taschenbuch Luftschutz, Teil 1; Leipzig 1961

Waninger, Carl: What the British found in Unterlüß in 1945, what they asked and what answers they were given. Translation of the Report: Secret Rheinmetall-Borsig A.G. Werk Unterlüß No 2/47; Combined Intelligence Objectives Sub-Committee G-2 Division, SHAEF (Rear) APO 413.

Zeidler, M   Reichswehr und Rote Armee 1929-1933; München 1993

Periodicals

Aero-Sport, Der Adler, Militärtechnik, Soldat + Technik, Die Wehrmacht. Particular Luftwaffe Regulations from various years.

LUFTWAFFE SECRET PROJECTS
Fighters 1939-1945

Walter Schick & Ingolf Meyer

Germany's incredible fighter projects of 1939-45 are revealed in-depth – showing for the first time the technical dominance that their designers could have achieved. With access to much previously unpublished information the authors bring to life futuristic shapes that might have terrorised the Allies had the war gone beyond 1945. Full colour action illustrations in contemporary unit markings and performance tables show what might have been achieved.

Hbk, 282 x 213 mm, 176pp, 95 colour artworks, c160 dwgs and c 30 photos
1 85780 052 4 **£29.95**

LUFTWAFFE SECRET PROJECTS
Strategic Bombers 1935-45

Dieter Herwig and Heinz Rode

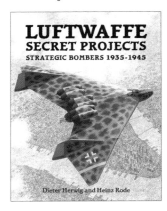

In this companion to the enormously popular volume on fighters, Germany's incredible strategic bomber projects 1935-45 are revealed showing the technical dominance that their designers could have achieved if time had allowed. The authors bring to life futuristic shapes that might have terrorised the Allies had the war gone beyond 1945. Careful comparison with later Allied and Soviet aircraft show the legacy handed on, right up to today's stealth aircraft.

Hbk, 282 x 213 mm, 144pp, 100 colour artworks, 132 b/w photos, 122 dwgs
1 85780 092 3 **£24.95**

LUFTWAFFE SECRET PROJECTS – Ground Attack & Special Purpose Aircraft

Dieter Herwig and Heinz Rode

This new addition to the series takes a close look at a varied range of about 140 ground attack and special purpose aircraft types including Kampfzerstörer (multi-purpose combat aircraft), multi-purpose and fast bombers, explosive-carrying aircraft intended to attack other aircraft, air-to-air ramming vehicles, bomb-carrying gliders and towed fighters, and airborne weapons and special devices (rockets, cannon, flamethrowers etc).

Hbk, 282 x 213 mm, 272pp, 154 colour illustrations, 168 b/w photos, 196 dwgs
1 85780 150 4 **£35.00**

Black Cross Volume 1
JUNKERS Ju 188

Helmut Erfurth

The Ju 188 was among the most well-known combat aircraft of World War Two from the Junkers Flugzeug- und Motorenwerke in Dessau. Developed from 1941 out of the Ju 88B-series model as an interim solution for the Ju 288, the Ju 188 incorporated the sum of all the military and tactical experiences of frontline pilots together with the technological design possibilities in aircraft construction and armament at that time in Germany.

Softback, 280 x 215mm, 64 pages
30 b/w photos, 6pp of col, plus dwgs
1 85780 172 5 **£8.99**

Black Cross Volume 2
JUNKERS Ju 288/388/488

Karl-Heinz Regnat

The Ju 288 was a medium bomber which first flew in June 1941. Several variants of the Ju 288 offering different speeds, ranges and bomb loads were envisaged, but only 22 aircraft were produced. The Ju 388 development began in September 1943. This was to be a multi-purpose type which could be used as a bomber, a night fighter or a reconnaissance aircraft. The Ju 488, first proposed in early 1944 was a four-engined heavy bomber.

Softback, 280 x 215mm, 96 pages
c150 b/w photos, 5pp of col, plus dwgs
1 85780 173 3 **£12.99**

ROYAL AIR FORCE GERMANY Since 1945

Bill Taylor

This detailed survey takes the lid off RAF operations within Germany and provides a detailed valediction of its exploits from the establishment of the British Air Forces of Occupation in July 1945 to the tense days of the Berlin Airlift and the establishment of NATO and its tripwire strategy which placed Germany firmly in the front line via its Forward Defence policy. This book serves as a timely study of a hitherto thinly documented era of RAF history.

Hbk, 282 x 213 mm, 240 pages
295 b/w, 59 colour photo, plus maps
1 85780 034 6 **£35.00**

GERMAN SECRET FLIGHT TEST CENTRES TO 1945

H Beauvais, K Kössler, M Mayer and C Regel

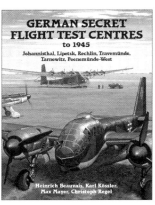

A group of German authors, some of whom were involved at the time have brought together a history and overview of the establishment and activities of government flight-test centres in Germany from its resumption in the 1920s until the end of the Second World War. Major locations included are the research facilities at Johannisthal, Lipetsk, Rechlin, Travemünde, Tarnewitz and Peenemünde-West.

Hardback, 282 x 213mm, 248 pages
270 b/w photos, sketches, 8pp of col
1 85780 127 X **£35.00**